Westminster Man

Westminster Man

A Tribal Anthropology of the Commons People

by AUSTIN MITCHELL

Research by Sharon Goulds
Cartoons by Les Gibbard

Thames Methuen

First published in 1982 by
Methuen London Ltd
11 New Fetter Lane, London EC4P 4EE
in association with
Thames Television Ltd
149 Tottenham Court Road, London W1P 9LL

British Library Cataloguing in Publication data:
Mitchell, Austin
Westminster man.
1. Great Britain. *Parliament. House of Commons*
2. Legislators—Great Britain
I. Title
328.41'073 JN677
ISBN 0-423-00380-1

Filmset, printed and bound in Great Britain by
Hazell Watson & Viney Ltd, Aylesbury, Bucks

Contents

Preface

So much has been written about the House of Commons that you cannot see the wood for the trees; the real House is almost unknown. The living realities of Parliament are smothered in facts, tables and analyses, then embalmed in pedantry and veneration, an attitude which brings out the worst in academics and parliamentarians alike. That small proportion of the public who are interested have to be passionately so, given the outpouring of material they have to wade through, much of it unreadable, academic, legalistic or boringly pedantic. This book tries to be none of these things. If it fails, then blame it on the subject. The intention in this case is not to write for an elite. They have enough books written to their level already. This is aimed at a wider audience who want to know something about the Commons and its denizens, but at present are offered only expensive picture books, mythology about a constitution we did not even have in the nineteenth century, or the self-serving hagiography and alibiography of senior politicians.

It is more important for the Commons to be known and understood than to be held in awe. Parliament has enough veneration already. Far too much emphasis is placed on the myths and the dignified ceremonial of the constitution, to both of which the House seems more central than it is to the real processes of government. We British are a peculiarly ignorant and ill-educated community. We are already too prone to believe in mythology, and the politics of decline which we are now going through will make us more so. Yet understanding demands a perception of reality. It is time to throw away the swaddling clothes of legend and ceremonial which distort the essentials of what should be a practical, workaday place into something unreal, and remote from the lives of the people. In any case our national vice of escapism tempts providence. Too many other British industries have done what the legislative business is now doing. Shipbuilding, engineering, cars, motor cycles, all indulged in similar fantasies and self-congratulation in the 1950s. Remember 'British achievements speak for Britain'?

The House of Commons not only relishes such treatment, it inhibits any other. Its formal activities are reported, its real doings are blanketed in silence. The babbling lobby correspondents pour out a constant chatter of analysis about politics and government. They become positively Trappist about everything else. Members themselves are difficult to silence on most issues. Yet when these egomaniacs talk about themselves as a collective, the clamps of convention and club rules come down.

This piece of participant anthropology sets out to provide a small antidote. Its subject is not the procedures of the Commons, Erskine May with less *son* and more *lumière*. Nor is it an attempt at political taxidermy, much as people might like to see such an art form applied to MPs. This book is an attempt to give a collective portrait of the people who are the House of Commons, the elected Members of Parliament. The aim is to show the House as it is, to concentrate on its human side, on what the people in it are like and what they do. There are 635 stories in the naked Commons and this is an attempt to tell them all at once. Illustrating that reality seems a greater service to a House of Commons in danger of becoming irrelevant than any attempt to encourage it to atrophy into yet another dignified part of our cumbersome constitution: a rowdier version of a City livery company. MPs are human, despite their own beliefs and all appearances to the contrary. To show them as such is a far better way of indicating what the Commons are really about, and what really goes on, than to embalm them. It is reality we need to understand, not mythology. I do not venerate the House of Commons. But it does have a very important part to play. It is not playing it adequately. Britain is the worse for that.

The material for this study, the pigment of the painting, comes from three sources. The origin was the interview material collected for Thames Television's programme *Westminster Man*, fifteen verbatim interviews, done on film and at some length, and forty more wide-ranging interviews carried out by Sharon Goulds in the course of selecting those who were to take part in the programme. This provided a series of different perspectives and diverging attitudes to the House and the job of MP. Next I used a series of questionnaires: one to all MPs, one to defeated Members, one sent out independently by an American research student to Members' wives. All these put the views of the smaller number who had been interviewed into perspective by showing how the fifteen MPs fitted into the overall picture. Finally, there is the interpretation, a piece of participant observation by an amateur Margaret Mead who has gone to live among the natives. This aspect of the book is based on the experience of one man, a Labour MP with most of the prejudices of the breed. No MP is typical, but perhaps the experience and attitudes of this one are less typical than most; the second last surviving Gaitskellite, with all that that implies in terms of attitudes, loyalties and feelings for the Labour Party.

I was elected at a by-election, which is the worst possible way of joining the Commons tribe for anyone who wants to be integrated. Those who come in at a general election share the same initiation rites and think of themselves, and are, as a Class of '59, '64, '70, '74 or, most unlovely of all, '79. I was a class of two. One of them flunked the practicals though he's now back again. A by-election also implies an abnormal entry process. Selection is much easier for someone of my rather peculiar background at a by-election than through the hard slog of hawking one's conscience and qualifications round constituencies, which would almost certainly have remained impervious to both in normal circumstances. Then winning an election in a glare of national publicity confers delusions of grandeur rapidly deflated on arrival.

The seat, which I inherited from Tony Crosland, is also unusual. Grimsby is not only the best constituency but pretty unique. The district council and the constituency share the same boundaries so I am a rare survivor of the species 'Borough Member'. Grimsby is also a self-contained community, not a slice of somewhere else, with a strong sense of local feeling and identity, as the reverse of the coin of isolation. It also has a Labour Party like Labour Parties used to be, where we actually get on with each other. Lastly, it is marginal enough to keep the Member on his toes but not so close as to require the continuous wearing of brown trousers, or wasn't until the combined efforts of an alienated electorate and the Liberal–SDP Alliance brought the joys of the lottery and uncertainty as a way of life to British politics under the guise of giving a new continuity. I often feel myself to be the luckiest man in the House of Commons – until I begin the 200-mile drive north or south. Finally, perhaps a background as academic turned journalist sets my experience apart, making me observer as well as participant. A corduroy jacket still hangs in this particular parliamentary wardrobe, memorial to that previous incarnation. Not that the two jobs are that different. The politician and the academic both dole out their own prejudices. However, the former does not need to prove his in percentage terms and support them with a paraphernalia of quotations and footnotes to absolve himself from blame.

This study, then, embodies all these prejudices and distortions. To offset mine there are those of all the others quoted here. There is safety, if not absolute truth, in numbers. There is, however, one real danger attending the exercise of having *Homo Westminsteriensis* writing about his own breed, or the inside dopester approach, to give it its proper name. There is the possibility of breach of privilege. As Parliament has fallen in public esteem it has become more and more cowardly about using the potentially horrendous procedures to deal with contempt. The arcane and eminently scrappable procedures have been left in abeyance to the point where outsiders can now say what they like about the House and its denizens. Several make regular use of this opportunity. Nothing happens. This is partly because outside views can always be discounted as ill-informed, but largely because the House has lost so much of its earlier confidence.

Parliament's own members are a very different proposition: more readily dealt with, more easily frightened. There is also a bigger incentive to trundle the machinery into action against them. Few have friends in the House but lots have enemies, a warmly affectionate band of fellow Members eager to seize any opportunity to help them on their way – downhill, and there are always party political arguments for trying to embarrass another side, as well as psychological motives for using one of the few powers MPs still have. So the question of contempt is invoked mainly against other Members. This cumbersome clobbering machine of parliamentary privilege is operated by elderly parliamentarians of enormous, and usually self-ascribed, dignity who have devoted the major part of rather stale lives to the institution. They handle it anxiously, like an old blunderbuss likely to explode in their faces: the nervous dealing with the unknown. The whole proceedings have the atmosphere, and a lot of the effect, of blind man's bluff. Some recent cases do give a rough idea of what is involved. Jim Callaghan said in 1965 that when he saw Members facing him as Chancellor, he did not think of them as the Honourable Member for X or Y or even Z:

> I look at them and say, 'Investment trusts, capital speculators, or that is the fellow who is the stock exchange man who makes profit on gilt edge.' I have almost forgotten their constituencies but I shall never forget

their interests. I wonder sometimes whom they represent, the constituents or their own or their friends' particular interest?

Patrick Duffy told constituents that in a recent censure debate some Tory MPs had been 'half drunk and disgusting to look at'. Joe Ashton told Jimmy Young in 1974 that there were MPs for hire by firms and interests outside the House. What was almost certainly true and what might have been permissible comment from outside became very different when uttered by the House's own. The heinous offenders were promptly reported by Sir Robert Cary, Sir Herbert Butcher and Sir Harmar Nicholls, all brave men motivated only by concern for the good reputation of a House of which they were particularly distinguished ornaments. The Privileges Committee thus trundled into action was concerned with the 'protection of the reputation, the character and the good name of the House itself'. It had to follow the Erskine May ruling that 'Reflections upon Members, the particular individuals not being named or otherwise indicated, are equivalent to reflections on the House'. All the Members who had spoken out so boldly apologised, grovellingly. They had little alternative. To produce proof would have generated libel writs. Justification has not in any case been entertained by the Committee of Privileges as a defence. So discretion is always the better part of valour.

Of course, such an approach on the House's part is wise and just. It is also absolutely relevant to the 1980s. No Member ever gets drunk, accepts money for any purpose from interests outside, or allows it to influence his parliamentary functions. All fulfil their duties to the very limit of their abilities. Those abilities are enormous. This author at least has nothing but respect for the House and its Members, and if anything in this book could be interpreted as in any way critical of either, it is the responsibility of those who have done the real work of the book. Reversing Mrs Thatcher's cabinet priorities, collective responsibility applies here for praise, not for blame. Furthermore, any such aspersions as may have accidentally crept in are the result of misunderstanding or infelicities of expression and are totally unintended, as well as being unfounded.

The book is set out as a manual of how to get into Parliament, and how to get on in it. That is the most convenient way of tackling a wide-ranging subject. I, for one, would have appreciated such a DIY manual when blundering into this madhouse in the first place. I still would if the Labour Party had not opted for being a spectator sport rather than a vehicle for ambition. They do not serve who can only stand and stare.

Information on the surveys on which the book is based is relegated to the appendix and the analysis is kept down to the very barest minimum. The interview material is polished by the omission of the 'er-um-ulps' and the constant 'I thinks' to which political speech is heir. To avoid a huge and pedantic paraphernalia, sources are cited briefly with that absolute minimum of footnotes necessary to distract attention from the inadequacies of the argument.

Lastly, the people who really made this book possible and did most of the work for it. In common with a number of MPs I have had the benefit of the help and enthusiasm of a number of American interns all working as researchers for British MPs for a limited period. It is a mark of shame for Britain that its MPs should have to turn to American educational institutions to provide help which their own country is too mean to give, but I have relied heavily upon them and found all the students who have worked in my office keen and enthusiastic. Nancy Aronson, Kelly Collins, Lesley Farhangr, Jennifer Gold, Tom Jessiman and Peggy Shohade deserve special mention because, with all their other duties, they also helped with particular pieces of research for this book.

I am also particularly grateful to Joe Ashton, David Butler, George Jones, Phillip Norton and Philip Williams for reading through the draft and helping to avoid those perversities I was not determined to plunge into. Naturally, they all wish to be disassociated from the result. Les Gibbard has brightened the book just as much as he brightens the *Guardian*. But then he is the best cartoonist in Britain. My friend and astrologer Joe Cooper helped me with the Zodiac. Adrian Barker, Micky Chittenden and Anne Holgeth organised the whole thing while Adrian did much of the detailed research. Caroline Elliston typed the 238 drafts before literacy dawned. Lastly, one person who can't be thanked enough: Sharon Goulds picked the MPs, interviewed them and did most of the real work.

Austin Mitchell
Grimsby
February 1982

PARLIAMENT
EMPIRE

1 Meet the People Tour

Between Parliament Square's traffic jams and the turgid Thames sits one of Britain's best-known tourist attractions. It occupies a prime eight-acre site which, in more enlightened times, would be dedicated to cheapjack offices or industrial dereliction. Even a mud-coloured patina matching the river cannot obscure the beauty of the finest Gothic revival building in the land. Earth has a great deal to show more fair, most of it less conveniently situated. So three quarters of a million hob-gobs tramp dutifully through every year. Their itinerary is like *rigor mortis*: once started, no going back.

'C'est un rêve en pierre,' said Tsar Nicholas I; 'a fairy palace, a marvel of the thousand and one nights,' said a French contemporary; Lord Clark of *Civilisation* called it 'a triumph of the Picturesque': all roughly what was intended by the architect, Barry, and Pugin the designer. They set out to create a Palace of the Arts and with 1,180 rooms, 126 staircases, two miles of corridor, eleven courtyards, their palace has everything to delight the eye: grandiloquent decorative ceilings, tasteless paintings; superb wood and stonework; magnificent views of a dilapidated hospital on the other side of the river. Like its occupants, the palace looks older than its years. Visitors fondly imagine that the great scenes of British history took place there. Before 1850 they didn't. They'd have had far more majestic stage settings if they had.

This magnificence has had to be put to uses never intended. Designed as a show-piece of empire and a home for an aristocratic debating society, it is now a legislative factory. Complaints began as soon as the Commons moved in: ventilation asphyxiated, speakers could not be heard, offices were 'a sort of cupboard', the upstairs committee rooms were inaccessible, the dining-rooms hopelessly overcrowded, and Members who wanted to bring secretaries were told by Sir James Elphinstone that 'he would just as soon think of keeping a pipe in the House. What was required . . . was to recur to the custom of our forefathers and have some place where they could keep a grid-iron and eat a good beefsteak and drink half a pint of good port wine.'

Such was the immediate grumbling. Now it is worse. Some 4,500 people work in a palace intended for a quarter of that number. The 1,151 members of the Lords maintain tradition in being apathetic attenders: on average, 292 peers pop in each day to collect their £46 for passing 'go'. The rest are more assiduous, for this is an employment growth point and an edifice which cost only £2,166,846 (three times the original estimate) now pays out nearly twenty times that sum in wages. So 400 secretaries are crowded into every available space, including windowless basements which would be closed if any passing Shops and Offices inspector were allowed in. Some 181 researchers are herded into Portacabin toppings added to the original buildings at any point where neither the public gaze nor IRA firebombs can fall. Nearly 300 attend to needs for food and drink (which is 3,500 meals a day). 1,186 run the place, 124 keep it semi-pristine, or stop it falling down, sixty-nine record the debates, 129 fuel them with library facts, and over three hundred work in the press gallery passing those facts on to the nation – after mutilation in the Chamber. Everywhere there is a sense of inadequacy, harassment, an institution under strain; majestic shell, sordid reality.

> If one all-purpose image could sum up the present state of British politics, it would be that of a packed division lobby at three or four in the morning in late July. The bell has stopped ringing, the doors at the end of the lobby have been unlocked, and a strange race of troglodytes has started to stumble through – red-eyed, whey-faced, grubby with stale sweat and disappointed hopes. They were kept up until the small hours today and the odds are that they will be kept up until the small hours again tomorrow: by now, few of them know what they are voting for and fewer still care. . . They are there because they're there because they're there – the poor bloody infantry of the democratic process, waist-deep in the parliamentary equivalent of Flanders mud.[1]

Not quite what Pugin and Barry intended. Like a stately home used for slum rehousing, their shrine to democracy has fallen on hard times. The pressure of numbers and the growth of business turn a palace into a factory, the kind of plant all too common in British industry: a legislative slum. The residents of the North Wing, 635 Members of Parliament, would angrily reject that description. They might see themselves as a tourist attraction, for the Gothic pile also features some of the best views of Michael Foot and of the North

[1] David Marquand, 'Farewell to Westminster', *New Statesman*, 7 January 1977.

Face of Cyril Smith. They would almost certainly see themselves as members of the best club in London, or part of London's rich tapestry of tradition, woof or warp. They might even point out that they are Britain's political elite, the pool of talent from which this government, and the next, will be selected. But slum dwellers?

Yet nevertheless, the club is run down and tatty, the ceremonial meaningless, the elite sub-standard. The Commons people do not see all this, partly because their noses are so close to the grindstone, partly because their lot is in fact better than it was. Like residents of an old house showered with improvement grants, they have spent money eagerly but not altogether wisely.

Payment for Members began before the First World War, a generous £400 per annum reaching a more mediocre £1,000 in 1945. By 1965 their pay went up to a dizzying £3,000 and in the 1970s the real key to progress was discovered: independent recommendations from the Boyle Committee on Higher Salaries, so as to take salary decisions away from the timidities of governments and the inhibitions of Members. This new system started well: £8,000 per annum was recommended. Incomes policy interposed itself. The Wilson Government provided only £6,000 and pensions geared to a notional £8,000. The real breakthrough was delayed to 1979 and another Boyle recommendation of £12,000 implemented in three stages, bringing the salary to £14,510, now plus a tax-free £4,100 for living in London, free travel to the constituency, free phones, free postage, all a better deal than ever before but still nothing like enough. Too little too late is part of British tradition. Increases bring maximum public embarrassment and minimal effect before they are eclipsed by inflation. The Civil Service grade to which parliamentary salaries were to be pegged in 1975, Assistant Secretary, now gets £23,288, well over the parliamentary rate.

MPs still aren't paid well enough to provide the backing they need to do the job properly. Nor do they get enough to discourage moonlighting, supplementing their incomes, diverting attention from the real job. They also lag well behind their counterparts overseas. Parliamentarians, or, in American sub-journalese, Solons, have been steadily improving their position all over the world. More professional, more effective, and more conscious of their needs and responsibilities than their British counterparts, they have become almost a 'new class', perhaps a ruling class. This advance has been characterised by a steady improvement in both pay and privileges, and an increasing emphasis on comparabilities reinforced by the building of links through the Solons and related trades unions, the International Parliamentary Union and the Commonwealth Parliamentary Association. In this worldwide development British MPs are the poor relations.

The legislative elite overseas developed first in the developing countries. Emerging elites who had led the struggle against colonialism took over both power and its trappings as the colonial rulers pulled out. Politics is power and wealth its reward. Today's Member of Parliament could be tomorrow's corpse, but great risks often go with great rewards and the politicians in developing nations were eligible for both. In developed countries, the rise has been slower, less spectacular, but more sure. As government has grown in importance, so have the pay and privileges of the governors. Solons are everywhere a new class, exercising the power of the people on behalf of the people, and rewarding themselves well for doing so. US Senators and Congressmen get £34,370 in salaries, and staff finance of £200,000 a year for Representatives and up to half a million pounds and more for Senators, depending on state population. They also get travel allowances bigger than a British MP's salary. Politics there is a glamour profession, featuring increasingly in films, even in *Playboy*. It is increasingly possible for politicians to become national celebrities in a way only Tony Benn has achieved here. European and Commonwealth countries tread the same path, more discreetly but only a few paces behind.

Parliamentary Pay and Allowances (1982)

	W. Germany	France	Australia	Canada
Pay	£21,139	£29,321	£19,230	£21,848
Allowances*	£12,684	£31,536	£7,339	£50,843

(* France and Canada include staff.)

These figures conceal much better pension provisions than are available in Britain, far more help with staff, better library and research facilities. Where we have three research specialists per hundred members, Canada has twelve, Australia sixteen, America ninety-four. The pay comparison also ignores much better accommodation, even better perks such as the free air travel for wives which Australian and New Zealand Parliaments provide, free telephones at home, free world travel on national airlines or, in Canada and France, by military transport, tax-free salaries amounting to a third of the total in Germany, accommodation, housing grants, even fifty official cars in Paris. None of this comes to British MPs. They are so much loved that there would be a huge outcry if it did.

As with so many aspects of British life, we have suffered from the amateur tradition. Paying peanuts got us not monkeys but gentlemen with little incentive to be really professional about what they were doing. British workers toil longer hours for less money. So do British MPs. Legislative output and hours have grown steadily, so more time is spent passing more laws for less money per law, per committee sitting or per page of the outpourings.

Parliamentary Averages 1969–74

	UK	Australia	Canada	France	Germany	USA
Average days sat per year	167	68	171	149	62	164
Average hours worked per year	1,528	720	942	510	313	766

Worse, Britain has fewer legislators per capita to tackle the growing workload which a complex modern democracy generates. More sensible nations have federal systems with central and state legislatures, and elected bicameral chambers. There are 8,066 elected legislators in the United States, or one for 29,000 people. In West Germany, with its ten Lander, there are 1,926, or one for 33,000 people; 987 in Australia with its six states – far more legislators per capita. Sweden, Israel, New Zealand and Eire, all far smaller unitary states, combine smaller and more manageable chambers with fewer electors per member than is the case here, where one MP represents an average of 88,000 people (67,000 electors), compared to 9,700 in Sweden or 20,000 in New Zealand. Thus British MPs get less money for more work and greater responsibility than in any comparable system.

We are a low wage country offering low pay for low skills so British MPs, priding themselves on their amateurism, and content to tramp through lobbies as brute votes, are merely conforming to a national trend. Britain is an elitist society with marked class differences. Its MPs are an elite with a prestigious job but its rewards are mundane because British politicians have singly failed to promote themselves up the internal hierarchy of their own society. They have demonstrated their own impotence by failing to defend their legitimate interests. In doing so they have flunked the only test of group competence in a competitive free market: improving their own lot and enabling themselves to do their own job properly.

Unfortunately they have also failed to gratify the electorate's self-interest. As politicians and governments they have not delivered the economic growth and well-being which all modern electorates expect, most have had, and a few are still getting. These failures have combined to produce a decline in their public standing which has few parallels overseas. Now that national pride has been transformed into a galloping national inferiority complex, the British discount everything about their own country. They have always assumed themselves bad at industry, lazy and strike prone, yet they have also been proud of their political institutions and indeed have tried to foist them on a reluctant world with much the same success as the heart transplant industry. Now awe and respect have given way to public hostility, indifference, almost contempt. Surveys indicate that people think politicians do not listen to them. Asking who MPs are 'out for', Gallup found 46 per cent saying 'themselves', 24 per cent 'their party', and only 19 per cent 'the country'. On honesty, MPs had a negative rating of −9 per cent compared to doctors who got an enormous plus rating of +72 per cent, police +52 per cent, university teachers, lawyers, engineers and even psychiatrists, all of whom got substantial plus ratings for honesty. 'Most MPs are sincere and want to serve the community,' said Market and Opinion Research International; 60 per cent promptly disagreed. 'Too much time in Parliament is wasted in slanging matches,' said National Opinion Polls; 76 per cent agreed. A similar explosion of natural affection occurs regularly on each parliamentary salary increase.

The concept of Member of Parliament generates a distant awe: Grimsby has plaques unveiled by a 'Rt Hon. Austin Mitchell MP' who is rarely right, only intermittently honourable and never on the Privy Council, which confers the title. Yet the workforce who do the actual job is neither respected nor liked, particularly in their role of politician. MPs are trapped in a vicious circle: unable to improve pay and conditions further because of the widespread dissatisfaction with the way they perform their job, yet unable to do that job any better because of their inadequate pay and conditions. Income, when politically determined, measures esteem as well as status. On either measure, Britain's MPs come low down.

The Commons people typify Britain's genteel decline. That decline has been obscured by our national pride, even pretension, which allowed Britons to withdraw into an increasingly unprovable assumption of superiority. The same is true of Parliament. Assumptions of superiority, vanishing in other fields, linger on in pretentious gobbledygook about 'mother of parliaments', 'great forum of the nation', 'bastion of our liberties' and in attachments to constitutional myths, as if we were still living in the great days of the eighteenth and nineteenth centuries which engendered them.

Parliament makes many claims but lives up to few. In theory, it is supreme: parliamentary sovereignty means that it can do anything except change a man to a woman, as the coy joke goes. In fact, society is less governable. Some laws can be passed until Parliament is blue, or red, in the face, but they will not be obeyed. In theory, MPs represent the community: in fact they are hardly a cross-section. The party which wins a majority loses popular support within months of coming in, the electoral system itself does not give an accurate representation of opinion, while organised opinion speaks through pressure groups or corporate organisations, and dynamic opinion speaks through polls, not the House. In theory, Parliament controls the Executive. In fact the Executive controls it, through the party majority. In theory, Parliament controls expenditure. In fact the sums are so massive it has no prospect of doing so. It merely grants money as demanded by government and quibbles about those sums which approximate more nearly to the range of its understanding: small. In theory, Parliament provides the stage for a great debate between government and opposition. In practice, few listen and many of those who do dislike Tweedledum–Tweedledee bickering which is all they hear.

Layers of pretension peel away. Most roles claimed for MPs are outdated or unrealistic and the public has little idea what Parliament does. A 1973 NOP survey showed 77 per cent confessing to knowing 'nothing' or 'not very much' about it, only 22 per cent guessing anywhere near the actual number of MPs, half knowing who their own MP was, and 17 per cent defining the guillotine as a penalty imposed on MPs for persistent failure to attend and mercifully last used in 1873. Asked about specific functions, they got them wrong. Some 60 per cent believed Parliament appoints the Cabinet. The Prime Minister does, and Parliament doesn't even appoint him. Over half thought it chose the date of the election. The Prime Minister does. They assumed Parliament makes the law. It merely ratifies the package deals cooked up by Cabinet and the Civil Service. The public assumes Parliament's functions are as they were in the nineteenth century. Reality has been kept from them.

Parliament can therefore be taken as a paradigm for Britain, the Commons people for the British people. Both lag behind the world; neither has a clear idea why or what to do about it. Britain is a nation in comparative, currently absolute, decline. Its Parliament is the not particularly efficient legislature of that not very important nation run on the cheap by harassed legislators who think they are doing something different from what they really are. People and parliamentarians both comfort themselves in their decline with the myths of the past.

It is easy to say what MPs do not do, far more difficult to say what they really do, or to describe what an institution we take for granted is really about. We think we know it because it is there. We excuse our ignorance by saying that Parliament is 'in transition'. It always is. Yet what is it changing from and to? The situation can only be understood by looking at the men and women whose whims and foibles, activity or indolence, give it life: the Commons people.

Their own perception is limited. They can more easily describe their situation in individual terms than give an overall picture. Their perspectives are distorted by a nose-to-grindstone view. It is even difficult for them to be absolutely clear about what they are doing, because to be a Member of Parliament is to have a choice among a Job Centre's worth of jobs, all to be performed under the roof of a beautifully laid out parliamentary enterprise zone where anything goes. The workforce is given minimal provision and set free to do what it chooses. A modern MP has to be legislator, lawyer, particularly the barrack-room variety, advocate for a cause, party man, organisation man, committee man, researcher, social worker, local ombudsman, constituency advocate, interpreter of government, orator and thinker, showbiz personality, father confessor, pressure groupie, lobbyist and lobbied, critic and defender, adult education lecturer, media man and demagogue. He cannot hope to do them all, so he just does what he wants, a few, several, or none, and how he wants to do them: superbly, well, badly or indifferently. He is the last surviving gentleman of independent means, free to fill his time as he pleases and paid £14,510 a year for it. Thus the nature of his job puts him out of joint with the times. In a specialised and sophisticated system of government, he is the jobbing labourer. In a collective and hierarchical system, he is the individualist. In a complex machine, he is the last crudity, as if a gang of navvies had been set to work in a computer centre.

Our political and governmental system has to be seen through their eyes, because they work it. They create, accept or reinforce its faults, and some of its strengths. They generate pressures for change through their discontents and frustrations. The political scientist's bright ideas can be another day a week for the backbencher. The lawyer's improved scrutiny means less time spent in constituency nursing. The accountant's improved control of public spending means less chance of keeping the local party sweet. An expanding role for Parliament is less time for family, mistress, the people who put and keep him there, or all three. To write about Parliament as an institution, and to leave out the views and the activities of those who man it, is not only Hamlet without the Prince of Denmark, it also leaves out Gertrude, Ophelia, Polonious, Horatio, Rozencrantz, Guildenstern and Step-Daddy too. In the last analysis, Parliament is a collection of human beings, harassed or underworked, underpaid or over-privileged, incompetent or devoted. Collectively, they constitute the Commons people, the living, breathing, sweating or skiving reality behind the abstractions. They make it work or fail. They give it its collective characteristics and its inhibitions. Parliament is 633 characters in search of a function. Mr Speaker already has one; Owen Carron doesn't want one.

BALLOT
VOTE ME
VOTE ME
EVENT No 1
POLL VAULT

2 Getting There

Top jobs become more challenging with every step up the ladder but Parliament is front-end loaded: getting the job is more difficult than doing it. There are 635 seats to fill. Last time, in 1979, 2,576 candidates stood for them, 324 more than the previous record, and a much greater number had stood for selection. Getting into Parliament is a lottery rather than a career choice, and not for the scrupulous or squeamish; a question of survival, a reward for sheer brass nerve, thick-skinned perseverance, or simply good luck.

Many people contemplate it to promote a cause or an ego, because it looks like glamour for those too dull for television, or for such misguided motives as a desire to run the country or help humanity. Most such desires pass with other childish dreams. Even among the more stubborn, the practical problems can be too intimidating. Few can honestly say they had the chance and turned it down, but many still assert it. Barbara Cartland, romantic fiction writer, said:

> I was keen on politics and after my brother died I was offered two safe political seats. But I had a husband and children. What you have to remember is no English husband will dine alone, they hate it. So they go off with a go-go dancer. And children need you, especially at night when they are going to bed, saying their prayers. Parliament is from three in the afternoon to goodness knows what hour. So when people ask me, 'What's the most famous and successful thing you've done?' I tell them, 'Being a wife and mother.'[1]

The motives of those who actually make the attempt are difficult to sum up. Some say they have politics in the blood. With Richard Body it seems almost like an hereditary taint:

> I've always been interested in politics ever since my school days . . . and some people say it must be in my blood and indeed it is. Forebears of mine have been in politics . . . from Simon de Montfort's time. . . One

[1] *Cosmopolitan*, July 1981. Ms Cartland added, 'It's so much easier to get power from the pillow.'

> or two were executed and others got hanged for it, but it didn't deter me. . . It's a congenial life, one that's always fascinated me. I love politics and political ideas, and I suppose if you have that love it's a very natural outlet for it.

The real transmission mechanism is that political involvement is fostered by the home background which means that inevitably there is a proportion, small but always there, of hereditary politicians. One such was David Marquand, who sat for Ashfield from 1966 until he deserted to go to the EEC in 1977.

> My father was a Labour MP and indeed a minister in the Attlee Government after the war, and I'd always been fascinated by politics . . . I was thrilled and excited by the '45 election and I think I always had at the back of my mind the idea that one day I would want to go into politics. . . I was working as a journalist on the *Guardian*, I became very moved by Gaitskell's whole stand in the Labour Party. It seemed to me he was trying to turn the Labour Party into the sort of party that I believed it ought to be. I felt that sitting writing editorials in the corridor of the old *Guardian* building in Manchester was rather too lazy a way of expressing one's views and one really ought to be a bit more committed and a bit more active.

Ambition plays a large part. Julian Critchley, Tory MP for Aldershot, once burned with ambition's clear bright flame. Which probably meant that he had to conceal it. Now, long years after his first election in 1959, he can admit it:

> It's a mixture of vanity and ambition, and it's not for me to say the proportion between those two, but, ambition, after all is the engine of the public good . . . so I'm not ashamed of having ambition . . . vanity? It's nice to have a platform and appear to be important. I think in the first place every MP who gets here for the first time sees himself on the front bench and as a minister, and perhaps in the Cabinet.

Trying to get in puts some off. For most, the process of trying to get in reinforces the desire to get there. Once on the rails it may be difficult to detour. That was John Ellis's experience. It took him from Easthampstead Rural District Council to Westminster, first as MP for Bristol NW from 1966 to 1970, then for Scunthorpe from 1974 to his second defeat in 1979:

> Well, I think you get mixed up with politics. I lived in a little village. There were various things wrong and I remember somebody said, 'Why don't you stand for the local council?' . . . and it was downhill all the way from there.

Accident can also play a part. Bob Litherland, a councillor in Manchester, had greatness thrust upon him when he came in for Labour in 1979:

> It really came out of the blue with the elevation of Harold Lever to the House of Lords. There was a vacancy in Manchester Central and a number of people approached me to throw my hat in the ring. Up to that point I was quite happy in local government so it really was people asking me to be an MP, rather than wanting to be an MP as a career. I think the thing that prompted me most was a comment my son made: 'If you don't go down now you may rue it for the rest of your life.'

There is even a sense of *noblesse oblige*. Alan Clark, Conservative MP for Sutton, Plymouth, and son of Lord Clark of *Civilisation*, certainly felt this when he came into politics in 1974.

> Kennedy said, 'From those to whom most is given much is expected,' and rich people can justify themselves by making more money . . . but I think you have a duty to try to take part in the guidance of the country that you belong to. . . So many members of the ruling classes have abdicated this. All they want to do is get in the gossip columns.

Finally, some are just naive. They think politics is the way of getting things done, as Chris Chataway did when in 1959 he set out on a political career which ended in some disillusionment in 1974:

> It was within about a year of leaving university that I decided that politics was what I'd like to get into . . . I really felt it was a good way of helping humanity . . . in a most unfocussed way I thought that I would make life better in all sorts of directions.

When Members were asked in our questionnaire at what age they decided to try to get into Parliament, 7 per cent, mainly Tories, said before sixteen. It was a matter of destiny. A further 6 per cent decided before twenty, and 36 per cent more had decided before thirty. After this, when accidental factors presumably became more important, another 36 per cent decided before forty, and the rest after that, rather like some mid-life crisis. Labour men, always more humble, were more prone to decide later: 59 per cent in their thirties or older, against 44 per cent of Tories. Lord Chesterfield said no man enters the Commons without secretly believing he will end as Prime Minister. True of some. George Cunningham was Labour MP for Islington South from 1970, and, since he left the Labour Party in 1981, became first the George Cunningham Party MP, then SDP. He set out on a hunt for the source of power:

> If you itch you've got to scratch and most of the Members that are in the House have had that desire to be here for a long time. For many years I was involved in government as a civil servant and I think it's natural that if you are inclined towards government you should also turn your mind to be involved in the political side of government. . . It is a natural thing for people to want to be involved in the big decisions that are being taken in respect of the country. The odd thing would be if people didn't want to do that.

For those bitten by the bug there are two routes. The realistic take the party path. Labour and Conservatives have had a stranglehold and those who eschew these labels take a much more difficult option: since the war 104 Liberals have been elected, twenty-one Scottish Nationalists and thirty Ulster Unionists, of the various varieties emerging since they ceased to be Tories with funny accents. There have been a few mavericks like Sir D. Robertson, Dick Taverne, Frank Maguire, Gerry Fitt, a few odds and some sods, two Communists, and a small number of others. The numbers indicate the problem: minority groups have a hard time breaking in just as other deviants have a hard time getting on, which is why the pioneer Social Democrats have wisely chosen the back door. By-elections are becoming easier for minority parties, so unenthusiastic are electorates about the major parties; but general elections have always been hard, and will remain so with the present electoral system. Liberals like Cyril Smith or Richard Wainwright have to put an enormous personal effort in to getting into the House and then must work harder at staying there, because the electoral fate of third parties is more unpredictable and they are more dependent on their own individual efforts: a dozen one-man-bands each trying to look like an orchestra, or at the very least a pop group.

Aspirants should set out young. Politics is a middle-aged profession: only 8 per cent of the MPs filling in our questionnaire got in before thirty, a quarter between thirty and thirty-four, another quarter before forty and a further fifth before forty-five. Most MPs since the war have been elected in their thirties or forties. Yet the trend is towards younger candidates. The average age of new Conservative MPs, ranging between forty-one and forty-two in the 1940s and 1950s, was thirty-nine in February 1974, thirty-seven in October 1974 and thirty-nine in 1979. For Labour, whose MPs averaged six years older two decades ago, the rejuvenation came in 1966, 1970 and October 1974. Then the average age on entry dropped to forty, forty again in February 1974 and thirty-eight in October 1974. In 1979 it was up to forty-three.

It is a man's world. A woman's chances of election in 1979 were one in ten, against one in three for men. In 1979 the number of women candidates at 208 was a record, twice the 1970 figure. Yet women have never been more than 5 per cent of the Commons and since 1918 only 107 have sat there. In 1979 only 4 per cent of Conservative candidates were women, against 8 per cent of Labour's. Conservative women seem to think that their place is the home, not the House. So when the Tories win the proportion of elected women falls. At twenty-one MPs, 3 per cent of the total, it is now the lowest since 1951 and lower than the 13 per cent of women life peers in an upper chamber, of which Gladstone once claimed that if peeresses were admitted 'the majority of peers would die of shock and the peeresses would die of boredom'.

Britain's proportion of women Members is one of the lowest in the world. The USA manages 1 per cent more, Eire 2 per cent more, while 8 per cent of Germany's MPs are women, 24 per cent in Denmark and 28 per cent in Sweden. The national accident of a woman Prime Minister conceals a reality in which women are severely disadvantaged. Lamenting this is fashionable. Yet few of those who join the chorus have any clear idea of how to improve the situation and hardly any of the MPs who parade their liberal sympathies by joining it would be happy with the ultimate consequence of change: the elimination of half the male MPs. Women face a basic dilemma: work through a party and accept its aims, objectives and condescension, or stand as women *per se*, and lose. Proportional representation is also urged as a solution. It would improve matters if a party list system of proportional representation shifted the basis of candidate selection from local to national levels, obliging the parties to make themselves as respectable, and their lists as representative, as possible. Yet even then the extent of change depends on social attitudes and there is no reason to assume that the improvement would be any more than marginal initially.

The basic problem is not that the Commons and its lifestyle are tough on married women with children. It is not that women do not come forward: talented women do try for selection, though of the 600 people on Labour's B List only fifty are women, with the same proportion on the Tory central list. It is not that the electorate is prejudiced against women candidates. Opinion polls, studies of by-elections, and Michael Steed's direct comparison of seats where women were brought in or dropped out at one of the 1974 elections, all show that the sex of the candidate makes little difference. The basic problem is that *selectors* are not enthusiastic about women candidates. They believe the electorate does not want them. They do not see women as having the same commitment as men. They do not know how to categorise them in the same easy way they can men. They fear that women might be unpredictable, and one thing selectors like is predictability. In short, they apply different standards. Angela Hooper, chief woman executive of the Conservative Party, admits:

> I have yet to hear from a selection committee, 'We rejected her because she didn't answer the political questions' – but often I hear, 'Oh, it was a pity she was wearing high heels – she was absolutely superb but you just couldn't imagine her at a dock gate in those.' And it's often the women themselves who do it.[1]

A view which Lynda Chalker endorses from her own experience in winning selection in the Conservative Party, always less inclined to select women:

> Women on selection committees, because they can't envisage so organising their lives that they could cope with a job as an MP, automatically assume that no woman can do it. . . When Wallasey came up I was going into that interview for the experience . . . when I got selected, I don't think anybody was more surprised than the Selection Committee because they started out firmly believing that they didn't want a woman . . . but I think now they're quite glad. I hope so.

Central organisations attempt to moderate these prejudices. Their influence is slight, though occasionally it helps women get on to short lists so they have a ticket in the lottery of selection. Jo Richardson, after years of working as Ian Mikardo's secretary, knew the political game and the Labour Party backwards. Yet when she tried for selection in Barking before the February 1974 election, she felt she won it almost by accident, creeping in from behind:

> It wasn't in many respects difficult to get on the short list because the party was always encouraging: 'Please put a woman on the short list. You don't have to select her but put her on anyway.' So I got on the short list . . . and I was doubly delighted when actually I got it by one vote on the fifth ballot.

[1] *Honey*, September 1981.

Even after selection, a woman's difficulties are not over. Sheila Faith, Conservative MP for Belper, warns:

> The association may react against their decisions and wonder if a woman will have the stamina to fight a long and arduous campaign. Grooming and clothes are under constant scrutiny. When my husband attended several functions my constituency association wondered if I was unable to manage without him, and when, later, he was too busy and appeared less frequently, they wondered if the marriage was breaking up.

More usually, the persistent pressure which is building up gets women nominated for unwinnable seats. In 1979 women were selected for under 2 per cent of safe seats; four women stood down from safe seats and were replaced by men, but they did better in getting selected elsewhere. The result is that women stand the best chance when the unexpected happens, at by-elections or in surprise general election results like 1945 and 1970, when parties win seats they never expected and bring in women as a consequence – involuntarily.

The proportion of women is likely to rise only slowly. Most of those who get there will be older and either single or childless or child-rid. Even in the House itself women may have some disadvantage. Most will detail their search for toilets which are all ambiguously labelled 'Members Only'. If they enter the male toilets they may find the extent to which they are being discriminated against, for Joe Ashton, Labour MP for Bassetlaw, points out the advantages occurring from pointing at a certain shape of porcelain:

> Women find it difficult to get to know what's going on in Parliament because most of the wheeling and dealing is done shoulder to shoulder in the men's urinal . . . which is why Mrs Thatcher will never make a good Prime Minister.

Yet female MPs may have certain compensatory advantages. Helen Hayman got enormous publicity for her efforts to breast feed her baby Benjamin, the most popular parliamentary spectator sport since Charles Bradlaugh's attempts to sit as Member for Northampton without taking the oath. Mr Speaker Selwyn Lloyd ignored Bernadette Devlin's efforts to relandscape Reginald Maudling's face. He later let her get away with unparliamentary behaviour when eight months pregnant on the grounds that he was not sure whether he would need the Sergeant at Arms or an obstetrician to stop her. The minimal regiment of women in the House also have an enormous gimmick value and, once in the Commons, women advance more rapidly than men because of reverse discrimination. Every front bench has to have its ornaments, a token woman or alternatively Norman St John Stevas.

Unfortunately those women who do get elected do not appear to work together with any great effect or even to get on particularly well together. Maureen Colquhoun says they would get together in the ladies room to nominate a 'Prick of the Week' and plot against the 'Maleocracy'. In neither capacity have they been particularly effective.

Women as a group outside remain the great unrepresented. Advance will not come easily. Women will be filtered into the Commons piece by piece, if they'll forgive the expression. They will receive hypocritical sympathy from male graduate MPs who are themselves the biggest beneficiaries of unrepresentative politics, and from a Labour left which is essentially chauvinist and secretly believes a woman's place is on her back, but likes to make the right noises. Yet the main litany of complaint is still that there should be more women MPs, that they are condescended to and asked to make tea, not policy. This is not the stuff of which great movements or strong pressures are made.

Until they unite and organise, swamp constituencies with women nominees and infiltrate, as the loony left, trade unions, even the Catholics, Freemasons and Jews have all done, the women's campaign will remain a whinging whining clique which does not even represent those they claim to speak for. Politics responds to power and pressure, not nagging. The women's movement is therefore caught up in a not very vicious circle. Until the movement really represents the mass of ordinary working women and housewives, and until that mass is better motivated and feels a real concern at its situation, the movement's effectiveness will be slight and women will remain the great unrepresented. Nothing comes as of right.

As well as being young and male, aspirants should be Anglo-Saxon. Jews were reputed to find difficulty, particularly in the Conservative Party. Yet at two score MPs they are a higher proportion than in the electorate and there are now a dozen on the Tory benches. However, non-white candidates find it almost impossible. Three non-white Members have been elected: a Liberal in the 1890s, a Tory in the 1900s, and the last – Shapurji Saklatvala for Battersea North in the 1920s – but none since, though non-white electors are 3 per cent of the population and on that basis should have twenty seats. If they are allowed to fight constituencies, which they usually are not, the indicators so far are that they suffer electorally. The only one who has come anywhere near a winnable seat, David Pitt (who contested Hampstead in 1959 and Clapham in 1970 for Labour), did suffer some loss of support and in fact was brought into Parliament as Lord Pitt of Hampstead. Their day will come and soon, even if through tokenism, but both parties will approach it gingerly and with a terrified dragging of feet. It may even be that the Tories, who can manage these things better, will get there first, in which case they will have done better for the non-white population than they ever have for the entire working class.

Politicians like to see themselves as courageous leaders and takers of brave stands. In fact politics is an exercise in group conformity. Politicians like – and need – to be loved. The inoffensive find it easier to get selected and the best candidate is normal and conformist, so as not to induce unease: it is easier to repel votes than to attract. This usually means wife, children, and preferably a dog (useful in election photographs), outward sexual normality and avoidance of scandal. Though, as Julian Critchley points out, with some constituencies it can be a matter of 'do as I say, not as I do':

> One friend of mine who'd been divorced went to a constituency . . . and the chairman said 'I see from your notes that you've been divorced. . . No good to us, you know. We can't possibly have you if you've been divorced.' So my friend left, rather depressed. But the joke is that within a week of that actually happening, that particular chairman left home with his *au pair* girl.

A bachelor is acceptable if he is young, particularly in the Conservative Party – where many of the selectorate are matrons with unmarried daughters. Even homosexuals can use this trick, since their propensities are not likely to be known in the constituency. However, bachelorhood is a wasting asset. The marriage card should be played before forty-five (Tory) or forty (Labour).

The rule for all politicians is to conform vigorously. The Labour candidate for Glasgow Hillhead started out as a massively overweight be-earringed Bennite, but by the time his 1982 by-election campaign ended he had lost two stone, the earring and a lot of surplus Bennery into the bargain. He also affected a suit. It didn't do him much good, particularly since his past included an abortive hunt for the Loch Ness monster. The first question at his press conference was whether he believed there was such a monster. Yet if the struggle to conform availed naught in this instance, it is still the road by which to travel.

Conformity also means moderate politics. A few oddities sneak through the net, usually by voicing popular prejudices: Harvey Proctor fought Putney in 1974 as an overtly racialist candidate, then was dropped from the candidates list, to be restored only when a new leader made prejudice respectable. Alan Clark had also been dropped earlier, reputedly for Powellite views, but he too was restored, selected and elected. More usually, extremists have to get in either as sleepers or as acts of ideological defiance in that small but inevitable number of Labour constituencies more determined to blazon their perversity from the masthead than to win the seat. In a general election some extremists have in the past been able to sneak in in this fashion. With a possible by-election it is far more difficult, *vide* the martyrdom of St Peter Tatchell in Bermondsey. Even getting through the selection is now no guarantee of winning the seat. Such kamikaze candidates are exposed to vicious attack by the Alliance. To even choose them in the first place is in any case more an indication of a death wish in the constituency party than an accurate assessment of electoral response. Liverpool Edge Hill and Brighton Kemptown, once Labour seats, the first lost to the Liberals in 1979, the second to the Tories in 1970, have given up hope of being Labour again with the defiant decision of their constituency Labour parties to select *Militant* candidates. So have the other *Militant* selecting seats. What could be smuggled in in days of yore and party-line voting, of the 'I'd vote for a pig if my party put one up' variety, is no longer possible with an electorate whose party loyalties are weakening visibly by the year. In any case minute numbers of extremists who do make the Commons are cleverly reduced to impotence. They find themselves talking a different language. They are discounted and ignored. The struggle of attacking a Dunlopillo mattress quickly drives them to childish gestures of defiance, drink, lovable eccentricity or all three.

Next, the search for a seat. Purchase is now difficult. However, Labour, as the more conservative and impecunious party, keeps the rotten borough system for sponsored candidates, though only unions are allowed to do the bidding. Most unions will provide financial help to constituencies which accept one of their sponsored candidates. This bribe, and the national network of union contacts on which they can rely, gives sponsored candidates a considerable advantage in selections. A total of 148 MPs are sponsored, twenty-one by the Transport and General Workers' Union, eighteen by the engineering unions, sixteen by the National Union of Mine-workers, smaller numbers by smaller unions or the Co-operative Movement. Terms vary. The NUM has made a conscientious effort to support miners and to bring in officials of the union, though they have often been clumsy about sorting out their own internal rivalries and have lost seats as a result. The engineers insist on 'workers only' and, in general, the sponsored element keeps the Labour Party more working class. Yet some manual unions recruit outsiders. The TGWU has such horny-handed sons of toil as John Silkin and Peter Shore; the National Union of Railwaymen such unlikely railwaymen as Phillip Whitehead (TV producer), Robin Cook (Workers Educational Association lecturer), Tom Dalyell (maverick) and Frank Dobson (local ombudsman office), while the increasing trend for the white-collar and public service unions to sponsor Members has also diluted the genuine working-class element in recent years.

Typically, the unions get a lot of seats for a little money. NUPE is the most generous: £3,684 to Roland Moyle's constituency, 80 per cent of his election expenses, and £100 to him personally. Most pay substantially less; usually between £400 and £1,500 a year to the constituency party, up to 80 per cent of election expenses, and nothing to the MP, but of course any help at all is manna to near-bankrupt constituency parties. Haggling about the scale of the bribe is forbidden before selections, but the knowledge that it will be forthcoming gives a sponsored candidate a substantial advantage. Once constituencies have had the money, they can become dependent because sponsorship is a cushion to failure, not a spur to activity. So sponsored seats tend to stay so, or, if they change, they switch to a new sugar-daddy, as Warrington did in 1981 when a Co-operative Party candidate was followed by the vice-president of the Association of Scientific, Technical and Managerial Staffs.

For their part, unions want to spend their money where it will give them the best return. They prefer winnable or safe seats and often get them. The proportion of sponsored MPs, currently 55 per cent, is therefore highest when Labour is defeated. It is also rising as more unions provide more sponsorships and more local Labour parties need them. In the past they got contributions from MPs – Gaitskell was giving £100 a year to South Leeds in the 1930s – but with the new breed of candidates these contributions are drying up and parties have to turn to the unions instead.

Yet neither side gets good value out of the arrangement. Labour's resources are concentrated where they are least needed, and selections are influenced by irrelevant factors. Unions pay heavily to get little in return except invitations to union leaders to dine at the House, which they like. If they forgot status and merely aimed at specific parliamentary services they could buy them much more cheaply. In the Tweedledum–Tweedledee name-calling of politics Labour is prevented from objecting to the more dangerous commercial arrangements on the Tory side because it has so many beams in its own eyes.

Conservatives have no counterpart. The contributions their MPs can make are limited. Their rotten boroughs and dynasties have gone. The Duke of Devonshire was one of the few who foresaw the Labour landslide of 1945. He did so because his son had been swept from the safe Derbyshire seat, which the family had represented for generations, by an Independent Labour candidate. This was the death of the dynasties. In 1958 Lady Iveagh commended her grandson, the young Paul Channon, hauled straight out of university to take his father's seat in Southend, which both she and her husband had held much earlier, on the grounds that it was 'good to know the stable where he was bred', but he is now the only direct inheritor. The fact that the Tory benches now have the pale progeny of the great Butler, Lennox Boyd or Hogg, and Labour's have Benn, Silkin and Foot, merely indicates that addiction to politics can be inherited. Like haemophilia.

Industry has considered countering the unions by financing and supporting politically ambitious executives. So far nothing has come of the suggestion, though individual firms are helpful with time off and will hold jobs open. The only real advantage of organised financial support from business would be to dilute the dominance of lawyers and professionals in the Conservative Party. Whether it would bring in a business point of view or the more desperately needed industrial viewpoint is more doubtful. Those with ability will want to climb the hierarchy. The less able and the more opinionated managers could be shunted into Parliament as a consolation prize and only subaltern executives would be likely to take it up, bringing all the loud-mouthed prejudices of the executive dining room, rather than the real insights of industry, to a House which has too much of that already. Managers in Britain are coming to see themselves as harried powerless individuals, a good preparation for life as an MP, but an even better breeding ground for corporate Poujadism.

One other traditional portal, election as the culmination of a career, has been closing steadily. In the past, ability gravitated to the great forum of the nation. Great agitators, Cobden, Bright,

Orator Hunt, great Labour leaders from Burns to Bevin and, in the early days of the Labour Party, a lot of older officials as well, great figures from local government, Chamberlain and Morrison, business leaders such as Mond or self-made men who used money to buy influence, such as Beaverbrook; for all of these a seat in the House was an accolade, an advantage, a goal to be striven for.

No longer. Society is more specialised, the age of entry is lower, the parties have a tighter grip on the process of selection. The few eminent outsiders, Frank Cousins, who moved in from General Secretary of the TGWU, John Davies from the Confederation of British Industry and two latter day heroes, Mad Mitch (Lt.-Col. Colin Mitchell, Conservative MP for West Aberdeenshire 1970–74), the man the *Express* picked out as the hero of Aden, and Commander Kerans, of the *Amethyst*, have all been beached whales puzzled by the House. And vice versa. The 1945 and 1950 elections brought in on a tide of new ability men such as Gaitskell and Wilson from the Civil Service, Powell and Macleod from the war. These were the last big infusions of new talent, the first for Labour, the second for the Conservatives. Today politics is more professionalised as a career in its own right. The aspiring politician has to start early and devote himself to getting in, rather than waste his time or an eager nation's by pursuing another career.

Those who can, do. Those who cannot go into politics. One MP admitted as much in a questionnaire answer: 'Parliament in general terms is manned by those (including myself) who have not made the top elsewhere.' Sentiments which anyone who has sat in the Chamber for any length of time must echo. In any case ability now has to be measured on the parliamentary ladder and in the even more indefinable field of political skills, not elsewhere, and the main way of measuring it is by self-fulfilling prophecy. The speed of climbing measures the ability to succeed.

The party ladder is the first to be climbed. This begins with local office in the branch or constituency, in unions for the Labour Party, professional and business bodies for the Conservatives. It goes on through council candidatures. Half the MPs had been councillors beforehand; Labour MPs were more likely to have had such experience than Conservatives but far more should have had it, on all sides of the House, since the preparation is invaluable.

Such apprenticeships demonstrate loyalty, reinforce it and draw the aspirant to wider attention. Parties are structures of relationships and contacts, display cases in which it is important to see and be seen, to speak and to appear to listen. Conditioned and hardened, the aspirant is then ready to set out on the selection trail, a process better organised, even planned, in the Tory Party, entirely based on individual enterprise in Labour. Success can be sudden: Don Concannon was down the pit on 4 March 1966, selected on 6 March (after getting the NUM nomination, a wise precaution in Mansfield) and in Parliament for the early shift on 31 March. Greville Janner's father stepped down in 1970 through the combined effects of ill-health and a dissolution peerage less than four weeks before the poll, when the 'Vote Janner' posters had been printed. More usually, getting selected takes years. In 1924 young George Strauss volunteered his services to the Labour Party and was sent to a seat no-one else would fight. He lost the election by twenty-nine votes. By contrast today's selections are crowd pullers and local parties stand by to repel boarders. Because of this pressure of numbers the whole process has turned into an Outward Bound course.

Both parties have central lists: Labour's A list is for the union-sponsored elite, the B list is for the handicapped who are unable to offer constituencies a useful bribe. Because this gives the B list the aspect of a set of perpetual also-rans, it is easy to get on with local party sponsorship, which is often given to pass their pushy troublemakers elsewhere. The Conservatives are more selective and periodically purge their 600-strong list. Being on it is not essential for selection but can cause difficulties afterwards. Cr. Raymond Pearson was picked by Halifax and then discovered to have been involved in an assault – as well as having some fairly hard-line political views. The local choice was not confirmed though it took quite a time to persuade the constituency to drop its man. Yet even the preferred brood, the vetted high fliers on the list itself, can include some curious choices. Huddersfield's two seats were proffered two rising young stars in 1979. One was sent to prison for drug dealing. The other was Geoffrey Dickens.

Those with less to hide and more to hope seek entry to the list: Keith Best, who was slightly surprised to win Anglesey for the Conservatives in 1979, had the same experience as other Tory aspirants with 'the list':

> It's this strange list that nobody really knows how you get on – or off. In fact you go in front of the Standing Advisory Committee which consists of some of those involved in the party outside Parliament and MPs. If they think you're a decent sort of chap and hold your knife and fork in the right way, you get on the Central Office list. From then on you are

> circularised with all the constituencies that are seeking a candidate and you tick the ones that you wish to be considered for.

Labour has no effective counterpart, much as it needs one, because no one ideological group trusts the others enough to allow them to control the blackballing process.

The Conservatives are more confident. This allows them to use local variations in selection procedures while Labour, more prone to ideological, organisational, union and even religious manipulation, and trusting each other less, keeps the rules tight. Yet both parties have the same basic system: a selection conference, speeches from up to six candidates on a short list drawn up by the local party, decision by vote. David Marquand, who was lucky as a university lecturer to be selected for the mining seat of Ashfield, where they had to take a speedy decision in 1966, still is not happy about the system which gave him the job:

> You get half a dozen people coming on a Saturday night. Each of them gives a speech of a quarter of an hour. You answer questions for another quarter of an hour. The delegates see you for a total of half an hour. Nobody would select somebody for a job of that salary, let alone anything else, on that sort of basis.

The Conservatives try to make the best of a not very good job by much more thorough prior checking. Martin Stevens won Fulham for the Conservatives in 1979 as an overweight Conservative, but not before his avoirdupois had caused him selection problems:

> The Chairman said, 'You're a bit fat and my Committee's not sure you're going to be able to manage all the stairs in bedsitter-land.' So I solemnly had to come downstairs and run up and downstairs while they watched. . . They saw about twenty-eight and a lot of us were unmarried . . . a chap there called Gordon Hemming was told that all the bachelors have got to be asked why they're bachelors, you see, nudge nudge. So when it came to me I said, 'If you're worried about me getting married, I'll make a pledge that if you adopt me as your candidate I promise not to get married before the next election.' So they all laughed.

They interview their victims more thoroughly and involve wives, a group which Labour ignores in embarrassment. Alan Clark sighs with relief:

> Plymouth were very merciful . . . they didn't ask the wives to say anything, but they did ask the wives to socialise and mix with the selectors on two occasions. In the third stage we were down to five wives

> and they had a coffee morning at which the five wives were kept in circulation very cleverly throughout the crowd and talking to the different people. People formed an assessment of them. I think that was very important. The wife's your other half, isn't she? I think it's a very good way of assessing someone, to see what sort of wife they have.

So does Julian Critchley, whose wife was actually asked to speak and managed to do better than the ritual 'My husband and I':

> Three weeks after I'd been chosen a very nice old colonel in Fleet came up to me and said, 'I bet you don't know why we chose you.' I thought, 'My God, truth at last coming out.' And he said, 'It was because of your wife. We asked each of the three wives of the three final contenders the same question and she was the only girl to stand up to answer the question. And a damn fine woman she is too.'

Labour has never tackled the problem of managing local parties for national purposes. Most overseas socialist parties give the centre a good deal of influence in choice of those who are to carry the party banner. Here head office interference is counter-productive; general secretaries haven't even been able to get themselves picked; regional organisers are now largely impotent; refusals to confirm the local choice are rare and can only be invoked if rules are broken so, if local parties choose walking disasters, or try to demonstrate their ideological virility rather than win votes, the leadership can only turn to the last resort of impotence – an attack in the Commons. Such a check is of fairly limited use. This lack of control also means that local abuses are more frequent. A bus-load of miners were paid 7/6d each by the NUM to attend the North-east Derbyshire selection and vote for Tom Swain when he defeated Morgan Phillips, then Secretary of the Labour Party. NUM delegates are still paid for attending meetings, so they usually turn up en masse, if rather erratically. Those seeking selection get particularly badly treated as a result of the local dominance. Thus the normal situation is that a plague of candidates comes out of the blue, vested interests tussle, union branches, individuals and ideological groups compete to promote or block candidates. Weeding out becomes a bitter process of mutual ball-blocking and then, because no one trusts the others to do any adequate predigestion or preparation, the final choice is made on the spot. The only surprise is that outright disasters are so few.

Aspirants bear the main burden of the inadequacies of both parties. They join a travelling circus, hawking themselves round like beauty queens from selection to selection. Instead of beauty and a bikini, they need a word processor to write endless letters and *curricula vitae*, a network of contacts worthy of a commercial traveller, plus a Huckfield-hide impervious to rejection, slights, even taste. A lot of bread has to be cast on some fairly murky waters. This demands organisation and intestinal fortitude of a rare degree. Only the ego-maniac and the pachydermatous survive.

A quarter of the MPs who responded to our questionnaire had not attended any other conference before the one at which they were first selected. Neil Kinnock was selected for Bedwellty on first try. Other first-time winners were Eric Varley, Roy Mason and Dennis Skinner, though one man's first time lucky is another's sense of grievance. Brian O'Malley, a teacher and Musicians' Union sponsored candidate (he played in a band part-time) was selected for Rotherham after the steel union had tried to treat the seat as its own by putting an older nominee in. When the selection conference deadlocked, O'Malley was rumoured to have scraped home because an indignant wife came in and fetched her husband home for his long-delayed tea. Similarly, when Hugh Gaitskell was first selected in Leeds, he was helped because the NUR treated it as a pocket borough, thus offending the constituency Labour Party. The less fortunate, a further third, had attended only one previous selection (though they may have tried for others), and a quarter two or three, leaving 7 per cent who attended four or five, and 9 per cent more than that. Neville Sandelson is perhaps the classic trier, selected for Hayes and Harlington in 1971 after a score of selections and eight unsuccessful elections. Within a few years his party was trying to drop him.

A planned strategy is impossible. Some go for every selection, and most winnable seats have over two hundred enquiries, and perhaps half that number of serious applications. Others adopt a raiding strategy of intermittent sallies, or the remote control procedure: prodding unions or other organisations to push local affiliates into action. The more rational, the less desperate, and the tyro should turn first to unwinnable seats where competition is less fierce. They can learn the trade and establish the necessary record of service. The Conservatives, with greater ability to encourage talent, or its political equivalent, go further in this direction. Hence the succession of merchant bankers and stock brokers bringing market economics to miners. Among our questionnaire respondents, a third (29 per cent of Tories, 43 per cent of Labour MPs) had been elected at first attempt, a third had lost one election, and almost the same number two or three, and the rest more – some as many as seven.

Progress beyond this point means a sensible choice of constituency. Do not try too near home: they all know you too well, and only outsiders can appear like knights in shining armour. Sheila Wright, MP for Handsworth, decided to try for a local seat. Her husband immediately wrote to the delegates telling them that if they didn't reject her it would lead to divorce. They did not. It did. On the other hand, David Marquand's experience as an outsider was much happier:

> I had the immense advantage of not being a local man in a constituency which consisted of a lot of small communities all very jealous of each other, in the sense that the one thing Sutton in Ashfield was not going to have was somebody living in Kirkby in Ashfield down the road. They'd far rather have somebody from London or Mars.

While not actually living in the seat, it is better to concentrate on your own region: 55 per cent of our MPs lived within fifteen miles of the seat for which they were first selected when they were selected.

By-elections are risky. A chance to get in but to lose next time can be a prelude to a bitter period in the wilderness, not an effortless climb to the top. Scan the lists of safe seats and the ages of their members, the 'Ghoul List'. Look at which marginals fell last time, the 'Best Bets List'. Calculate which are likely to come back aided by social change or the sexual aberrations of the Member. Then cultivate contacts. Among our MPs only 38 per cent admitted to no connection at all with their first seat, the same proportion had personal contacts, and around a tenth each had had business or trade union contacts there. The rest were either resident or had some other connection.

There are the easy accidents. In 1959, Dan Jones was telephoned in Wales and told that the Labour candidate had pulled out of Burnley. He got a noon train to reach Burnley by 7.30, without even having time to telephone his wife, and beat Joe Gormley for the nomination. In 1976, Robert Rhodes James resigned from a United Nations job and came back to England. Within months he was selected as Conservative candidate for the plum marginal of Cambridge against 250 applicants and was back in the House where he had once worked as a clerk. But do not count on such lucky accidents. Organise as if they will not happen so as to be around if they do. It is particularly dangerous to be, or to appear to be, the favourite. Having opponents listed in the press as favourites is, therefore, a useful tactic which is not intended to help them. The press does not do the selecting, it builds up antibodies, and favourites do get nobbled, particularly in the Labour Party. It becomes the central aim of every other candidate and group to stop them.

Prepare the selection ground well. On the Labour side, have a father who passed through the constituency on the Jarrow March and made friendships enduring to this day. Conservatives prefer an uncle who owns large chunks of it. Yet neither is essential. Politics is a world of casual mateyness and local contacts are quickly cultivated. Phoning councillors' wives and posing as a journalist who really wanted to talk to their husband yields huge quantities of valuable information about the state of personal hatreds in the local party. Talking to the press (editor for Tories, journalists for Labour, delivery lads for Liberals), or to local members of national organisations, yields even more about the constituency and its problems, the issues and the preoccupations. Julian Critchley swotted Aldershot fairly thoroughly when he was on the come-back trail after losing Rochester and Chatham in 1964:

> This particular friend who was very wise said, 'Go and spend a day or two days in the constituency; talk to the editor of the local newspaper and learn something about it.' So I did precisely that. And when I came to perform I knew more about the problems of Aldershot than the Selection Committee did itself . . . the Selection Committee was so pleased that instead of somebody who had come from London to tell them all about the iniquities of Mr Wilson's Government, here was actually somebody who'd taken the trouble to come down to them and learn something about them and their problems. And they were immensely flattered by that.

Britain should have a primary system of selection involving the mass of party membership. In practice, that mass is excluded, except in occasional Tory selections. At the last Sevenoaks selection, aspirants went to three successive meetings in different parts of the area. Every party member could attend and vote. But this is very exceptional. Most would-be candidates have to appeal (or not) to the selectorate, that leadership nucleus which keeps local parties going, and gets few other perks in return. They are an unrepresentative group. To be interested in politics and prepared to play a continuous part in the steady boredom of party activities is abnormal, as Julian Critchley recognises:

> A constituency Conservative Party – and this must be true of any political party – is made up of a small number of relatively unrepresentative

> people who feel so strongly about Conservatism and politics that they're prepared to give up a proportion of their free time and work at being in a political party. I think one recent study had it that less than 3 per cent of the population actually joined a political party. . . So they start off by being relatively unrepresentative in that they hold rather curious views very strongly indeed.

The balance in the Conservative Party is to the right of the parliamentary party, a gulf which has got wider since the political enthusiast, small shopkeeper, lower professional, money manipulator, small businessman elements become more important in local associations, which used to be the fief of land and the professions. There is now little *noblesse* and no *oblige*. Labour is further to the left, particularly since the steady infusion into the party of the Class of '68, the polyocracy and the yap professions (those who are paid to talk for a living, whether in the language of social work, education or the box). Yet most constituency Labour Parties are very mixed – middle-class home owners pursuing pure socialism while making themselves a fortune through home improvement or price escalation, and sitting cheek-by-jowl with the old lady contingent, which lingers on in most parties until the New Model Army drives it out by interminable discussion. The three main blocks are the articulate middle-class left, the solid ranks of councillors, union officials and their families, and the make-weight of normal Labour folk. The dominant trend is for the left to grow, the last group to drift away, encouraged by the politics not of perpetual revolution but perpetual yammer and resolutionary socialism.

The balance of prejudice is usually modified by a sense of political realism. This has traditionally been stronger in the marginal seats where every advantage has to be mobilised. Both parties are ideologically divided and these divisions become building bricks for majorities at selections: 'You need a prejudice for every one of your audience' is the Tory adage. In the less winnable seats it is possible to take a strong, even extreme, ideological line and be guaranteed both selection and electoral defeat. Elsewhere it is better to talk the party code language, to navigate between shoals and to avoid confrontation by using trigger words to which everyone can attach their own meaning and which commit you to nothing. More selections are decided by blackballing than by positive enthusiasm.

An all-purpose speech is now necessary for branches, house meetings and preliminary conferences. Conservatives tend to want to hear about the candidate and if possible be socially humiliated in the process. Labour wants to hear about his ideology, though the end result in Labour selections is to combine both approaches suitably dressed up for the prejudices of the local party. This is the first training ground for the art of the politician, so go not for a lecture but a clever manipulation of symbols, a striking of chords which will bring a predictable response. Suitable frameworks are:

LABOUR

Labour likes an ideologue: that's their image of politicians. They like being told loud and clear what you think, even if it's total rubbish:

1. Pathetic gratitude for being given the opportunity. Chance for you and them to strike a blow for socialism (preferably left undefined).

2. Emphasis on winnability of seat (or, if this is glaringly apparent, on dangers of losing it to Liberals, Social Democrats, Nationalists, any passing party).

3. Their prospects depend on your unique contribution. Panegyric on previous /present member if Labour. They will almost certainly loathe him by now, but appearances count.

4. Decline of Grimethorpe East: unemployment, factory closures, housing conditions (without indicating what everyone knows, that it's a dump, or attacking the council). All this is not the fault of locals but of national decline, callous government indifference, lack of public spending.

5. Expect nothing better from Tory Party. Attack on its attitudes, record, private wealth, friends, history, lack of parents, tendency to divorce each other.

6. Attack on EEC /nuclear weapons /media or all three.

7. Need for new thinking in the Labour Party. Your own particular policy prescriptions. These should include planning everything (except incomes) and throwing large sums of money at the aged, sick, schools and Grimethorpe East.

8. Invocation of better future for working class and Grimethorpe East. Mention socialism at this point, otherwise it will be held against you. Also emphasise Bad Old Days and importance of them never returning. On disputed issues be vague. On those few where

the party is now clearly of one view, be absolutely clear and specific. If they can misunderstand your views they will.

CONSERVATIVE

Being too clever is a crime. Be the plain man who may not understand all that much about economics but knows what is right.

1. Gratitude for being considered, knowing the wealth of talent they have had to choose between. Hope to be worthy in a world where there is all too little feeling of moral responsibility. Let fall the fact that Mary Whitehouse is your great-aunt fourteen times removed.

2. Emphasis on connections with Cheltenham Central. Vast numbers of friends there. Frequent visits when a child. Importance of encouraging everywhere the same thrift, diligence, independence of spirit and decencies of family life which have made area what it is today.

3. Gratitude for inspiring leadership of Margaret Thatcher (if she lasts that long) or A. N. Other leader and criticism of disloyalty of those not fulsome in her/his praise. Need for leadership in these uncertain times. Mention of Churchill: it may be an unpopular view but we are not afraid to lead.

4. Condescending reference to pathetic state of Labour Party combined with warning of mindless militancy in the unions, constituency parties, and possibly Central Electricity Generating Board, North Thames Gas etc. Mention 'East European-type state' (but not Poland) and make a little joke about not knowing whether Marx or the Marx Brothers is now the biggest influence on Labour.

5. Basic problem of changing national attitudes: overmanning, restrictive practices, loss of will to work, giving management the power to manage. Set private enterprise free and make all except paraplegics stand on own two feet (unlike audience). There is a case for aid to Hotel Keeping/Farming/Lace Making (insert name of industry) to see it through temporary difficulties. Real problem is enormous burden of public spending, bottomless pits of nationalised industries grasping demands of Snurple Water Authority and soaring rates.

6. Need for sacrifices, particularly by workers. Won't be easy. Years

of socialism to undo. Encourage small business – entrepreneurial spirit. With leadership and willingness to work together we can recreate British greatness and make country worthy of Conservative Party.

For both parties, questions then follow. Supporters feed their man. Opponents try to trip him up or gather ammunition. Treat even the most fatuous as a penetrating insight. The only real problems will come with:

Standard Question One Will you live in the constituency?
Answer You want to because an MP should be close to his constituents and in continuous touch. You are looking forward to it and have looked at a few possible places. It is, however, important to talk it over first with your wife. She's not a Women's Liberationist, but these days it has to be a joint decision.

Standard Question Two Where does your ultimate loyalty lie: to constituents, local party or national?
Answer It is vital that an MP keeps in close touch with his constituency. The local party is the only real way of doing that. I don't foresee any disagreements, though I know you'll want me to think for myself. If you didn't, you wouldn't be looking at someone like me in the first place. You'd want a puppet /computer terminal /mindless robot /talking dummy /cardboard cut-out. Don't push this analogy too hard. This is exactly what some do want.

Standard Question Three Hanging? Corporal Punishment? Vandalism? Abortion?
Answer Need for traditional values, old basics and discipline, particularly in other people's homes. Indication that pendulums have swung too far. Need for a new hard look at problem.

There is less chance of winning people in a rush of enthusiasm than of alienating them and creating prejudices which may count against you. Politics is the art of striking chords and veiling real meanings. The more astute observers in the audience will be looking for this skill just as they would look for the ability to fit washers in a plumber.

To have done all that is humanly possible is no guarantee of selection but can act as balm. Lose well, 'fair fight', 'hard decision', 'hope to come and help'. Never recriminate however monstrous the fiddling, the character assassination, the duplicity. The chosen candidate may after all drop dead or be discovered *in flagrante delicto* with a battalion of guardsmen. Otherwise, offer a private prayer for selectee and selectors to rot in Hell and do not hang around to embarrass people. You would not have liked the dump anyway.

It could be worse. You could have won. As a prospective party candidate this means a future of thrusting yourself into dreary local functions where you are usually an embarrassment, trying to get the local press to print your releases, keeping your name before the estate agents without actually spending money, trying to pretend that you are the MP while he's on trips abroad, stabbing him in the back while he's down at Westminster. This is the worst limbo of British politics. Career, family life, bank balances, all suffer: the unspeakable in pursuit of the unattainable. It is a necessary purgatory if an expensive one, since few parties have the decency to help candidates with travel and other expenses, and fewer candidates dare ask.

The election campaign is a sad disappointment. Arguments have been developed, ideas saved up, catchy phrases fine honed, resentments have festered. Then there is no time for any of them in a three week ordeal which tests bodies not brains. Another Outward Bound course, but as Alan Clark admits, not an intellectual one: 'You have to talk an awful lot of tripe really, and you get sick of doing that. The level at which elections are fought is a little artificial.'

The problem is essentially one of physical survival, as Martin Stevens found in his Fulham campaign in 1979:

> Turn off your brain, because you haven't any more thinking. That's been done and you just run . . . I mean literally run, because you can't hope to canvass door to door. So you do this business of doing six or seven streets at a time and you have a team of three each side of the road who go and fetch the people out. You must have a councillor with you, because what screws the whole thing is when somebody comes and says, 'Will you come and look at my back kitchen?' so you have to say, 'Councillor Tomkins is a great expert on leaking roofs. He'll come.'

Electors participate in the election campaign through television. Candidates interrupt it by knocking on doors, or trying to cajole them to ill-attended meetings. The real objective is to survive, not only physically but also without dropping any major clangers, libelling opponents, assaulting electors, suggesting that murderers be left in their cells with razor blades, or making allegations about the Liberal candidate's attitude to dogs. Survive, and appear to relish it. Compatibility with politics is under test. Maintain a high visibility. See and be seen everywhere, move about constantly, create a mood of activity and *élan*, smile and press the flesh. Increasingly, the candidate is the campaign, locally at least, because the parties are becoming less active. Full-time agents are a dying breed: the Labour Party had 300 in 1950, now seventy, while the Tories are down by half. Party membership is a third of what it was in the Labour Party, half in the Conservatives, and they do less work: in 1951, 53 per cent told Gallup they had been canvassed, in 1979 only 15 per cent; while 3 per cent of them said they had been to a meeting, 24 per cent in 1951. Only 2 per cent of votes are postal but this and the other organisational factors can be crucial in marginal seats, though only a few of them. For the rest good organisation is more an outward and visible symptom of political good health than a decisive factor.

Politics are extraneous to an election campaign. Politicians, parties and politics are under a cloud. Avoid any association. Instead, candidates must be dynamic, active, friendly, approachable and non-political, like Alan Clark:

> I fight an election at a purely personal level. That is, I try to meet as many people as I can and get around the streets and go on the doorstep as much as possible. The day of the big political meeting – the 'I say again' stuff – is over. . . But they do want to meet the MP or the candidate.

Because of the physical strain, speeches have to be prepared in advance and deep frozen to be warmed up and served. Elections are no time for thinking. The real difference is not between Labour and Conservative. The other great variable of British politics, Ins and Outs, is now far more important.

In power

1. Praise of leader: pilot who weathered the storm. Single-minded determination and statesmanlike reluctance to clutch at popularity. Difficulty of task. Scale of inherited problems. Courage of strategy.

2. Fruits now coming. Rise in standard of living (if any), fall in inflation (if any), decline of speed of increase in unemployment (if any), improvement in number of telephones, washing machines, or food mixers per capita (if any). Reduction of deaths on the roads or increase in number of nurses and policemen. All figures adjusted to

most favourable base date, possibly 1926. Increase in spending on health service /education /defence, using cash figures or real terms or percentages as appropriate.

3. Knife-edge situation. Need for continued firm leadership and warning of disasters to come if opposition elected. Divisions in opposition. Dangerous irresponsibility. Huge cost of programme (with figures).

4. Denunciation of 'glittering' promises. Fruits of victory shortly to become available in increased pensions, spending and other developments. Not promises. Guarantees.

5. Talked straight. Anything else would be insult to their intelligence and integrity. We are talking of the future of a great nation, not the sordid vote-buying of the other parties.

In opposition

1. Promise of no personalities as preface to a sustained attack on Prime Minister and Cabinet. Government out of touch with the people. Policies based on simple class prejudice.

2. Decline of Britain in the eyes of the world, allies, Nord Deutsche Rundfunk or visiting grandmother from New Zealand. Increase in the cost of living /unemployment /decline in investment /industrial production /moral standards over the last four years. Using absolute figures or percentages and different base dates as appropriate.

3. No easy answers. No promises. Answer lies in increased spending on industrial support, particularly for local industries, welfare, pensions and housing. Not buying votes but simple economic common sense.

4. Decisive choice now facing the country between further decline and stultification combined with selfish sectional policies or a determined co-operative effort 'working together' to regenerate and rebuild, providing basis for better pensions, benefits, more roads, hospitals, prisons, schools or whatever it is constituency most wants.

Liberal/SDP

Attack on Government record (as above). Attack on irresponsibility of Opposition (as above). Attack on pursuit of sectional interest and invocation of national interest; one nation; working together. Proportional representation /EEC /co-ownership /decentralisation /

regular brushing of teeth (or any three). Need to break the mould and liberate the energies of the British people. A time to dare. A time for niceness. A time for known, tested policies and people. Mention Shirley Williams and, if possible, loft insulation.

The candidate has no way of judging how well or how badly the campaign is going. He sees nothing of the national campaign which will decide his destiny. Personal reactions are unreliable: people are always nice, even perhaps particularly to fools. Canvass returns are the prejudiced reading the evasive. So candidates can only suspend judgement and keep going. After the last ballot paper has been stuffed into the last box, one speech remains.

Victory/defeat all-purpose speech

Thanks to the returning officer and his staff. They have almost certainly been sullen, unhelpful and overpaid for their intransigence. Yet you may need them again. Thanks to the police. You have to drive home, drink taken.

Thanks to Party workers/united team. Almost certainly untrue because the work has fallen on your shoulders and the party members have squabbled and sulked. Yet it's too late to do anything about it now. There's always re-selection.

If lost

The people have spoken. We must accept their verdict (ie, it's no use trying to overturn the result in a court, even Tony Benn couldn't).

If won

Offer to serve all the people. Commiserations to your opponents. They've been spreading the most slanderous lies about you which you have nobly ignored, but whatever hatreds four weeks of fighting an unseen enemy have built up, thanks for a 'clean fight' are essential. Like detergent adverts, it's all relative, but nothing creates a worse impression than a speech as magnanimous as Doug Hoyle's at the Warrington by-election declaration.

Win or lose, it has been an experience, and usually not one to be missed: four weeks of elation, excitement, compulsive activity and heightened unreality. You could have had a long LSD trip but this will make you fitter and the four weeks will stay with you forever, even though everyone else forgets. To lose is to be an entry in *The Times House of Commons*, part of history. To win is to graduate to *Dod's Companion to Ego-Maniacs in Parliament*, the authentic fatstock listing. From here on, it is all downhill.

3 The House is Not a Home

The ordeal is not quite over. Settling into the House of Commons is the most difficult part of membership, a process designed to make the new MP conform to Parliament's peculiar norms without requiring any concessions from the institution itself: like being thrown in at the deep end. Except that the pool is frigid. This necessary ordeal is worst for by-election victors coming in on their own and adjusting to a situation in which everyone else knows the ropes. It is toughest for that rare commodity, a Labour by-election victor, such as Bob Litherland, who came in for Manchester Central when Harold Lever went to the House of Lords:

> They show you your coat hanger and your little pink ribbon to hang your sword on and if you haven't used a sword for the last few months you know then you're in trouble . . . But it's this public school atmosphere that frightens you in the first instance . . . where you were born to come to the Houses of Parliament and you should know your way about once you get down here . . . When you first come down you're absolutely lost and there are different people who will show you different things like introducing you to Tony Benn . . . while you were just wondering where you were going to sleep that particular night . . . they get all their priorities wrong . . . it was absolutely the unknown. I had nowhere to live and I found this a very daunting experience . . . I borrowed the flat at Stratford of one of the wine waiters of the House of Commons . . . and apart from that I had the possibility of going to the Salvation Army Hostel . . . I phoned a lady round Cleaver Square who was asking £110 with fitted carpet, some antique furniture and central heating, and when I asked her the cost she said, '£110.' I said, 'A month?' she said, 'No, that's a week. It's exclusive.' I thought it must be exclusive at those prices . . . [I found somewhere] where the lady had sub-let the front room of her flat. She was originally a secretary for one of the MPs and they write in to the whip's office and you go to the noticeboard . . . and follow them up . . . In London if you've got somewhere to sleep that's everything . . . I normally get home very late and I don't like to disturb the lady of the house so . . . I come in and make a cup of tea, listen to

the radio, do some reading and fall asleep . . . it's a very lonely world, this bedsitter land in London.

Election winners come in in droves, a Class of '74 or '79 which retains a bond of identity through its career. By-election winners come in with far more publicity but alone. Bob McTaggart was elected for Glasgow Central after its MP fell off a bus:

> I'd visited the House of Commons before, but . . . I had no idea that one had to go through the procedure of being introduced into the House. I had two sponsors who were teaching me the steps and bowing my head before the Speaker. The whole thing was pretty awesome to me . . . The Scottish members who I met were very helpful indeed . . . They were showing me the things which I should know but you can't really take it all in. You may as well be learning about two things in the first day – where you sit and where you do your work from. I was shown round a very very beautiful building in which in the first week I got lost three times.

Tories like to pretend that the new world is already familiar to them. For some it is. Martin Stevens had had friends and gone to meetings there for years. On the other hand, Liberals are in a similar situation to by-election winners. David Penhaligon won Truro in 1974 and had to ask his way to the Commons, never having been there in his life. He arrived at 8.45 a.m. Even Richard Body, who should have been well prepared, was terrified when he first came in as a young barrister to represent Billericay in 1955:

> I can well remember the day before appearing in the Court of Criminal Appeal before Lord Goddard who was rather a terrifying Lord Chief Justice . . . and not being frightened at all . . . But coming here I was completely overawed. There's something about the House of Commons, the Chamber, the whole atmosphere, that does make it very nerve-racking for a newcomer.

Go in boldly. You can now reach the parts other visitors cannot reach. Once you have a pass. Physical geography is the first hurdle. Work location the next. Horror stories of underprivileged MPs having only lockers to work from are always useful to jerk a tear in the constituency. In fact, most Members now have a desk, a phone and something less salubrious for their secretary. In my ignorance, on first election I just took an empty desk and camped there for months until the indignant owner turned up. More properly, offices are allocated by the whips so a certain amount of patronage is involved, yet offices are not now an overwhelmingly scarce resource. Half of our MPs, usually the more senior, had a desk in the main building, usually several to a room, over a quarter in what used to be Scotland Yard in the Norman Shaw buildings, North and South, where conditions show a contrast worthy of the Brandt Report: North with its lush decor, deep carpeting and enervating atmosphere, South shabby and poverty stricken with rooms looking like the cells and interrogation rooms they must have been. All the money allocated for the renovation of both wings was spent on one, until Nicholas Fairbairn, who once gave his interests as 'making love, ends meet and other people happy', decided to do so by complaining about the lush working conditions. A further 16 per cent are behind Westminster Abbey in Abbey Yard. The remaining 3 per cent, relegated to a locker, are there for preference: their real work place is elsewhere.

You must also pick a place in the Chamber, because the Speaker likes to know where to look when he calls people. Remember two things. In picking your place you are making a statement about your politics. If you are out of line or a minor party, sit below the gangway. Sopping Wets should sit in the marshlands behind the PM: knives are easier to put in backs from there. The loyalist and the ambitious should cluster round the leadership as protection. Secondly, pick somewhere uncrowded or you will have to face humiliating 'bum wrestling' for seats as the House fills up. Tories have even been known to plonk as heavily as possible on people's knees. On the Labour side, bums reserve places and they are less likely to budge, even for ex-Prime Ministers to sit in their traditional seats on the front bench below the gangway. Yet there are also some strategic bombers there. Andrew Faulds plonks where he pleases. So do not sit next to him. You would soon go deaf in any case.

Now lose your virginity. Frank Maguire was never a maiden speaker, and others might have been better advised not to, but most get it out of the way in the first month: thirty-eight of the 102 new Members of February 1974 had taken the plunge by the end of March. An ordeal for those without public school confidence or debating society experience, the whole procedure is as formalised as a ritual circumcision. Disraeli managed three hours of elaborate metaphors, affected mannerisms and foppish dress, and ended by shouting above the laughter: 'I will sit down now but the time will come when you will hear me.' With some modern Members that would be more of a threat than a promise. Margaret Thatcher managed half an hour, but the modern record is Koni Zillicus at thirty-nine minutes. Styles vary. A few plunge straight into controversy like Nicholas Fairbairn, not the best of precedents. Stuart Holland began with a joke, 'Accustomed as I am to public speaking,' and went downhill from there. Michael Morris managed a boring history of Northampton, a town already boring enough. The Earl of Ancram had a homily on livestock prices. Yet most conform to a pattern: ten minutes, beginning with a few nice words about the previous Member, often the most difficult part, a description of the constituency, an indication of the Member's own (parliamentary) obsessions, and concluding with a passing reference to the subject in hand. The next speaker then produces a ritual encomium, however little deserved, and the ordeal is over. For the House as well as the novice. Next time he can be interrupted, shouted down, slept through and generally treated like an ordinary Member.

After this, the new MP can now ignore the Chamber for a time or for ever if he is that way inclined. It is the biggest time-waster for backbenchers. Newcomers like Bob Litherland have to sit there and fume.

> There are some subjects that you really want to speak on and you get in the Chamber and you can sit there from half past two to late on . . . and one or two Right Honourables who may be front bench spokesmen on other subjects will come in and get priority over you. It's tremendously frustrating. You've done all the research and you've got your speech, your adrenalin going, and somebody strolls in, makes a brief interlude into the debate and then goes out . . . And outside the public think these are the people that are doing the work but they don't see the people in the committees that are going right through the night and coming out mentally and physically exhausted, because they're not newsworthy.

So beginners can save their time by concentrating on the urgent and important, such as getting some freedom to plan life by finding a pair: a partner in the crime of absenteeism or a Member of the other party with whom to play licensed hookey. This system allows Members to escape voting on two-line whips, which is why, of 500 divisions from 1979–80, the average English Tory voted in only 318 and his Labour counterpart in 264. It can bring other benefits: a brace of pheasants for anyone paired with one of the Tory sporting brigade, a Cup Final ticket from one of Labour's football figures. Where were you in the revolution, Daddy? I was paired. As Keith Best found, the search can become desperate:

> I think if I'd had my first few days again in the House of Commons, I

> would do nothing but concentrate upon getting a pair. I wouldn't bother to find out where the cafeteria was, where the Members' toilets were or anything like that. I would home in entirely upon that one thing because undoubtedly . . . having a pair can make all the difference to the way in which you're able to exist . . . some of my young colleagues who were elected for the first time in May have been able to get pairs. Some of them inherit pairs from their predecessors. It's a strange thing, it's left entirely up to the individual.

Pairs make life bearable. Every week each Member gets a Whip setting out next week's business. Each item is underlined. Three lines means 'Be there' and the frequency of three-line whips, now averaging at least one a week, has increased steadily over the years. In the late 1950s there were few and Members could even pair for periods of weeks, certain there was no need for their votes. Now, as parties become less united, they put more and more issues to this test of party loyalty. Absence on three-line whips requires the express permission of the pairing whip. This is not readily given, though anything from fifteen to thirty on each side do get it. Two lines is interpreted to mean not 'Stay unless you've got a good excuse' but 'Go if you can pair', so Members find a like-minded partner from the other side and they both agree not to vote. One line means 'Why bother?' Most don't.

Opposition Members, because fewer, have more power to pick and choose. Conservatives are usually more desperate than Labour, if only because the Dennis Skinner syndrome of nonco-operation leads a score or so of Labour men to refuse to pair at all, or to do so only covertly, so keen are they to clock up votes, even against their own party.

Next locate the leisure facilities, which is the safest description of the tea room, for Labour Members; the smoking room, for Conservatives; the bar, formerly SNP territory; and the family room, for those misguided enough to allow spouses to intrude. All these, but particularly the tea room, serve as the great gossip exchange, the place where backbite meets bullshit to form a characteristically parliamentary blend. Members put this in romantic terms: 'the walls of Parliament have ears and the stones speak', which may be true, but the tongues are human and they mainly wag in the tea and smoking rooms and the House's nine bars. However, the more factual grist for the House's espionage mill comes not from gossip but from confidential papers left in committee rooms or Xerox machines or, in a few cases, lifted directly from rooms. These were the ways that

Tory plans for coal-pit co-operatives, the details of the '92' group and the Owenite plans to break away from the Labour Party, before the actual rupture, all came to light.

Compared to this, the tea room and the bars are more of a garden fence or a launderette for information exchange. They are also a way of life, being the last hiding place of the workers and the old left, and hence a culture of their own. Backbenchers and leaders are both advised to see and be seen in these places, initially to absorb the atmosphere, then to prove that they are not suffering from an acute dose of uphimselfism. This demonstration of humanity is best afforded by having an ability to put up with prolonged doses of the mindless meanderings of the regulars and the stale stodgy food. Be seen there. Get the gossip and find out what's going on: there will be many only too eager to tell you. At length. Do not hang around. Brain rot can result.

Members are then ready to get on with the job. Unfortunately, there isn't one. An MP has no defined role, no daily scale of duties to run. He is handed a build-your-own-job kit and a salary, and left to get on with it. He finds his own feet, usually by observing his fellow Members and then doing the same. He is essentially a self-employed entrepreneur, the last surviving Jack-of-all-trades. For the presupposition of the system is that MPs are all-purpose laymen, bringing untutored commonsense to bear on issues too complex for them to understand. Here the whole system is geared to the lowest common denominator; everything is designed to keep MPs pristine and ill-informed. Unfortunately they live in an increasingly specialised age so they must also keep up with several subjects, do the reading, know the problems. The schizophrenia is unbearable. So is the accumulation of roles for the MP. He is legislator and lawyer, accountant and economist, orator and committee man, behind-the-scenes fixer, front-of-curtain soloist. He is constituency representative, pressure group spokesman, party propagandist, social worker, sectional advocate, spokesman of the general will, interpreter of the locality to the centre, the centre to the locals. In all these jobs he is unskilled. To all the parliamentary Peter principle applies: the skills necessary to get in are of little relevance to the job.

As a new Member, Julian Critchley was detected reading a book by Charles Hill, later Lord Hill, and advised, 'it does not do to appear clever. Advancement in this man's party is based firmly on alcoholic stupidity'. Times have changed; work, even reading books is now essential. Any Member coming in and finding his job easy is not doing it. The range of jobs he faces is compounded by the flow of information: the outpourings of the Stationery Office, Hansard, pressure groups, vested interests, specialised research bodies, not to mention the public prints and the specialised press. Then there is the mail. Most get between thirty and fifty pieces of mail a day, usually transferred from envelopes to wastepaper basket. Unfortunately some demand answers, for at least a quarter comes from the constituency. Some of this is, of course, 'fabricated' mail, for British pressure groups are now mastering the technique of getting supporters to rewrite standard letters and send them in as their own. This produces sudden deluges, which is easy for those with electronic offices, where word processor shall speak peace unto word processor without a brain intervening. For the great majority it poses more problems. This mail, like all the rest, has to be answered even if it is done laboriously in longhand. The tide never stops. Neglect it, and it builds up and engulfs you.

All this demands the powers of Clark Kent to change into Supermember. It also demands an ability to be in more than one place at once, for the House of Commons is increasingly merely the venue for a continuous series of meetings. Continuous creation of meetings has become a lifestyle. Thus, just to give an illustration in the week starting 25 January 1982, there were seventeen meetings of all-party groups plus one film show (on El Salvador), a Heritage Group visit to the Victoria and Albert Museum, and a mass lobby of 750 about Manchester schools. There were also twenty-five meetings of Conservative Party groups, including meetings with Ian MacGregor of British Steel, the President of the National Farmers Union, the Director General of the Institute of Directors and both Nigel Lawson and James Prior discussing the policies of their departments. The Labour Party had eighteen group meetings and both major parties had their full party meetings on the Thursday. The Liberals and the SDP are not under the same pressure, having only their weekly party meetings (6.00 p.m. on Wednesday for the Liberals, 4.00 p.m. on Thursday for the SDP) though the subject chairmen in the Liberals do meet with panels from outside the House to formulate policy, and the SDP also had a regional group meeting and a steering committee meeting. The Welsh and Scottish Nationalists are so reduced in numbers that their party meetings can be held in any convenient telephone booth. George Cunningham, since he went into splendid isolation, takes his party meeting around with him. All this activity was in addition to all the usual run of meetings with pressure groups, firms and constituents, which go on anyway, and the committees of the House and the requirements of the Chamber when there were three-line whips on the Monday, Wednesday and Thursday. It also ignores all the meetings which Cabinet and Shadow Cabinet members hold with backbench supporters to build up support and drop a few crumbs from the Cabinet table.

'Specialise and stay out of the bars,' Prime Minister Attlee advised the young Roy Mason. The two are not necessarily alternatives but the advice is more than ever true. The only key to success is to narrow the focus and concentrate to know more and more about less and less. So take one or two subjects, keep up with the field, then build up the expertise, the useful contacts and the files. It is possible to have a flair for publicity and look as though you are doing the lot without bothering to do anything at all, but ignorance is not normally bliss and will eventually be exposed. Then observe the basic rule of parliamentary success: be there. Not everything comes to he who waits, but something will, even if it's only a trip to Fiji. Much of the art of politics is that of hanging around. Actively. So never give up, choose your furrow, plough and persevere. In the first flush of enthusiasm many Members assume that having written the letter, made the speech, aired the problem, the job is done. This is to subscribe to the great public myth that a superintending angel hovers over Parliament. Members might as well be talking to themselves in the lavatory. Words have to be kicked home. The machine is too complex, too slow and too wrapped up in itself to produce instant action. It is much better equipped to provide reasons for not acting than to do anything. Before becoming a one-man party, George Cunningham felt that success was a product of co-operation and hard work:

> Any new MP has got to realise that he doesn't alter anything just by tabling a motion or asking a question. He's got to work at it. He's got to talk to them in the tea room. He's got to put articles in the newspaper and that sort of thing, and gradually people start to say, 'Oh, well maybe he has got a point.' That was the work done by Tom Dalyell on the devolution issue over the years. He educated Members by his many speeches and the House works when Members are educating each other to the difficulties of some issue.

Learning the job is a four-year course although naturally the super-smart think it is over in weeks and the dullards keep flunking the practicals. For most the learning process is complete about the time the new Member is eligible to be thrown out. Research, gathering information, concentrating in the House of Commons is like working next to a fun fair. Roll up, roll up. See the Chamber and the side shows in committee. And get distracted from the job of being an MP. The work imperative also conflicts with the need to make friends, to become known and trusted, to hang around the tea room or the smoke room, to attend the endless meetings. The best channels of influence are often behind the scenes. There is a general feeling that the noisiest Members are the least effective. As Richard Body puts it:

> If you want to get the Minister to change his mind about something, you don't confront him and try to make him a fool publicly. What you can do is to take him to one side, have a drink with him or a meal with him, talk to him in the Lobby, give him the idea, persuade him, let him promote it as his idea.

There is a lot to learn. Curiously, everyone learns something different. Martin Stevens early on discovered a rather unusual technique which not many others have used:

> I didn't realise how much power we could have if we played it right in a positive way . . . it's simply a question of learning the technique . . . I found that you can get changes made in the law much more easily through the House of Lords than through the House of Commons. So I go waddling down the corridor with my amendments and new clauses and get a friendly peer. They're all computerised. If you're wondering who's interested in capitalist trash cans you just press the button and out comes all the names of all the peers who are interested in that subject, so it's quite easy to do . . . and so you go to them and say, 'Look, will you introduce this on the committee stage of such and such a bill?' . . . you usually find someone who will, if it's sensible, because they're much less rigidly whipped than we are. It often gets through and we almost never reject House of Lords amendments. So provided you're willing to be anonymous and nobody knows it's you except you, you can get an awful lot of new stuff in.

An MP is given not a job, but access to a tangle of wires and levers: some to pull, some to push, and a long learning process about which is which. There are 634 ways of reacting. Some learn the ropes with enthusiasm, then find the game isn't satisfying. Julian Critchley did that:

> I remember when I first got in in '59 when I was 28, and the Conservative

> benches all filled to listen to Aneurin Bevan, which was the only speech I heard him make before he died. I remember he wagged his fingers before us and said: 'What you have to look forward to is hours and hours of exquisite tedium and boredom.' We were all shocked at this – we didn't believe it. But by God it's true.

Others, like examinees, attempt all questions and fail. Those who thrive on activity get plenty – leading to futility. Others live on their wits and improvise, dashing round like fire engines arriving too late, putting up a spectacular spray to obscure the fact that the fire has a firm hold, then moving on, bells clanging, lights flashing, to the next holocaust. Most find their level and stick to it, a few find a niche and hide in it.

The time demands are considerable. The Boyle Committee's 1978 research showed an average working load of forty hours in the House and a further twenty-seven on constituency business: a sixty-seven hour week, though 5 per cent of backbenchers and 11 per cent with ministerial office did over sixty hours in the House alone. Yet, surprisingly, many Members still find time for second jobs. Excluding Ministers, 54 per cent of our sample had paid second jobs, 8 per cent of these as 'parliamentary advisors' which can cover anything from Brian Walden's £5,000 a year as 'the highest paid bookie's runner', to a fifth of that sum to be nice to, or about, the Federation of Snurple Manufacturers. Indeed it could, by a stretch of the imagination, cover the £2,300 Will Owen MP had pushed in his pocket (against his will of course) by the Czechs from 1961 to 1969 for telling them about 'Britain's democratic way of life'. Then 48 per cent are in the professions, 34 per cent in business, 4 per cent in industry, 5 per cent in farming. A minute number write books, which is also a second job, if less rewarding. The Boyle Committee's findings were similar: 70 per cent of non-office holders with second jobs: more of them old boys than new. Only 33 per cent of these moonlighters (or, in parliamentary terms, post-prandials) were working ten hours or more per week in session, which leaves some of them such as those lawyers working as recorders or those who have managed to get on the European Assembly gravy train (with two salaries and Europe's much lusher expenses) doing much more than ten. The proportion putting in over ten hours a shift rose to 55 per cent in recess. They are mainly professional and business people. Miners are unable to do a morning shift in central London. Manual jobs require more hours for less money. Labour men are more likely to see their parliamentary salary as a step up. So Labour has a lower proportion (30 per cent) with second jobs, compared to 70 per cent of Conservatives.

In 1974, the Boyle Committee found that two thirds of the 70 per cent of MPs with other jobs got over £1,000 a year, one third over £3,000, a fifth over £5,000, most of the latter having constituencies in or near London. Yet it is possible that some do these jobs for interest, not the money. Certainly in our survey the rewards are not substantial: 17 per cent claimed that their MPs salary was under 50 per cent of their total income, 36 per cent of that it provided 50–90 per cent of the whole.

Financial need, diversification of interests, the search for satisfaction, activity as an end in itself, even boredom, the motives are mixed. So are the justifications the MPs dredge up for not doing their real job. To Julian Critchley it is all a question of the right rate for the job:

> A lot of us do not just one job, but probably two or three, and this is the real point of argument about MPs' pay, for as long as you pay MPs the same amount of money as a Ford car assembly worker with overtime, you will find them doing an additional job or even an additional second job, making three altogether, which suggests that all three jobs are done perhaps less well than they might otherwise be. Which further suggests that you, the public, are cheating yourselves.

But others who do two jobs are bolder about it, justifying their moonlighting by the need for experience and staying in touch. John Stokes, elected for Oldbury and Halesowen at the almost geriatric age of fifty-three in 1970, kept his job:

> I have recently retired from my job after twenty-one years, but my constituents knew I had a job. I was a selection consultant in industry and commerce and they felt that put me in touch with the sort of lives that they lead as ordinary people. And also of course I can bring that knowledge and expertise to the Commons. I only used to do mornings really here, and occasional afternoons. I was usually in the House for every Question Time and every evening when we're there and the constituency most Fridays and Saturdays so they didn't suffer. But I did know what was going on in life, what the effect of the laws was. One of the troubles in the House still is we have too many lawyers, too many public relations men, and too many people whom I call verbalisers, who can talk the hind legs off a donkey. But can they actually do anything? Have they done anything?

Others, like Keith Best, present their defence as a plea for sympathy. They may be doubling a reasonable salary but they really have to work at it:

> It means that I have very little social life to speak of. I find myself in court in the morning. I go into the House of Commons when it sits in the afternoon at 2.30 and I find myself there till midnight . . . I then go back to my place and I get up at six in the morning anyway to get on with the work for the next day so it means that I'm living on, I suppose, about four hours' sleep during the week, and at the weekend I don't catch up on that because having a constituency which I cannot reach during the week . . . everything that would otherwise be done in the week has to be truncated and placed into two days, Saturday and Sunday.

In the USA where neither Senators nor Representatives are as prone to spread themselves into second jobs as here, where an elected Representative's task is much more demanding, and where the House of Representatives has a strict ceiling (recently doubled to $18,000) on outside earnings, there have still been several problems of conflict of interest, even corruption. The 'Koreagate' scandal of Tongson Park bribing Congressmen, or the Abscam operation, in which the FBI offered bribes from pretend oil sheiks and found takers, both indicated that the complaints had substance. We like to convince ourselves that corruption is an American tradition: the honest politician there is one who once bought, stays bought. Yet in recent years concepts of the acceptable have become more flexible here. Three MPs, Reginald Maudling, John Cordle and Albert Roberts ('I was paid for my ability'), were on the Polson payroll. Nothing terrible happened. Sir Peter Emery's diving school had a very profitable contract from the Manpower Services Commission which was strongly criticised by the Public Accounts Committee, though clearly his knighthood is a public forgiveness. A happy trio of John Nott (christened John Nitt by Sir Ian Gilmour), Peter Rees (as a tax lawyer) and Tom Benyon (Abingdon) were all reported by that scurrilous defiler of pristine reputations, *Private Eye*, to have associations with the Rossminster Group, merchandiser of dubious tax avoidance schemes. So long as they are kept quiet such affiliations are accepted. Once they become public knowledge the House lumbers into its best hypocritical form and 'fringe benefits' and outside retainers are treated with moralistic censoriousness. MPs have little scope for the kind of fiddling on expenses, fringe benefits and job perks which so many other professions take for granted. Thus, when they stumble on them, or on the real world in general, their reaction manages to combine the shock of discovery with pure envy.

The problem is certain to get worse, not only because modern MPs are a different breed, representing a society with different standards, but more because there is an increasing tendency for interests to be represented in the House. MPs, for their part, find it useful and certainly convenient to look for extra income, not in sweating in some legal chambers or an office in the City, but in doing things they would do anyway in the palace itself and being paid for them, or, better still, in being given a fairly undemanding watching brief for a firm or an interest, to keep them informed of things coming up in their area and to put the case for them as required.

This process can spread to national government. Though only one MP is down in the *Register of Interests* as having such a capacity: the late Sir Ronald Bell, who had an advisory retainer from the Transkeian Government, the efforts of the Greek military regime to improve its political image in the past did spill over into Parliament and some MPs have had close contact with regimes overseas, either through the Anglo-Snurple groups which abound or more directly. Albert Roberts had close contacts with Franco Spain, Ben Ford with Namibia, Tories with South Africa, and several on all sides have been on visits sponsored by governments overseas, some of them very dubious regimes indeed. These are the ones most anxious to become respectable.

The published figures from the *Register of Members' Interests* show about a fifth of the non-ministerial House supplementing their parliamentary incomes in this convenient way, even ignoring the trade-union-sponsored MPs and those who act for various employee or professional associations, as Eldon Griffith does for the Police Federation. A total of thirty-six Members, (five Labour, two SDP, twenty-nine Tory) listed themselves as consultants or advisers to various trade and industry associations; 102 (nine Labour, three SDP, ninety Conservative) had the same relationship with private firms, some of them the firm or the legal partnership they had previously worked with; and fourteen (three Labour, four SDP, seven Conservative) were 'consultants', some occasional, in their own right and therefore presumably plying for hire. Here, then, is a useful bandwaggon for the new Member to get on as he acquires experience in the House and, with it, both a growing need for money and the ability to convince people that what he does is important. The demands are not onerous, asking a few questions, perhaps hosting a few overpriced receptions at the House to awe customers, meeting some unpleasant and sometimes dubious people. In return he gets an extra income which can range from a few hundred to a few thousand, though the figures are not known because the *Register* imposes no requirement to give them. So few do. On top of this there are also the occasional retainers from professional lobbyists, a new breed who make very extravagant claims. Firms such as Lloyd-Hughes Associates have claimed 'major' political successes for clients; exemptions from the Trade Descriptions Act here; the Queen opening a major installation there; the creation of an all-party group of forty; introductions to ministers. David McDonough and Associates more prosaicly promise working lunches at the House of Commons (presumably as a form of punishment) while Charles Barker Watney and Powell boast of providing the secretariat of several all-party committees. To get all these benefits for clients no one would suggest that any payment is made to MPs, but the firm itself does make a charge. To clear the air it would be a good idea to require registration of payments and affiliations. Indeed it would also be useful to implement the recommendations of the 1976 Royal Commission and bring attempted bribery of MPs in their parliamentary capacity within the criminal law.

Until then, avoid temptation. Representation is not a job for the squeamish or those with principles. That means that there are always lots of Members willing to take it. Its consolation is that it helps to pass the time and make the political art of 'being there' more comfortable; and you can always justify it as defending the time-honoured right to lobby MPs. You are defending freedom. Particularly your own.

The practice would undoubtedly be more widespread were our MPs either more salable or more powerful or both. The sensible organisation, business, or pressure group will realise that MPs are of little importance and can do little for them, except add a wholly spurious dignity. So the real criticism of the growing practice of retainers, like the long-standing tendency for Members to have a second job, is not that either is corrupt but just that both are wrong. They are both distractions from the real job of Member of Parliament. Neither job is done well. An increased burden falls on the remaining MPs. The House is held back from desirable reforms and from any increase in its powers and functions. Which doesn't stop some from justifying the unjustifiable, as in this questionnaire answer:

MPs should be paid less, not more, and they should have external employment as a matter of course. Research workers are a gross waste of public money. Parliament sits for too long, it passes too many laws and shows little inclination to do anything about it. Now that MPs are so well paid and receive shockingly excessive redundancy pay, it really matters to them if they lose their seats. That only binds them further into the party system and makes them lobby fodder. About 70 per cent of activity at Parliament is futile and the new select committees are just making things worse.

Governments are happy to maintain the status quo. Second jobs check the clamour for better pay. Overworked MPs aren't troublesome. If energy, talent and ability were focussed on the Commons, ministerial life would be much more difficult. A Member can manage on his salary, though he cannot live well. So those who take second jobs are really saying that money is more important to them than the job they were elected for. There is nothing to stop them. The public's interest is limited to opposing better pay, or indeed any at all. The 1971 Boyle survey of public opinion confronted people with two statements: 'MPs should not have jobs outside Parliament so that they can concentrate on the job of representing their constituents,' and 'Working on a job outside Parliament gives an MP wider experience and helps him keep in touch.' Majorities agreed with both.

There is no audit of how well or badly MPs do their real jobs. David Penhaligon points out that many do not:

> I've always said you could divide the House into three categories for how hard they work. About a third work very hard, really very hard, a fifteen hour day would be the norm and they're workaholics really, but the other two hundred probably do a reasonable day's work, and there's two hundred that if you can discover anything they do, let me know.

This situation is implicit in the job. An MP is a man alone, deciding his own priorities, his workload, his destiny. Whatever choice he makes, selfish or altruistic, he is well protected. Few constituents have any idea of what the job involves, so electoral judgement will be little influenced by accurate assessment of either effort or performance. Members themselves are a mutual protection society: privately gossipy, publicly protective. The House cossets because it is a club. Clubs are protective societies and traditionalists like Alan Clark find this one of their best features:

> It's the most wonderful thing. Chips Channon I think it was who

described it as a 'tawny male paradise' and it hasn't changed at all since then . . . it's a marvellous club of course. It's a mixture between a common room and an officers' mess. But it's most like a school, with pecking order, gossip, sneaks, good boys. It's a closed male society. There are a few ladies . . . but it's real charm is the closed club-like atmosphere.

Clubs protect Members against wives, mistresses, creditors, and the outside world. This club has a resident fifth column of leakers to *Private Eye* or Paul Foot, but it still provides the same protection even, perhaps particularly, from constituents. The theory is that the House insulates its flock to allow calm deliberation. That service is irrelevant in an age when to govern is to adjudicate between conflicting pressures. Yet together with the 'law of silence' it is a useful shield for those who do not do the job. Only a strong sense of duty pricks cossetted MPs on, and the surprising thing is how hard the majority do work at what is still a voluntary activity. Work with specific duties and timetables imposes its own imperatives. An MP's consists of bits which can be postponed, ignored, reassembled at will. Authors have a book written, lawyers a brief defended; an MP has only a continuous process of living on his wits.

This fragmented penny packet nature of the job is complicated by lack of continuity – some of the week in London, some in the constituency, some at home. Part of the year Parliament sits: three months it does not. Part is spent overseas, where an average of a third of the House goes each year. A typical week in a session might show this pattern:

Monday

Tribal migration day. Members converge on the House, Scots by air, northerners by train, midlanders and southerners by car, which is also the resort of the less well organised who use it as a travelling desk, dustbin and suitcase. A two- or one-line whip can allow Monday to be postponed to Tuesday, though most come anyway. The post continues every day. Secretaries have to be kept busy. Some feel lost out of Westminster. A light day in work terms. The twenty or so group meetings which are listed on each week party whip, and the similar number on the all-party whip, are rarely called on Monday. This leaves time for encounter groups such as the Tribune group meeting, in the Labour Party, or for Select Committees.

Tuesday

Committee morning for those unable to escape. An average of eight committees in the morning, four in the afternoon, and a committee corridor thronging with secretaries taking dictation from Members, civil servants avoiding it from anyone, pressure group representatives, and the odd school party indicating that this is also a school visit day, a rare pleasure for anyone north of the Humber, an ordeal for those below. Other visitors of all kinds pour in steadily, and usually expect their MP to guide them, get tickets for them (a time-consuming chore) and generally dance attendance. Lunch can be at the expense of some pressure group, firm, embassy or any organisation unimaginative enough, or ill-informed about political realities, to want to impress MPs. In theory, it is possible to go all week without buying a single meal. 'Gastronomic pimping', Aneurin Bevan called it. This requires thick skin and thicker stomach, so most will average one or two lunches or dinners a week, and some will claim they are slimming for the rest to excuse paying for their own. Economists know of no such thing as a free lunch, but politicians see it as a tribute and have a shrewd idea to the last Mouton Rothschild what each organisation is worth, a propensity heightened by the unattractive and expensive food in the House itself, although a sharper assessment would be that if organisations think they are buying MPs with food they must estimate them at bargain basement level.

Back to the House for Prime Minister's Question Time, a twice weekly taking of the political temperature. The constant preoccupation in politics is with short-term measurement: how well or badly we /they did this week and Prime Minister's Question Time is a guide. Then party committees, starting at four, each lasting for an hour. After a meal, either work in the office, browse in the library, or chat in the tea or smoking rooms or the bar until a ten o'clock vote. This is usually followed by another at 11.30 pm, but many members, particularly from minor parties, do not hang around to find out.

An example: Tuesday, 16 February 1982, the Rate Support Grant: a major issue, a three-line whip. At ten o'clock 308 Tories voted 'Aye', one 'No', fourteen paired with Labour, ten were absent unpaired. Labour: 222 voted 'No', fourteen paired, three absent. Liberals: eight 'No', four absent. SNP: all absent. Welsh Nationalists: both 'No'. SDP: nineteen 'No', ten absent; while all the Ulstermen of all varieties were absent bar Kilfedder, the sole UUP Member. By

11.30 the votes dropped from 562 to 523, largely because nine more were paired, five more Labour men had sloped off (though more Tories had been found) while three more Liberals, sixteen more SDP and Kilfedder had vanished into the night. The three SDP who remained split: two 'Aye', Dickson Mabon 'No'. All this is laboriously calculated and tabulated by hand in each party office each day.

Wednesday

Some committees. More a catch-up-on-the-post morning. Whatever the MP is doing, the post pours in every day, building up backlogs. The Chamber is also probably less demanding so more work can be done in the afternoon. An evening of meetings and rap sessions with the groups which gather round Ministers or leading figures in the Opposition, even Tory dining clubs. Labour Members, less keen on status and strong on saving, prefer the downstairs self-service cafeterias. Two late votes. Home.

Thursday

A repeat of Tuesday, but gathering pace in the attempt to clear up the week. Committees in the morning, perhaps another institutional lunch, Question Time followed by another highlight – the business motion – Shadow Cabinet, Cabinet and whips all know everything one to two days in advance but this is the opportunity for the rest to be told what is happening to them next week. Diaries are filled in on the spot. This late notice of next week's demands is a major inhibition on outside activities, unless, like the law, they can be crammed into the mornings. Six o'clock is party meeting time. The Chamber is left to a skeleton staff of Members desperate to speak. The great majority converge on the 1922 Committee (the Conservative backbenchers' meeting, described as 'the longest running show on earth' by Humphry Berkeley) in Room 14, or the Parliamentary Labour Party ('collective cantankerousness') in Room 10. Divisions are usually carefully timed to have nothing with more than two lines after ten o'clock, because of the clamour of the Scots and other far-flung MPs to get sleepers. Others drive through the night or go home to the digs, everyone making, in his own way, his own summing up of the week. For his party and himself.

Friday

A notional parliamentary day. Those who live in London or can't bear to leave the House have unwhipped business: Private Members' motions and bills, uncontentious government business. This provides a chance to speak for those who have been squeezed out of the big pool; ritual dullards' days when the House prides itself on being able to give more leisurely consideration to matters. This always means boredom. Staple subjects are abortion, indecent displays, Sunday trading or other matters on which the job of the House is now not to do anything but to recycle the arguments endlessly in order to persuade lunatics outside that all is not lost. Rather more Members are in their constituencies or getting on with their work. Friday is a chance to visit factories and farms, to speak at universities to pathetic audiences, to talk to local parties up and down the country or to the Member's own constituency organisation.

Saturday

Surgery morning. Other public engagements in the afternoon: fêtes, some of them worse than death, football matches. MPs can then either leave the constituency, or if they have the misfortune to live in it, go home and raise the drawbridge to allow wives or children to work out their accumulated resentments. Bob Litherland describes one of his Saturdays:

> A couple of Saturdays back I did two advice bureaux, starting at 10.30 Saturday morning and finishing at 2.30, went along to assist with a garden party at an elderly persons home, drew twenty-seven raffle tickets, and to listen and applaud a pipe band, then go on to give a talk to the Co-Op Movement in Deansgate, Manchester. Coming out of there at 5.30 I found that the police had towed my car away and it cost me £27 to go and get the car back to go home to the family. So that's one day in the life of an MP back home.

Sunday

For all the saints who from their labours rest. A chance to look like a family, for those who remember how it is done. Or do some work. Or read. Or just sprawl around devouring Sunday papers or falling asleep over *Weekend World* and *The World at One*. But it is also a busy day for some: church parades, marching teams, amateur football, even visiting the pubs and clubs. It all depends on the constituency. And the domestic situation.

This basic framework offers scope for a great deal of variety. Some rarely venture to London. Tories make special efforts to drum in the city brigade from time to time, usually to listen to the Prime Minister. Others, Dennis Skinner, Bob Cryer, Tristam Garel Jones, the whips, are House of Commons freaks: there from first to last. John Ellis was, too, particularly in his whipping days:

> I was a bit of a sticker, I mean, all right, you can look at my division record, both as a whip or not, and I believed in being there; if you were a bit sick or had a lame leg, if you could not walk to the House of Commons, you crawled because that was your job.

Walter Harrison could beat him and indeed anyone. In 1974–5, of 333 votes he voted in all of them, 1975–6 on 264 out of 266, 1977–8 in 202 of 204, and 1978–9 in all forty that took place in the aborted session.

Social Democrats are bad attenders, never very good when they had whips to mobilise them, worse now that they decide their own destinies, but then they do have to be up and down the country denouncing Parliament and the party system. The Liberals and minor parties are also bad attenders, having to work harder at keeping the party in the country going, and at their own constituencies which they seem to find more important than most because their survival is more at stake.

An annual pattern is more difficult to define. Most MPs reach the end of the session in late July or early August in a state of exhaustion. The rush to complete business piles on the pressure. After a quick constituency visit to establish that the MP is still alive, August is escape time. September is overseas trip or, for the unlucky, nursing the constituency time, some MPs even going in for autumnal canvasses, 'Just to say hello,' others taking up visits and contacts postponed during the rest of the year. Those with commitments outside Parliament are free to devote themselves to them full-time. In October, politics revive from hibernation: the party conferences: the House resumes. MPs wash up the old session and start the new one by the end of the month. The parliamentary grindstone turns again.

By their jobs shall ye know them. The nature of the MP's job accounts for much of our politics. Forced to be Jacks of all trades by the nature of the job, the constant pressures, the flow of new issues and subjects and the ragbag nature of the work they become intellectual grasshoppers, never really mastering anything. They need to specialise but have not the time to. They scatter their efforts across too many subjects with too little backing. As a result they are weak against a government which controls the facts and the specialists. They are harassed, as anyone must be who attempts too much. They are inefficient and difficult to organise. In the last analysis, they are individualists: they stand or fall by their own efforts. They decide what and how much to do. And the odds are loaded against individualists in a battle with the corporate system of government. Governments take care to see that things are weighted that way by keeping MPs deprived of the staff necessary to do the job. In the 1960s, secretaries had to be paid out of the Member's own salary, as did phones and postage. Now the last two are paid for and a secretarial allowance of £8,750 will support one secretary and a part time researcher living on chips. Yet this improvement has no more than kept pace with the growth in the workload as constituencies get more demanding, and the volume of mail grows – a growth rate which some MPs assess as doubling every five years. Nor has it brought anything like the profusion of help and backing in other parliamentary systems. In America, Senators have staffs of up to thirty-five, Congressmen nearly as many. In Germany, staffs of five or six are not uncommon. In Canada and even in tiny New Zealand, a better research backing is provided by teams of researchers servicing both Opposition and the Government.

The inadequacy of our provision is illustrated by our survey: 60 per cent of the MPs had full-time secretaries, three quarters of them in London, the rest in the constituencies. A third used their wives, this time mainly in their constituencies as secretaries. The remainder relied on part-timers. Only 5 per cent had a full-time researcher, a further two-fifths a part-timer. A fifth spent only part of their secretarial allowance, 61 per cent spent the whole of it and 18 per cent (21 per cent of Conservatives, 13 per cent of Labour) supplemented it out of their own incomes. A similar pattern prevailed among defeated MPs in their questionnaire: just over half had had full-time secretaries when they were MPs, 41 per cent of them part-time, while 11 per cent had had a full-time researcher, 24 per cent a part-timer. When they were asked how many staff they considered necessary, nearly all thought that a staff of two, or in the case of 15 per cent of the sample, more, was necessary to do the job to their own satisfaction. They are being too modest.

There is a widespread feeling in the House that the resources now provided are inadequate to do the job. Like many another, Martin

Stevens, used to something different, found the Commons a sad descent:

> I have a full-time secretary because I pay her £2500 a year out of my own pocket to supplement the state grant which is based on half a secretary. Valerie Wallace typed seven thousand letters to and about Fulham people in our first year. I hired for her a brand new IBM electric typewriter and when they came to service it after twelve months they said to me, 'Why can't you give her a decent typewriter instead of this old thing . . . it must be six or seven years old!' . . . Now I'm hoping to have a one day a week research assistant which will be a tremendous help . . . but for the most part one is dealing with hundreds and hundreds of approaches every day, with telephone calls, telegrams, messages, about a hundred letters a day in the case of a London MP, slightly falling off now but in the first year it was a hundred, more than most medium sized businesses get in a day . . . I've been a big businessman and a small businessman but I've never had every single detail of the day being a struggle because you've nobody to look up a telephone number, nobody to be there so that people can ring you back, nobody to check a library reference, nobody to get you a cab . . . it keeps you humble, I think one can say that. Most Members of Parliament are very modest people but that is largely because they are face to face with the realities of living in a way no business person is.

The library provides excellent briefs on most subjects with a few days' notice, and an adequate clippings and Xeroxing service. There are also the researchers attached to the Opposition. Both sources are dominated by Opposition front benchers, who use the library as a counterbalance to the Civil Service and take over the Opposition researchers as their own. The library particularly is under too much strain to provide either the detailed and continuous service or the instant service that disorganised Members require.

An essential minimum provision would be a secretary and researcher in the constituency to cope with the problems there, particularly the social work aspect, which is growing, a secretary and researcher in the House to allow for parliamentary duties, and a minder /fixer /major domo to keep the moving centre of it all on the go. All necessary to tackle the role of parliamentarian, but making no allowance for the failing provision from political parties, nor for helping MPs to do their jobs as politicians promoting their own careers in an increasingly rickety and inadequate system. Even this might be inadequate to help MPs keep up to date with the many and varied subjects they must tackle, for on each of these the major time waster is the process of catching up on the latest state of play each time the subject comes up. In America, each subject can be delegated so that one expert can be responsible for it, in touch with the material and the people, and ready to brief the legislation as necessary. That should be possible here. It is not. In a desperate attempt to move towards it, some MPs, particularly Tories, get research assistants provided through fringe organisations, from the Freedom Association to Central Office. Others pay for their own. Nearly seventy MPs on all sides benefit from American students provided at no expense by American foundations. The provision is useful, though in a limited way, because the students are learning on the job. They are treated with base ingratitude by other Members, either envious or incapable of understanding what a research assistant does, by secretaries who complain that they overcrowd the inadequate space and resources, and by a Services Committee which infers that they are a security risk, as if MPs had access to anything that had not been in the papers weeks before. There is a risk. It is only that run by the young girl students from the not quite paternal attentions of some MPs and the rudeness and self-importance of others. Indeed, the whole issue of student 'interns' really shows the House at its worst: incapable of providing adequate backing, resentful of anyone prepared to fill the gap.

The real effect of the totally inadequate staff provision is that the public are not as well served as they should be, MPs work less effectively than they should and the powers that be, responsible for these cheeseparing decisions, demonstrate that they take neither MPs nor Parliament seriously. MPs who allow this make the same assessment of themselves. For all the argument over reform of Parliament, new committees and new powers, the best way to strengthen both the institution and the men who run it is to allow them to do their jobs with some semblance of competence.

The MP has been thrown on an assault course to test his physical stamina, his adaptability, his survival instincts, all prime requirements for ministerial rank. Office is strain. MPs are being tested for it and conditioned to it. They are being trained for a job they might not get. Yet if they come through the parliamentary apprenticeship they will have shown that they might at least be able to survive it.

Members are made, not born. It takes years to know the job and all its complications, and make an MP competent to serve his constituents, but those who do achieve mastery – and not all do, for there are so many aspects to it – face the problems of what to do with the skills. Can they bear a limitless future as a backbencher (semi-skilled) or do they want to climb the slippery pole? The House previously had a substantial proportion whose answer was clear. The knights of the shire neither wanted office nor sought it. The solid trade unionists were too old for it. Legend credited both groups with great influence – even wisdom. Each had a rueful admiration for the other. In so far as either really had influence, it arose from experience and status, undiluted and uncomplicated by office or expertise. It was always a commonsense perspective. Both groups linger on but much reduced in numbers and influence. Today's House is harder, more competitive. By a Gresham's law of politics the pushy drive out the dutiful, the professionals eclipse the amateur.

Whether the backbencher's job is sufficiently demanding and varied to offer sustained satisfaction to that majority who will never secure office is an open question. David Marquand praises with faint damn:

> Quite a lot simply become super local ombudsmen, which is not a thing I'm trying to decry. It's very important and satisfying . . . Then you have a very small group – the kind of backbench hero figure. Michael Foot was the obvious case in point in the 1960s. In a rather different way, Brian Walden was a kind of semi-backbench hero . . . people who play an active part on the floor of the House, harassing the Government . . . and becoming significant parliamentary figures even if they don't have any great national acclaim . . . Yet another one is the sort of parliamentary ferret which . . . concentrates on wrongs to be righted . . . scandals in the administration, failures of the system to work properly . . . if you have the right kind of appetite for detail it can be a very rewarding role for those who play it. But most backbenchers, given the existing system in the House of Commons, are wasting their time, and this is the real truth of the matter. They're not really achieving very much. Either they realise this and they become very frustrated and fed up, or they don't realise it and they're living in a kind of fantasy world.

Young Members are not quite this realistic. Almost to a man they spend their first few years proclaiming their satisfaction with the job. Yet the process of learning itself is much of their fulfilment. The endless pursuit of trivia, the struggle to keep up with the general issues, and to learn more and more about less and less, begin to pall after a time. Then MPs have to resort to a whole series of self-justifications to comfort their impotence. A few, like George Cunningham, take refuge in a romantic return to the past. Things should not be this way, and, with a huge amount of effort, they need not be:

> There is no doubt that MPs, when they wish to do so, when they have the will to do so, and they're prepared to organise it properly, are not only very influential; they possess all the power there is. Now they have to be prepared to put up with the frustrations, they have to be prepared to attempt things without being able to get a majority of their colleagues to support them and to fail . . . but the notion that the MP is really a powerless cog in the wheel is nonsense . . . It was during that period '74 to '79 that the House of Commons really was working as it ought to work. The seat of power in the House of Commons is lodged in 635 different places . . . and if it is concentrated in the hands of the Prime Minister or in the whips or whatever, it is only because the Members have abdicated voluntarily their power to somebody else . . . I've no sympathy at all with those people coming here and saying, 'now if I don't become a minister pretty quickly then the whole purpose of my coming here is ruined.' If that's their object in coming into the House then they might make good Ministers, but they make bad Members of Parliament and the public is losing the watchdog over government which it's entitled to have.

Some learn the lesson that while MPs have little positive influence they have enormous nuisance value. In a soured middle-age they can make a career of this and exploit it to the full. The more positive and devoted are content to become specialists, acclaimed in a limited circle. Others devote themselves to obscurantism, amateur Maxwell-Hyslops or professional Michael Englishs. Some tortoises take pleasure in tripping up the hares as opportunity arises. They become 'House of Commons men', outwardly pompous, inwardly soured, obstinately attached to the dignity and privileges of the House because these are useful weapons against men who have outdistanced them and because their life offers nothing else. Larger numbers vent their frustrations by seizing on issues of formal importance but not at the forefront of the party battle, and holding them up by inordinate displays of pedantry, concern and simple malevolence. Lords reform, devolution, a Canadian constitution, these bring out the worst in the House and give it and its Members a chance to get their own back for having to do what they are told on everything else. Most just feel passionately, or dimly, that something is wrong. The job does not fulfil. So governments in power for longer than seven years (formerly, now two as everything becomes more frenetic) find an increasing restiveness. Oppositions feel frustrations bottling up.

The House survives. The opportunities opened up already are one safety valve, the hope of more is another and second jobs are a sublimation. Yet mostly it survives because the frustrations will be submerged, denied, and turned inwards. Few are honest enough to say with Julian Critchley: 'When you've got to middle life and you've got nowhere it can be a very frustrating place indeed. And there are times when one wonders whether one shouldn't leave it and go out and do a proper job.'

MPs don't even have the satisfactions of friendship. In the last analysis an MP is on his own. A largely male institution has an atmosphere of casual mateship. A very very few have intense relationships with fellow MPs, heterosexual or homosexual, musical, cultural, even political, but such trust is extremely rare. Most are as friendly as is necessary to smooth the path of life, thus far and carefully no further. Friendship across the party lines is rare and rather frowned on: MPs thrown together on trips and deputations do not resist the tendency to fall apart afterwards in the segregated lifestyles of the House itself. Inside parties, Members are competitors rather than brothers. They get on at someone else's expense, they regard those of a different viewpoint or another section of the party with ill-concealed impatience. Ask Members who they hate most and they will invariably give the name of someone in their own party, usually Tony Benn in the Labour Party, and, among the Tories, Sir Keith Joseph, who is disliked for his new politics, his 'Dracula on Valium' behaviour, his intellect (always something of a crime) and his impatience, for to be important and rude and get away with it, you must be either right or Prime Minister. The job itself is appropriate for a loner, for MPs appear to belong everywhere but in fact belong nowhere. Instead they are balancing between a local party, a constituency, a parliamentary party and the House itself, playing one off against the other, ultimately belonging nowhere, forced to get on with fellow Members but ultimately having little in common with them except gossip, the same job, and an inconcealed impatience with the way others do it. The outward appearances are matey, the *House Magazine* always praises Members, describing the most stupid as 'genial', 'amiable', 'popular', but real attitudes are shown in the pent-up malevolences of the gossip. The House is the greatest gossip exchange in the land. Anything relating to other Members is heard with eagerness, particularly if it relates to their downfall, a situation best illustrated by the old adage among the press lobby 'attack one MP and win 634 friends'. A Member of Parliament represents 67,000 electors and is essentially alone.

4 Power: Getting and Spending

Parliament is a nursery. Some are groomed or groom themselves for stardom in government, others wait in the wings, lurking figures or quick flashers in the corridors of power. The House usually contains half a dozen potential or future Prime Ministers, as well as some who will become Prime Minister without that qualification, plus a hundred actual Ministers, two hundred replacements, trainees and people who know they could do the job better. The great game is about power. Admission tickets are widely distributed, but only to Members of Parliament. An American President can pick the best available talent, a universe of choice which makes actual allocations the more puzzling. A British Prime Minister is restricted to the parliamentary ranks: so the surprise is the other way: that good Ministers can emerge from such unprepossessing material.

The great majority of Ministers come from the Commons and the odds on getting office are good: 31 per cent of all MPs from 1945 to 1974 held some appointed office. Margaret Thatcher chose ninety Ministers (including Assistant Whips, Under Secretaries and all the rag-tag-and-bobtail) from the Commons out of a parliamentary party of 339. Harold Wilson in February 1974 chose ninety-six out of only 301. The odds are even better than one in three for new MPs are excluded from the choice unless they are retreads returning after a period out of the House. Thus Margaret Thatcher really chose from 262 re-elected Members in 1979, Harold Wilson from 252 in 1974. Even among those returning MPs there is a sizable contingent of the incompetent, the irredeemably stupid, and the copybook blotters who failed in previous governments or in more interesting ways. The real chances of getting some job, however puerile, are one in two. Equality may not have made much progress in British society but it has among MPs. Governments are bigger: Attlee had fifty-five Ministers and a Cabinet of twenty in 1945, as against Harold Wilson's seventy-five Ministers and twenty-one in the Cabinet in 1974. The appropriate Conservative figures are sixty-one and sixteen in 1951 and sixty-eight and twenty-two under Margaret Thatcher. Alternations of government have also become more rapid, improving the average chances even more. The thirteen Tory years were a bitter, wasteful period for a Labour Party rich in talent. The less impressive party of the 1970s has not had to face such a dire prospect though that of the 1980s is organising well to bring it back.

Ministerial office is the second prize of parliamentary career. The first prize is power. All the rest is mythology, sublimation and 'highly commendeds'. David Marquand realised early on that backbenchers were impotent. The only way to achieve things was office. Unfortunately he got it in neither the 1966–70 government, nor in its 1974 successor. In Lynda Chalker's view not all MPs want power, but some do, very much:

> I think possibly people fall into two or three categories. Those who are perfectly content to be an MP and do a very good constituency job and to pursue those things they're interested in in the House, and pursue something else outside the House. Then you have what one might call the obvious other end of the scale who are extremely ambitious and sometimes I wonder about them. Then you have the people in the middle who would like to do more because they would like to advance the cause they represent . . . and actually believe that they could advance that cause better as a Minister. Many people believe that you have much more power as a Minister than you effectively do. I certainly think that there are many people who really think they're going to change the world.

Richard Body is one of those who have reconciled themselves to not holding office. He consoles himself with the view that his role is still useful:

> If I'd wanted to be a Minister I'd have played my cards very differently from the way I have done. It would have been fine to be in the Cabinet I think, but to get to the Cabinet you've got to be a Junior Minister for a number of years and I don't think I would be very good at that chore . . . I think a number of older ones take a much more relaxed view about it and know that once you've been here for a while and know your way around, you can influence a lot of decisions concurrently. If you're in a Cabinet post you have tremendous power within that department but as a rule you have very little power in any other department. Now if you are a backbencher and know your way around, you'll know how to achieve results.

Others are more frank. Geoffrey Robinson has never held office, coming in from a top job as chief executive at Jaguar, but winning

Coventry NW only in March 1976 too late for office in the last Labour Government. He would still like it:

> Most politicians are ambitious people, that's clear. Others go in because they have a crusade or a particular cause they wish to promote at a national level. There must be something that drives you to be a politician because it's not an easy job. In my case, yes of course I'd like to try to get into a Cabinet . . . and that would be my aim. If in the future it's clear to me that I won't, I would reconsider my position. But I hope I can . . . I don't think I'm a natural backbencher . . . but we shouldn't infer from that any overwhelming ambition on my part.

In George Cunningham's view, Robinson is not alone. Everyone wants office but not necessarily just for reasons of ambition. Many want an end to their Jack-of-all-trades lifestyle:

> For practical purposes every member would rather be a Minister and partly that has to do with the very different way of life. Most of us come into this place from a structured career where there were things that actually had to be done that day and you didn't generate them yourself. In the House, that's not the case. You don't have an in tray of things that have to be done that day. You decide yourself what speeches you're going to make, what points you're going to try to get through and so on, and it gets very weary sometimes, that sort of life. And so the prospect of being in a job where you have a staff and there are things that actually have to be done and all you've got to do is to take the decisions, that is a very attractive thing . . . And the other thing is simply the ability to take decisions on the matters that don't need parliamentary approval.

The man who avows that he has no desire for office is a very rare bird indeed. Julian Critchley affects cynicism but even that could melt if Mrs Thatcher suddenly asked him to take over Defence, or the Home Office, but not some other jobs:

> It can be no joke being Parliamentary Secretary to the Department of Health and Social Security, stuck in some slum in the Elephant and Castle, actually having to answer the sort of constituency questions and letters that we send on to them . . . appearing in the House of Commons to make a speech two or three times a year, having to deal with Question Time and having to work extremely hard. Having to be at the Ministry at nine o'clock in the morning and having all the nonsense of the House of Commons at the end of that, and at the end of the day . . . next to no money at all.

Most Members are ready to play the great game. Some have a much better chance than others. Both parties seem to put up their most presentable candidates in marginal seats, but safer seats stand the best chance of office. Their denizens are always there to be chosen and best equipped with the highest parliamentary skill: being there. A seat that is fraught means a career that is more so. Teddy Taylor lost Glasgow Cathcart in 1979. He got back in months for Southend but too late for a ministerial job and ruled out for a Scottish job by 250 miles. A freeze frame illustrates the odds. After the 1970 election, 54 per cent of Conservative MPs in seats with a 10 per cent majority or more had already had ministerial experience, 73 per cent were to get it again. The figures for those in more marginal seats were 17 per cent and 53 per cent. Of the latter 44 per cent were defeated later, only 6 per cent of the safe seat incumbents. Among Labour MPs 5 per cent of the big majority men were later beaten, 22 per cent of those with majorities under 10 per cent, an obvious impairment of their chances. In this respect politics is like horse-riding. The major requirements are good luck and a good seat. Fortunately most seats are safe. The 1955 redistribution lasted out five elections. Only 160 of the seats ever changed hands; three quarters stuck with one party.

Other basic laws are difficult to discern. It is sensible not to do a Kilroy-Silk, who arrived after his election and immediately proclaimed an intention of being party leader in fifteen years. An assembly suffused with ambition finds it convenient to condemn its open avowal just as people at orgies do not talk about sex. So try and take other people just as seriously as you take yourself and if such a tall order is impossible at least appear to try. However pushy you are feign modesty, a desire to serve, and moderation. In all things. It is more important to be sound than sensible. It is also vital to decide your line. Dick Crossman believed that the way to the top was either to follow the party line slavishly or be such a nuisance that you have to be bought off. Today rebellion is allowed but it has to be selective and discreet, and the inside track is still the fastest, for the would-be nuisance first needs a strong position from which to exercise his nuisance value; but if he does it too vigorously, he then faces a difficult re-entry problem to get back on the ladder without betraying his old friends and associates too bitterly. Bevan and Foot managed it. Tony Benn might face the same problem as Enoch Powell and get stuck in orbit. Some betrayal is inevitable. Margaret Jackson as a left winger is still attacked for replacing an Education Minister who resigned against the cuts. Tony Benn is criticised for having replaced Frank Cousins when he resigned as Minister of Technology. It is best therefore that it should be kept down to the ordinary level of knife in the back competition and not exacerbated by being made a question of principle too. That guarantees long-standing bitterness.

In the promotion stakes there are three broad types. First the workhorse brigade, either too stupid for office or so deep in their own furrow that they are not glimpsed. In the Tory Party they end up with a knighthood, though these days even that is not untainted, for Mrs Thatcher has handed out some very curious rewards for hack work and her honours lists have not always shown the same fastidious concern for the first word of the title as, say, Harold Macmillan's. In the Labour Party workhorses can get to the Lords in a bad year but are more likely to get a rolled gold watch. Next the ideologues. They disqualify themselves from office by the purity of their ideology. This failure then reinforces their paranoia and makes them even more vigorous oppositionists. Finally the 'ministrables'. They can hold any opinions, as long as they do so reasonably. The Tribune Group, once happy to be the conscience of the party, is now three factions: the intransigent Bennites, the old Tribunites, and the young ministrables – Robin Cook, Frank Field, Martin O'Neil, Jack Straw, an alliance so unstable that only a desire to retain the goodwill of the business keeps them together. That goodwill is vital in promotion, for Cabinets have to represent all sections so ability in the Tribune Group is certain to reap a disproportionate reward for its representation and rarity value. Similarly the right has to be represented in Conservative Cabinets.

Some ministrables are superministrables. Each party has its share of the 'really quite extraordinarily able' (in Mrs Thatcher's words) Leon Brittan self-raising syndrome: Jack Straw managed to get his photo and a headline in the Leeds student paper in his first week at university and has built up from there. Among the Social Democrats David Owen is a good self-raiser; indeed that party may only have his services because, unlike the other Red Sea, the Labour waters did not part to make way for him. John Pardoe was one of a similar breed in the Liberal ranks though, as a darker horse-cum-tortoise, David Steel is now well ahead. Parliamentary reputations are fragile flowers, blossoming in one Parliament, dying in the next, and the only one to linger is one for 'bottom' or *gravitas* which is really a condemnation: the possessor is not going anywhere and is no threat. So it is difficult to maintain the image of unstoppable brilliance in the House itself. It comes mainly from the right contacts, particularly in the media but also in the party's higher reaches, and from carefully calculated publicity. To be constantly tipped as a rising young man, 'able' or 'someone to watch', does not guarantee promotion. It does, however, ensure places in publicly touted lists and thus ensures attention, as well as requiring party leaders to at least think about the individual before turning him down.

In the Commons no one looks under bushels for lights. So let them shine before men. Particularly leaders, and in the Tory Party, whips as well. Leaders choose but whips advise. So both should be given the maximum possible opportunity to get to know your charm, ability and ruthless desire to serve the party. Do not be inhibited or feel you are creeping, that is the only way to advance. Speaking is essential, provided it excludes ego and intransigence. The aim is a reputation for having something to say, not to bore the House stiff with it. You must have sound judgement, not be a ranting raver, establishing yourself as a 'good House of Commons man', a clubbable chap, incapable of *chie-en-lit*, who threatens no one. It is also important to establish a reputation in the party by speaking at party meetings in the Labour Party, at committees in the Conservative Party, and by working for office in one of the party groups: Stephen Dorrell seemed to become vice-chairman of the Economic and Finance Group of the Tory Party before his voice broke. This attracts the attention of the people who appoint and builds up a party reputation. It is also necessary to build up wider support: politics is a gregarious art. The maverick is distrusted, loners rise slowly and are disposable, as the career of Norman St John Stevas (as memorable – in Lloyd George's words – 'as the whiff of perfume on a silk handkerchief') clearly show.

Each party has to prove itself representative and normal, when it is in fact neither. Edward Heath became leader of the Conservative Party because he was a grammar school product and therefore assumed to have an ordinary, democratic image. Thus Heath's law now states that minorities are better places to be than majorities.

Women in politics have much better promotion prospects than men. So do Celts: 31 per cent of all MPs held office from 1945 to 1974, but 36 per cent of Scots and 43 per cent of Welsh MPs in the same period. Scottish and Welsh Tories get on best of all: three times better than the English because of their rarity value, just as dying species are preserved in game parks. In the Labour Party southern seats confer a similar advantage increasingly for the same reason. A working-class Tory would have a meteoric career, as would a black Member in either party, while the horny-handed son of toil also has a distinct advantage in today's middle-class Labour Party. Each party is at pains to make itself politically, as well as socially, representative.

Margaret Thatcher included all sections of the party in her Cabinet, though putting her men in key posts and reinforcing them there as time passed. Harold Wilson was famous for Cabinet balancing acts. The left in the Tory Party has – until the 1981 reshuffle – been stronger in its Cabinets than in its parliamentary parties. The same craving for balance has given Labour's left Cabinet seats which it might not attain on grounds of IQ, and while the right has preponderated in both Cabinets and the PLP, its adherents will find it more difficult to get places than those wearing a 'left' badge which is now meaningless but more respectable.

Those unable to establish minority status should recognise the importance of court politics. Courtiers flatter monarchs, claimants attach themselves to courtiers. So leading figures have cliques, except for loners like Denis Healey: which is one of his key weaknesses. Few others are so abstemious or incautious. As they rise their associates move to junior office, unless the leader's displeasure excludes them. It parted Jim Prior and Barney Heyhoe, quickly deprived Prior of Jim Lester, and moved Jim himself to the political equivalent of the Siberian power station. Yet Margaret Thatcher's admiration for James Prior is perhaps exceptional in the warmth of its frigidity.

The toughest part of ascent is the Parliamentary Private Secretary's. This first training ground is essentially a kind of public school fag, a 'gopher' since he has to go for this and go for that, carrying messages to and from the Minister, sticking behind him like a shadow and having as much to do, and generally suffering all the *Angst* of pre-ministerial tension. The Conservatives make better use of PPSs than Labour since they provide offices in departments for them, take them about, have them to sit in at meetings, all practices less common under Labour. Yet basically their job depends on the Minister. Some use the PPS only to fix pairs for themselves. Others try to bring them into enough things to give them a sense of being involved, as well as put upon. The next step up, the Junior Ministers, are the dogsbodies of government, and there are quite a pack of them, currently twenty-seven Ministers of State and thirty-two Parliamentary Secretaries and Under Secretaries. Like Boy Scouts they must be clean in thought, word and deed, as well as loyal to a party and departmental line on which they have little or no influence. Unable to resign because no one would notice, yet unable to push themselves up, unable even to make a success of the department because they have so little independent scope, they are doomed to wait for another turn of the wheel, another ministerial funeral, staying out of trouble, building up their images if they can find anyone interested. On the Labour side they must vote the payroll line in the PLP. There is also a built-in tendency for Prime Ministerial computer dating systems to mix and match in deadlocked pairs (Bob Cryer with Eric Varley; William Waldegrave with Sir Keith Joseph) rather like making St Francis ADC to Genghis Khan. The result is not so much apprenticeship as purgatory. Junior Ministerial ranks were a hotbed of discontent under the Labour Government, yet when they attempted to organise to gain influence, their efforts were immediately vetoed by Harold Wilson and sabotaged by their own cowardice. Junior office is therefore a necessary hell through which the ambitious have to pass and in which, such is the log-jam of ambition in our increasingly competitive system, they can expect to spend longer and longer periods. As George Cunningham points out, the prize which looks so glittering can crumble to dust:

> The Minister . . . is a member of a team and he has got to accept that he stands by the policy of the team . . . The backbencher, by contrast, I always think of as licensed pilot on the high seas. He picks his politics for the day, for the month, for the year. He watches for his chances and then he shoots . . . As a Minister, you become a second-class citizen, because you are not as free as the full MP, you lose the ability in Parliament to do what you think is right, and so it's not just a Member who therefore loses out a bit, it's also his constituents. There were things I could do for my constituents not being a Minister in the period '74 to '77 which I would not have been able to do had I been a Minister . . . A Member normally has to step on to the first rung of the ministerial ladder pretty low and pretty powerless too, and pretty thankless before he is thought suited for senior ministerial office, and many of the Junior Ministers in the period '74 to '79 really felt quite envious of those of us who did not have ministerial office because they felt they had nothing. They didn't have the power of a backbencher and nor did they have the power in Whitehall of a senior Minister.

Yet Lynda Chalker, whose liberal instincts were hardly fully satisfied working as a Junior Minister in the DHSS in a climate of cuts and cheeseparing on social security, still found perseverence worthwhile:

> I'm not sure it's all that bad . . . If you believe very firmly in what you're

> trying to do, then you talk with your own Secretary of State and your fellow Ministers. We have a jolly good relationship. We meet twice weekly as a group on our own, we also talk to other colleagues and I think it's a mistake to think one doesn't have powers. If you approach the issue from the right angle you'll be able to persuade people to follow what you want to succeed in . . . If you really want to succeed you take the rough with the smooth . . . I must say, late at night sometimes I think, 'Is it all worth it?', and then I think of the person receiving the letter sent on by their MP that my officials and I have gone through when we've tried to improve their situation, and yes, it is worth it.

Once Ministers have struggled through the foothills to base camp, they are ready for the final assault. Not all can get to the top, nor can they afford to relax on the way. Reshuffles have become a habit, and a way of demonstrating Prime Ministerial virility. Particularly Mrs Thatcher's. In two years she has had two reshuffles. Between 1964 and 1970 there were changes of personnel or of portfolio on fifteen separate occasions, and in 1974–9 on eight. Thus, of the thirty-four people who held Cabinet office at some stage in that last government, the mean average tenure of posts was only two years and thirty weeks – not long to attain mastery of one of the most difficult jobs in the land. This game of musical chairs leaves a few Ministers undisturbed, as thirteen were in the 1974–9 Cabinet throughout, including four in the same post, but it makes the life of the rest uncertain and weakens Ministers as against the departments. Only the very senior men are secure.

Is the game worth the candle? Not to Chris Chataway, who would almost certainly have got Cabinet office again had he sat out the period when the Conservatives were in opposition from 1974–79:

> You do work tremendously hard and it is tremendously engrossing . . . I always did my boxes in the early morning. I always got up at half past five and I really worked, worked hard against the clock till eight o'clock. Then throughout the day you're busy with Cabinet committee meetings or seeing delegations of one kind or another or in policy meetings and then you're probably in the House until fairly late if you're not at a dinner making a speech. So you don't get much time to question what you're doing or assess its importance. But when I'd finished the job I said to myself, 'What have I actually achieved which nobody else would have been likely to do?' and, giving yourself the benefit of quite a lot of doubt, it still comes to a relatively short list. Power is, of course, concentrated in government in relatively few hands. Perhaps half a dozen people at the outside really take the major decisions in any government, and I wasn't one of the half dozen.

The benefits are rewards and status, power and a seat at the top table. The first two are directly measurable. Neither is substantial. A car, and driver in London regularly, and elsewhere for official occasions, is hardly a great perk by business standards. The Minister's private office, half a dozen staff devoted exclusively to his purposes, is certainly better. Yet with his own money he could buy undivided loyalty and greater effort. No civil servant can ever give total commitment to a temporary master on whom his career does not depend. Financial rewards are pathetic by the standards of even Britain's shabby capitalism and the perks in housing, children's education, health, loans, top hat pensions, travel, or other fringe benefits in flesh or kind are virtually non-existent in our puritanical (and highly exposed) political sector. Paying peanuts and getting monkeys is not the image. In the public service power is measured by virtue, abstemiousness and austerity.

	1974	*1977*	*1981*
Cabinet	£8,500	£19,650	£23,500
Minister of State	£5,625	£12,635	£16,250
Parliamentary Under Secretary	£3,750	£9,625	£12,350

Power is certainly there. Denis Healey has held more of it than most:

> There are two sorts of politician and you can see them all around you. There are those who want to be something and those who want to do something. I want to do something . . . I did change the status quo enormously when I was Defence Secretary. I changed the priority given to defence spending so we spent more on education than defence. I took us out of east of Suez and I revolutionised the way in which we pay our armed forces. I did a lot of other things which are probably less interesting to the party but which were entirely innovative. I can't think of any other Defence Minister who's done as much. As Chancellor I had to spend far too much of my time simply dealing with the problems of jobs and prices, but of course that's what most people in our movement wanted me to deal with. I was quite successful at that if you compare the first year with my last year . . . We managed to find money for a new disablement pension and for the highest increase in old age pensions we'd ever had. In the circumstances of the time that wasn't too bad.

Those who get this far up the slippery pole are within reach of the top: the Cabinet, entry into the inner ring of half a dozen which dominates all governments, even the premiership. A career now is either self-sustaining or self-destructive, but Parliament is only one of the influences at play. The main one is still luck just as it always has been. With a narrowing pyramid and intense yet fairly equal competition, it does more to determine success and failure than most other factors. Yet there are other influences, best described in electrical terms:

Parliament: negative. Enoch Powell has claimed that, 'No man can occupy any position in the politics of this country who has not learned to deserve the respect and to govern the attention of the House of Commons.' He must really mean 'in the esteem of J. E. Powell Esq.', since in practice few Ministers have much ability to command either respect or attention in the House, and those who do are usually outsiders who are allowed both because they are no threat to the rest. At this late stage, reputations and careers can be destroyed in Parliament but rarely made and a little part-time enhancing is the limit of the possible. The careers of Ernest Bevin and Frank Cousins, both General Secretaries of the Transport and General Workers transmuted into Ministers, point the lesson. Bevin made his impact in government first in the war-time coalition and then in Attlee's Labour Government. He was unimpressive in the House but it hardly mattered because his mastery of power was demonstrated. Cousins too was bad in the House but this ruined him because he had no base to build his stature from. Sir Geoffrey ('Mogadon Man') Howe is also a disaster in Parliament but he has the backing of the Prime Minister whose policies he is implementing. Perhaps such a situation calls not for histrionic talents but the interposition of a bag of cotton wool between Parliament and policy. Sir Geoffrey does that job excellently. Most Ministers are well briefed and backed and if the Minister is something like on top of his subject and moderately aggressive, he will easily acquit himself in Parliament; well is another matter but that is in any case rare. Yet it is no longer an essential springboard for advancement. Denis Healey and Sir Geoffrey Howe are both strong Chancellors. Healey's parliamentary performances were uninspiring, Howe's disastrous, but neither made much difference to their standing. Balfour was a master of the Commons, not a bad Prime Minister, but a disaster for his party. Margaret Thatcher takes after him in that last respect if no other. The media and particularly careful massage of the lobby are far more important in building up reputations than actual performance. With Ministers, as with film stars, we are in the myth-merchandising business.

Stature: neutral. Stature within the party is more an earth, deflecting bolts of lightning, than a positive charge. Ministers like Willy Whitelaw or Jim Prior are there because they are there and because they have a base in the party. So were Albert Booth or Stan Orme in the Labour Party. This guarantees place, but not advancement.

Death: (hopefully of others) positive. In death there is hope, as David Owen and Lord Barber can testify. Only the Grim Reaper has more power than the Prime Minister to make vacancies in the jostling scrum of ambition.

Prime Minister: positive and negative. The fount from which all blessings flow can also distribute curses, as Selwyn Lloyd, Douglas Jay, Norman St John Stevas and Sir Ian Gilmour are aware. Power in our system is still highly personalised. Even Junior Ministers, nominally working to and dependent on their departmental heads, are also dependent on the Prime Minister. The degree of consultation within a department and the ease of relationships depends on the Secretary of State – a strong Minister can do what he wants. Roy Jenkins was usually able to gather a jeroboam of Jenkinsites round him, particularly at the Treasury; Keith Speed would probably still be at Defence if Francis Pym were Secretary of State. Yet most Ministers are not in that position, so an ambitious Junior Minister needs to keep in with his Secretary of State (which Bob Cryer, Alex Lyon and Michael Meacher found difficult enough) and with the Prime Minister, for to turn both against him guarantees a prompt exit as Alex Lyon found when his former boss became Prime Minister. In promotions and demotions, Prime Ministers are influenced by the advice of the Chief Whip, the party talent scout, grapevine and gossip manager, by their own reading of the newspapers, and by personal likes and dislikes: Jim Callaghan was as immune to the charms of Tony Benn as Margaret Thatcher has been to those of Jim Prior. All aspirants, once on the ladder, remove themselves from 'country' to 'court'. Talent can establish itself in the country. At court nearly everything depends on the whims and decisions of the elective monarch. The present one is very much a woman alone, her own mistress, trusting no one, making her own mind up and treating colleagues as enemies or worse, which they inevitably become. Unless they want promotion.

Ministers are the elite of Parliament. They sit, envied, at the top of the tree, having the trappings of status, the black cars, the private offices, and the envious jealousy of the pack pounding behind them.

Ministers have arrived where the great majority of parliamentarians really want to be. They hold what the game is all about: power. Or, rather, they seem to. In fact the status is slightly tawdry, while there are major restrictions on individual power. Power is held only under certain rules and conditions. The Minister is not a free agent using the department as his agency. There are enormous collective and departmental constraints so that he can have a happy time chugging round the departmental empire feeling important but doing things is another matter and far more difficult.

In theory, Britain has Cabinet government. In fact, full Cabinet has always been more of a battle-ground than a focus for policy and strategy. It is now turning into a second chamber. The real decisions are taken in a much more flexible way by committees or by floating groups in and below Cabinet, while the main body has all a second chamber's pleasure of confirming the inevitable. Beneath the Cabinet itself there is a full panoply of Cabinet committees. Mrs Thatcher has refused to give details of these committees to Parliament, though she is perfectly prepared to announce both their names and her chairmanship when she wishes to take the credit for the decisions. The Civil Service is forced to keep closing stable doors after horses have bolted, for the details of the Cabinet committee structure are widely known: indeed in Commonwealth countries they are officially published. Here everyone has to pretend they do not exist. The cabinet office has five secretariats, Home and Social, Economic and Science, Overseas and Defence, Foreign, and Security. Cabinet itself has five types of committee: standing committees of ministers or officials ad hoc committees of either and mixed bodies. The standing committees consist of four basic committees, each with sub-committees, and known by an alphabet code, such as 'E', the economic committee, which was James Prior's sop for going to Northern Ireland and which Mrs Thatcher took the trouble to pack with her own men in the September 1981 reshuffle; E (NI) a new committee on nationalised industries so Margaret Thatcher can frighten them; OD, Overseas and Defence; or OD (E) for the EEC. Then there are the miscs: Attlee created 396 in his period as Prime Minister; Margaret Thatcher has run up just over sixty. So far. This elaborate structure keeps the machine going and co-ordinated. It predigests Cabinet business but the real decisions are taken more informally and higher up by the Prime Minister working with a floating nucleus of senior Cabinet ministers. The committee and Cabinet system is the way of formally ratifying them and initiating action. Thus the strength of any particular Minister depends on his placing in the team or the Cabinet committees he sits on and, most important of all, on his relationship with the Prime Minister, always edgy these days. Trusties have control of policy, as Sir Geoffrey Howe has had in Finance, with such enormous benefits to the nation. Michael Heseltine at the Environment has been viewed with rather more suspicion which means he has had to try harder. On the other hand, the real outsiders face an uphill struggle as well as the constant bolts of lightning unleashed against them by the Prime Minister: *vide* Tony Benn under Labour, Jim Prior now. In either case the Prime Minister is the spider at the centre of an enormous web of gossip and information, reading the press avidly while pretending not to do so. Ministers are often judged and condemned in absentia on all kinds of irrelevant grounds, often without knowing what is being held against them.

Most Ministers find their influence restricted to their department and its affairs. Few have either the expertise or the time to make a significant contribution to Cabinet's general discussions and their role on committees is largely one of defending their Department, its finances and its interest. Even a concerted collective effort at protest at government policy, such as that built up by Tony Crosland against the IMF-inspired cuts in 1976, though it won all the arguments and probably had a majority, ultimately foundered on the inability of Cabinet to overrule a Prime Minister in a matter of central importance. The growing doubts in the Conservative Government about Thatcherite economics will run into the same problem. Thus Ministers exercise collective power only as one of a team. Given the size of today's teams, the dilution is considerable.

The departmental constraint is more complex. Departments, indeed the entire Civil Service, can hardly be regarded as neutral agencies. They are a vested interest. The numbers and scale of the Civil Service make it a force to be reckoned with, and its self-interest either as civil servants or as a department, always has to be taken into account, as when a departmental view becomes empire building or when civil servants use their power to protect themselves from cuts by pushing them on to building workers, local authorities, anyone but themselves, and by protecting their own vested interests, financial and otherwise, from ministerial intervention. Departments also have views, or at least patterns of thought. The Home Office, incestuously related to institutions of authority and order, is conservative in instinct. Social Security is innovative. The Foreign

Office defends the EEC as the condition of its new found strength, and feels as paternalistic about that bastard institution as it once did about the remnants of an empire it now can't wait to get rid of. The Treasury is even more divided than usual: wherever five economists are gathered there will be seven opinions, three of them the Treasury's, and, oddly enough, two of them will be the most pessimistic and the most optimistic. For their part Ministers vary in ability and in their standing with the Prime Minister: Tony Benn might not have developed the views he has about the impotence of Ministers had Harold and Jim loved him more. Barbara Castle was perhaps the most effective Minister of recent times because she had the good will of Harold Wilson, determination, and a willingness to pick the best brains and take advice, yet it all went phut when Jim Callaghan came in. Governments, too, behave differently at different stages. They come in determined to impose their views, becoming more amenable to sense as the mainspring runs down towards the end. They are also more inclined to listen to advice as time goes by because their own reserve tanks are quickly exhausted. Many thought Sir William Armstrong had become an extra Cabinet Minister at the end of the Heath Government, so closely aligned were Ministers and machine.

Departments have a series of techniques for getting their way. Learn to recognise them. They will certainly be used against you. The ties that bind will be detailed in *Questions of Procedure for Ministers*, the standard manual of 140 sections which Ministers are asked to memorise and then eat on taking office. This is intended to restrict the Minister to acting only as one of a team. Thus he can neither take his own decisions, push his own barrow, nor go out and drum up support for his own causes. This is the first step to neutralisation. After this the ploys begin. They are:

The Confrontation with the Facts Scenario

Let the Minister stew in his own juice. He may want to cut aid for ailing industry, but leave him alone a while, keep warning about the disasters which follow collapses and even the most obtuse ideologue learns. Running heads against brick walls has not been a great British political skill until the Thatcher Government, but all eventually learn. To supplement the process Ministers should be exposed to as much ear-bashing by pressure groups as possible. Leaking information to those interested groups with whom the Civil Service lives incestuously can mobilise them against the Minister.

The Counter-Briefing Balance

Colleagues, who are not always warmly sympathetic to a fellow Minister, can be briefed against him through official channels in the old boy network. Suddenly and apparently spontaneously, he will find the oddest colleagues saying, 'What's all this about . . . ?' before launching into powerful critiques of things he did not know he had even contemplated.

The Experts Rule KO

Decisions need expert advice. The Civil Service has it. The Minister is dependent. Even bringing in his own two advisers (who are mainly 'fixers' and 'scurriers' in any case) is not sufficient to outweigh this.

The Maverick-Isolation Ward Manoeuvre

A Minister who is a nuisance has to be undermined. The impression is therefore given that he is unreliable, hasty, not a team chap. He took this decision without consulting anyone. Doesn't listen to advice. Very odd. Of course some are. Yet it is difficult for the outsider to distinguish and most of this battle is by leak and innuendo.

The Predigestion Ploy

Ministers are fed with papers prepared by interdepartmental official committees on which they do not sit. With no input to this structure those wanting a quiet life can and do accept its output. They have little alternative. The others find themselves fighting a Dunlopillo mattress.

The Selection Screen

Ministers cannot know everything that goes on in departments. Not even departments know that. So filtering is power. Unless the officials go for the opposite technique of submerging the Minister in paper or keeping him happy touring the country or the world while the department gets on with the job of flogging off the houses /dockyards /factories he has visited after he has been there.

The Timing Tactic

Papers can be kept back, arriving too late to be useful. Work asked for can be delayed for all sorts of reasons. Feet can be dragged on the Minister's pet schemes but hop, skip and jump on those he is less keen on.

The Unhappy Marriage Manoeuvre

A Minister paired with a Permanent Secretary or an Under Secretary with whom he does not get on or whose views are very different can just be left to stew. He has after all no power to change him, much as he might plead with a Prime Minister, who might well want him checkmated.

All these ploys can be and are used. Which does not mean either that this is a conspiracy of Civil Service hanging on to power, versus Ministers fighting to recover it, or that a strong Minister cannot run his department. Tony Benn has made an important point in saying that the Civil Service is not a neutral tool full of neutral tools. Yet it does not follow that the manifesto a party comes in with is perfect and should be implemented with every i dotted and every t crossed by a compliant Civil Service. The people did not vote for all of the manifesto with equal enthusiasm. Indeed they may not have voted for it at all, and most of them did not. In any case circumstances change and the job of the Civil Service is to put the practical problems. They speak for continuity, the national interest as they see it and the interests of the government as a whole rather than the enthusiasms of a particular Minister. Government is a battle because politics is about conflict of views and interests, and climbing the ladder is not a means of escaping by reaching near-Olympian heights, but, on the contrary, a means of intensifying the whole struggle. There is not only no point in pretending otherwise but no way of running the machine otherwise. No reform will get round the fundamental problem: tension between Ministers and departments must be there. A Minister with proper political skills and strong views gets his way even if he has to fight for it. Indeed Mrs Thatcher has regularly got her way even when she should not have, and it is difficult to argue that the Civil Service runs the country when government has been able to impose an economic policy entirely its own over the ill-concealed hostility of most of the departments involved. On the other hand, a weak Minister without clear priorities does not get his way. Perhaps he should not do so. Departmental lines are at least considered, predictable and usually sensible, even right.

Even so there is no reason why Ministers should not be strengthened and several why they should be, if only because better argued decisions are usually better decisions. Political advisers have brought a new channel of advice, another pair of eyes and ears, and a greater degree of political sensitivity. Allowing each Minister to set up a ministerial cabinet of advisors, experts, and backbench MPs would further strengthen the political head and inhibit the inevitable tendency for him to be absorbed though at the acceptable risk of more friction and a less loyal Civil Service. Argument may waste time. Unfortunately that is what democracy is about and it is often the imposed ideological decisions which have been the worst, from the 1971 Industrial Relations Bill through to EEC entry, or the famous Planning Agreements, to Thatchernomics, the most disastrous of all. Here the critics of the Civil Service are really saying they want it to resist those measures which they oppose but expedite those they support.

The world of *Yes Minister* is cynical myth, ignoring principles, policies and political will. The real problem is the closed circuit. Debate goes on; the more the better. It should be reinforced and made more open so that more points of view can be articulated and brought to bear, and so that the outsiders can participate on a more equal basis. As the great educator of the nation, Parliament must have a standing in the real debate. The House could establish its own through select committees, the governing party by involving MPs with Ministers, thus invoking the collective strength of party. Both would be more realistic than our present insistence on having the machine driven by a coterie at the top, managing a one-class stagecoach and excluding five-sixths of the people's elected representatives from everything. Power, like muck and information, has to be well spread.

All this would make government even more cumbersome, even more argumentative but eventually better. It will also make Parliament, and hence the public, better informed, as well as making MPs, and the public for whom they act, more powerful. British government can be strong government: it was in the Second World War. Three years of determined implementation of entirely wrong-headed economics under Margaret Thatcher show that it is still effective with a strong drive from the centre. Without that drive the system is weak against major interests, compromising and dissipating its strength like a dithering giant which manages to get the worst of all worlds by giving the appearance of bullying inconsistency. What is in doubt is not so much the potential strength but the quality of the decisions. The public, because they understand neither the decisions nor the reasons for taking them, and because they are not involved in the processes, react negatively, a situation which guarantees increasing instability. What is lacking is not strength but light, information and dialogue. If that means slower decisions, then there is every possibility that they might be better ones.

OK BOSS
NO
NO
NO
OK BOSS

5 The Fun Factory

Like a huge nineteenth-century cotton mill now turned into a plastics factory, the public views Parliament in terms of its heyday, not the more sordid present. The more deeply involved and the better informed tend to view it as theatre, though they are unable to agree whether it stages high drama or simple farce. It is one theatre which has been given very mixed reviews, particularly from those who have strutted or fretted a few hours on its boards:

Shirley Williams: 'It's an old man's club and the sooner the place changes the better . . . I won't pretend the Commons is a club I enjoy . . . it's terribly outdated: there's too much spare time boozing and too many old men . . . I just don't like the Commons.'

Lord Bill Blyton (MP, Houghton le Spring, 1945–64): 'It's got good walls, a good roof and there's no water. It's the best pit I've ever worked in.'

Cyril Smith: 'Parliament is the longest running farce in the West End.'

Roy Jenkins: 'A splendid place to leave.'

Those who write about it, as distinct from having to work in it, are more awed, more inclined to veil its role in circumlocation. Its powers are potentially enormous, actually minimal, but commentators pay attention in almost inverse ratio. Bernard Crick subtitled *The Reform of Parliament* 'The Crisis in British Government', seeing the one as central to the other. It is not. Most authorities restrict their analysis to saying nothing very much but doing so at length and with the maximum use of convoluted imagery. This seems the only way to describe the indescribable:

Geoffrey Smith:

> Parliament is a constitutional giant: but under normal circumstances the government of the day is the brains of Parliament: a small part of the body determining how the limbs should be used.

Aneurin Bevan:

> The House of Commons is the most unrepresentative of representative assemblies. It is an elaborate conspiracy to prevent the real clash of opinion which exists outside from finding an appropriate echo within its walls. It is a social shock absorber placed between privilege and the pressure of popular consent.

Norman Shrapnel:

> The essentially feminine role of Parliament in the constitutional process does indeed put one in mind of the traditional wife in a male (or government) dominated national household. What the master says goes. Parliament may advise, complain, criticise, protest, delay, nag, scream its head off but it does what it's told in the end.

Gerald Kaufman:

> The Commons will make you miserable when they have it in their power to do so. If you regard Parliament as your highest priority, and take the trouble to let it know that you do, you will experience in it the most fulfilling moments in your ministerial life.

British government works behind a huge protective mechanism designed to sidetrack discontents by obscuring who rules and focussing attention on who does not. Parliament is central to this conceit. Its nominal functions seem to be total power: granting taxation, passing legislation, authorising expenditure and checking its use, protecting the subject, controlling the executive, all safeguarded by the ultimate power of voting down the government. In fact the rise of political parties since the 1860s has put a new reality in the old shell. The people now choose a job lot of Prime Minister, Cabinet, programme and built-in majority of serfs to carry it out. Thus Parliament loses its power. Government proposes, Parliament disposes. Its legislative role is reduced to tinkering and maintenance just as distributors check over new cars from the factory, hoping to make them roadworthy. Parliament grants money, but what the government asks for it gets. Parliament can vote down the government: it did so in March 1979. Yet this was the only peace-time government to be brought down by a vote of the House since 1924 and the Commons had that power only because their ultimate masters, the people, had not spoken in 1974 but mumbled. When the people speak clearly, as they did at seven of the eleven elections and for eight-tenths of the years since the war, Parliament can only fret, fume and comply. When that happens the Commons are really a legislative machine driven by government. Over a third of its time is devoted to government bills, another tenth to government motions and the only other sizable category is the further tenth devoted to supply days largely used by the Opposition.

The House can still have its moments of greatness. It did on the Falklands crisis of 1982. Yet like so much else in British government these are formal and ritualised. Even then the crisis showed the House at its worst as well as its best. The House emerged well because widespread public attention focussed on it, dramatic special sessions captured the mood, members displayed a sure-footed sense of history and occasion, Labour slipping into their traditional role of speaking for England and Tories into theirs as the voice of Empire (R.I.P.) and a serious issue was treated in appropriately serious fashion by the great Forum of our angry nation. Yet it also managed to emerge badly. From the crucial first landings the news services were providing more up-to-date information than the government was giving the House. Much of the rhetoric about the rights of British subjects came hypocritically from a government and a House which had refused to allow them British passports the year before. In the desperate attempt to recreate great moments of the imperial past it was forgotten that Britain was fighting for islands it had been anxious to get rid of until the moment of invasion and that it was the energetic pressure group activities of the Falkland Islands lobby, men like Sir Bernard Braine, advocate of all dying causes and James Johnson the labour imperialist, which had forced governments to go about their sensible efforts to de-fuse the problem in covert hole and corner fashion and thus given 1,800 Falklanders a veto on British policy. Perhaps the House needs a touch of hypocrisy to fuel its moments of greatness. They are, after all, rare enough.

The traditional functions and powers which remain get disproportionate attention. Private Members have twenty Fridays a year for their motions and bills, around one fifteenth of the House's time, a concession granted by government which can be, and occasionally is, swept away as convenience demands. A huge amount of effort, interest and concern goes into what is a safety valve rather than a useful function: over 80 per cent of Private Members bills founder. Backbenchers have considerable powers to raise matters, but none to pursue them. The backbencher is suspended between two worlds. He is a party man there on a party ticket, yet his party is too badly organised to give him any real influence on policy. So deprived of influence where it could be effective, he has to concentrate on his functions in the old world of Parliament, attached to them because he is conditioned to think this is his prime role, rather than because they have any real value.

We have government by party. So Parliament provides the stage on which the party battle can be fought out, the case for and against the government can be put, the arguments fired like accelerated particles into the nuclear mass outside to start more haphazard reactions there. Eventually, so the theory runs, the community decides on the basis of the arguments put before it in that great mass of a thousand decisions in one which is a general election. Parliament is therefore a theatre: what the political scientists call an 'arena assembly' as distinct from a 'transformative' one, like the grown-up legislative world of Congress. David Marquand, who transformed himself from academic to MP, then back to academic via Brussels, sees his former home in this light:

> I think that the theatre side of Westminster is higher quality than it is in most other parliaments . . . This is in a way the ritual side . . . but at least it's . . . quite high-quality ritual. I think there's more drama in a big debate at the House of Commons than there is in, let's say, the Italian Parliament, but as far as the day-to-day routine work of Parliament is concerned, I think that continental parliaments give much more scope to the individual ordinary MP than the Westminster Parliament does. The continental systems all really concentrate on committees where backbenchers do have a job to do and they don't have anything like the party battle which is the sole thing that matters here. The combination of these two things, the lack of the public party battle and the importance of the committee system, does make the actual floor less of an occasion, less something that the press and sketch-writers are going to write interesting articles about. But on the other hand it makes the whole thing much more meaningful.

Good theatre sustains the attention. The Commons has highpoints, particularly the start and the end of major debates. Yet it has far more *longueurs* when the attendance plummets, and however brilliant the contribution it is heard perhaps by a dozen, all more anxious to prepare and deliver their own speeches than to listen. Up to the reforms of the late 1960s the House could be counted out if attendance was low enough, a tactic the Tories frequently used against Labour after its narrow 1964 victory. Now the quorum rule requiring forty to be present is gone and the House can, and does, shamble by on pathetic attendances. It has become rather like a continuous orgy. The young and enthusiastic join in a lot at first, some older ones sit and watch, but gradually everyone finds better things to do, except a few oddities who never grow out of it or who find some perverse satisfaction in what is going on.

Like other West End theatres, the Chamber is dying on its actors' feet. Attendances, even for the major debates, are substantially down and often pathetic. The growing burden of other work, greater commitments upstairs on committees, and the attraction of offices to work in, all lure Members away. Even when the Whips make their periodic sweeps to increase attendance, they bring in only the old familiar faces of the tea and smoking rooms. The rest are immured in offices well away from whipping. Aside from ritual occasions, such as Prime Minister's Question Time, major debates and the Budget, the Chamber is becoming like the House of Lords prior to the transfusion of life peerages. Members stay away in droves, and the work falls on a diminishing number of work-horses who shoulder it for reasons of ego, ambition or lack of imagination. With other legislatures this might not matter. It could even be an indication of health, a sign that so much legislative work was being done elsewhere in committees which have always been more important in other countries. Here, because the centre – the Chamber – is really most of what there is, the decline is disastrous. Parliament now needs a transfusion. It could get it from procedural reforms transferring more report stages to enlarged committees upstairs and reserving the Chamber for issues of principle. It could secure it by an enlargement of the House. It could win it by admitting television. Things must get worse before the House is persuaded to do any of these things.

If the Chamber is the theatre of government, it is traditional: strict rules, proscenium arch, no ad-libs, highly ritualised and stage-managed by the whips. Surprises occur from time to time but usually business grinds on remorselessly to a predictable conclusion. Frontbenchers give the lead and set the tone, Privy Councillors having a precedence, which is the oratorical equivalent of a heavy goods licence, bog it down in pedantics or David Owen, then backbenchers plod through their own dull and deep contributions as people shuffle out. Finally, the whole thing is rounded off in a more lively mood, as Members return noisy and excitable from dinner, an obstreperous and boozy audience which usually only Michael Foot can command. At moments like these Sir Geoffrey Howe sinks without trace, bringing the House alive only when he loses his notes.

There are serious exchanges on the issues of the day. There are thoughtful contributions, often from government backbenchers expressing their doubts about policy. There are effective interruptions. Yet in the main it is a predictable trading of stock arguments for stock answers. It can even sink to this kind of Welsh rarebit:

> MR ROBERTS: I hope that Hon. Members will excuse me for not allowing them to intervene. I have already allowed one intervention and there have been about twenty-four *sotto voce* interruptions . . . The people of South Wales have already anticipated the sort of speech they would have heard and the sort of interruptions they have heard from the Hon. Member from –
> MR ALEC JONES: Will the Minister give way?
> MR ROBERTS: I will not give way on this.
> MR JONES: The Minister's speech is a disgrace.
> MR ROBERTS: They have learnt . . .
> MR ROWLANDS: Answer the debate.
> MR DEPUTY SPEAKER: It is customary for speeches on the adjournment to be heard in silence.
> MR ALEC JONES: This rubbish should not be heard in silence.
> MR ROBERTS: Such comments would be better made in the bar than in the Chamber.

Even when the Opposition makes a massive effort of resistance it can neither hold up bills nor get useful coverage in the media. It is indulging in the ultimate form of masturbation: posing for itself. The 1971 fight against the Industrial Relations Act was the most bitter of recent times. Several suspensions, several guillotines, on one occasion twenty-two consecutive divisions over five hours, accompanied by the (bad) singing of *The Red Flag*, a report stage of twenty-one hours, the longest since 1881, 238 divisions in the Commons, 138 in the Lords and thirty-four more when the Commons considered the Lords' amendments. Yet all this accomplished absolutely nothing except to let the bill go through with many clauses unconsidered and unscrutinised because of guillotines, and to discredit both Commons and the Opposition. The bill passed as the government wanted it. Its failure was due to its own in-built inadequacies and the refusal of the unions, for whom the whole display had been put on in the first place, to co-operate with it. Opposition is impotent and displays of virility only bring out that fact more clearly.

Most institutions lament the giants of yesteryear. Always they departed some years ago. This is clearly true of the Commons people: Pygmies rule not OK, and Julian Critchley is particularly disillusioned:

> First of all oratory is dead and . . . most of us make speeches with our hands in our pockets as if we were at some symposium or other. Orators are few and far between. Secondly, nobody reads Hansard. Thirdly, the small number of people in the Chamber are listening only because they know they are about to be called. As soon as they make their speech and they listen to the speaker who follows as a courtesy, out they go in order to seek refreshment. Fourthly, the press . . . are dreadful because all the press is interested in doing is reporting Question Time. None of these writers who can write most amusingly about politics ever report anything that happens after tea time. At five o'clock they knock off and go and have a cup of China tea and a dry biscuit and write their copy.

Most MPs show their attitude to the Chamber by staying away from it. Some, yet to rise, share Alan Clark's awe of it:

> The Chamber is very important because if you can perform well in the Chamber, and you can get a reputation for being lucid and pay respect to what it requires, but not be pointlessly controversial or publicity-seeking or deliberately provocative, ie: if you can be a responsible House of Commons man, it will be reflected in the esteem in which you're held.

Jo Richardson is rather more put off by the mumbo-jumbo tradition of an institution which moves in a mysterious way but without performing wonders:

> I sometimes look up into the gallery of the House of Commons . . . and there's a lot of jargon going on and a lot of this ritual addressing of each other and all this sort of thing, which you get used to, you can't avoid it, and I look up and I think, 'I wonder what they really think of us.' I'm sure it's a great mystery to all of them.

The most realistic view is that of George Cunningham: cynicism tinged with sentiment:

> What is the point of a day spent on an issue perhaps . . . some great issue like employment. We all know what the vote is going to be at ten o'clock at night, and yet you hang on with people making ritual speeches, they're really only dictating pages for tomorrow's Hansard, only waiting in the Chamber until someone else shuts up and they can get their chance to talk. We waste an awful lot of time on that . . . I suppose if one wanted to be rude you could say that the Chamber is like an old folk's home with everyone sitting round waiting for something to happen, but it justifies its existence because occasionally something does happen, and in any case it's the only place where it can happen.

A harder working, more professional, more cynical and more doctrinaire audience is less open to the witching orator, more likely to be influenced by the manipulation of facts and statistics. The only giants left are Enoch Powell and Michael Foot, both fallen on hard times and past their prime, both looking dated, particularly when dealing with economics, now the central issue. John Biffen is capable of a calm and rational exposition of arcane ideology, Peter Shore of passionate sub-Churchillianism. Edward Heath, now deprived of his notes, is eloquent without them. Yet the general level is mundane. Margaret Thatcher shows her most generous feature to those behind her as she reads out undergraduate essays at accelerating speed. Her voice, that monument to the unknown elocution teacher, rarely attains the husky timbre television audiences have come to accept as the cue that serious subjects are being discussed. In the House she hectors. Denis Healey blusters, Tony Benn is preoccupied by his own (current) obsessions and is not much there since his time has to be devoted to telling audiences what they want to hear. Such audiences are not in a House where young Tory whippersnappers pretend to discern the flash of white coats when he speaks. Willie Whitelaw waffles. Very few – Phillip Whitehead, Stephen Dorrell, Robin Cook, Chris Patten – have the unique ability to think on their feet and make sense of the process. Fewer still, perhaps only Neil Kinnock, can now orate. All the rest are either professional bores, the rejects of the yap professions, ham lawyers, or readers of substantial and usually dull essays which could come from the gamma delta of any decent university. On a few subjects – law, education, Commons procedures – debates reach a high level. On major modern preoccupations, such as industry or economics, it is poor, swamped by lawyers, accountants and ill-gotten Keynes. High points are few. The average level is a rehash of old arguments put badly and rescued only by extensive correction for the record.

Even allusions are recycled: the road to Damascus is as much used as the M1: Chinese generals baptise with hosepipes; Caligula's horse, Frederick II's treaties (never respected and frequently violated), all regularly make their appearances. So do gods making mad before destroying. Wit is weak, humour dying. The comic turns, such as John Stokes' defences of the nineteenth century, which have at times become so impassioned as to earn him the party label 'Stokes (Ancien Regime)', Arthur Lewis's carefully cultivated image as the layman's layman, or Mick Walsh's nightclub routines about his wife are now all too rare. There is, however, still the occasional spectacle of Willie Whitelaw floundering endearingly through a half-understood brief, accusing the Opposition of going round the country 'stirring up apathy'; or halting in the face of uproar, precipitated by reading a page of his notes twice, to observe benignly: 'I realise that I have repeated that passage. I repeated it because I thought it was important.'[1] Or commenting impatiently: 'I should like to say yes and I should like equally to say no. I think that it would be appropriate for me to start again . . .'[2]

Spontaneous interjections generally hover about the level of Eric Heffer's 'Get lost' and rarely reach the intellectual penetration of Denis Healey's 'You fucker' to Dennis Canavan abstaining on the cuts. Most are mercifully recorded as '(interruption)'. But not all. Nicholas Fairbairn was once observing, apropos of St Paul on the road to Damascus, that he was stoned. Russell Kerr interjected, 'So are you,' and brought the House down. It does crumble very easily. Most spontaneous demonstrations seem carefully planned, particularly when elections are due in Northern Ireland and stirring Ian Paisley and the fellow members of his God, Show Biz and Related Trades Party, or other elections to Labour's National Executive are in the offing. However, something else has to be invoked to explain Michael Heseltine's finest hour when, in opposition, he angrily grabbed the mace and swung it to demonstrate his anger and embarrass his party. Even the efforts of Bernadette Devlin clawing Reginald Maudling, or former boxer Tom Swain punching a Tory, have not yet raised violence as a parliamentary art form to Kop levels. The Commons Kop, below the gangway where the malcontents sit on both sides, has become rather sanctified by the invasion of the Nice Party, the SDP, on the Labour side, scrabbling for seats with Tribune MPs, and almost deified by Ian Paisley (MP for the Balcony and All Points Higher) on the government side.

Humour is mostly unmemorable. Michael Foot in full flow suddenly invited all Tory Government supporters who approved of its policy to put their hands up. Six hesitant hands went up. Laughter. More usual is the studied insult, such as Denis Healey's description of Sir Geoffrey Howe's efforts as 'being savaged by a dead sheep', or of Mrs Thatcher's special relationship with President Reagan as 'the parrot on Long John Silver's shoulder'. On a claim that Social Democrats believed in solving problems by 'being nice to them', Healey commented *sotto voce*, 'Not while David Owen's around.' More lovingly, but outside the Chamber, he remarked about Tony Benn, 'Today Tony announced that he is Deputy Leader.

[1] *Hansard*, 22 June 1981, col. 31.
[2] *Hansard*, 21 January 1982, col. 409.

Tomorrow he is parachuting into Scotland to hold peace talks with the Duke of Hamilton.'

Rather more parliamentary humour is entirely accidental: Geoffrey Dickens, 'I am seeking, Mr Speaker, to do a favour for every woman in the United Kingdom.' (Laughter.) Mr Speaker: 'Order. It was well worth calling the Hon. Gentleman. I await the rest of his point . . .'

Finally, even the stimulus of exciting speeches, original opinions, a new twist of thought, is largely lacking in debates. The wit and wisdom of the *Daily Telegraph* on one side is countered by aerosol *Guardian* from the other, while at the lower level of the Kops the *Weltanshauung* of the *Daily Express* and the *Daily Mail* are banded against the *Daily Mirror* and the *Daily Star* in exchanges as stale as yesterday's newspapers. When Jeremy Bray attempts to lift the debate to the level of the *Journal of Econometrics* the House shuffles in boredom. Radicals have always accused the Commons of damping the fires of dissent, dulling the desire for change. In fact most of those who get there are conventional in opinions: to be so is the price of getting in. This might be heightened by the rubbing off of awkward corners and the muffling effect of the club after getting in, but conformity is more a matter of group think by those who are fairly sheep-like in the first place. Safe opinions are boldly asserted as if to do so was an act of great courage. Those who stick out usually do so because they find it a useful show-biz routine, like John Stokes's Church and King Tory Romanticism or Dennis Skinner's much-loved truculence, or even Enoch Powell's parody of Enoch Powell, rather than because of any blinding originality. Those who assiduously canvass parliamentary opinion hardly find it very original. In 1981 the RSPCA sent questionnaires to 492 MPs. They were rewarded by such gems as the amazing discovery that 74 per cent favoured more controls on experiments on living animals and 65 per cent wanted to ban the sale of pets in street markets. None confessed to kicking dogs, or hating animals. An Opinion Research and Communication survey of 100 MPs found that most Conservative MPs believed that its economic policies would succeed, while Labour Members 'overwhelmingly' believed that they would fail. Most surveys produce the same result: putting the obvious in percentage terms. Never look to MPs for exciting or original opinions. Never hope that the Chamber will yield anything beyond fashionable nostrums or dull reflections of concerns widely voiced outside. Never expect anything beyond the regurgitation of pressure group handouts, newspaper articles or, at the very best, bowdlerised rehashes of books or ideas fashionable a year ago.

Even the most vaunted of Chamber occasions are not what they used to be. Question Time typifies the transformation, having been changed from important event into public show. Each department comes up by rota every four weeks usually for fifty-five minutes, the Prime Minister twice a week for fifteen. As a way of probing it has been replaced by television. By contrast with that intimate studio theatre, Question Time is music hall, as if Robin Day, Alistair Burnet and Anna Ford (suitably aged) all had to bob up among a posse of football hooligans to bawl one question in convoluted language before someone else changes the subject. In television studios one against a hundred always wins. So it is in the Commons. As a method of examining the activities of departments, Question Time is useless, compared to investigative journalism or select committees. As a method of raising grievances, it has been entirely swamped by the party dogfight. It is, therefore, useful only to ventilate issues, grab headlines and make or ruin reputations. As Rab Butler observed, 'The law of the jungle prevails. If they see you limping they're after you,' even, perhaps particularly, those who limp themselves.

In departments, enormous effort goes into preparing for the four-weekly ordeal. Meetings prepare stooge questions for distribution to tame MPs. As a PPS I used to put in some twenty questions for friendly backbenchers on the assumption that some at least would be drawn either to allow a breathing space or detour the discussion on to what the department wanted to talk about. This process becomes feverish, on both sides, at Prime Minister's Question Time, when the slogan is 'let a hundred plants blossom'. Mike Thomas organised a pool when Labour was in power with Members signing forms in advance and questions being agreed for those who drew lucky. Today, the similar questions are more sycophantic as the Prime Minister gets deeper into the mire, but the number of volunteers appears to have shrunk. Indeed, present progress could leave only John Butcher last, loneliest, most loyal, asking such questions. Until that day happens, sympathetic questions will still be farmed out and those on the government side who draw lucky in the Prime Minister's days will still be approached with suggested 'interesting' questions.

The next stage is departmental meetings to prepare the answers for those questions which are drawn in the lottery. Answers start at civil servant level and work up. Meetings a week before and on the day give the political varnish and a final gloss, and also provide material to give the tame recruits on the same side politically a suitable supplementary. Thus the best brains, both Civil Service and political, are devoted to preparing suitable replies, sussing out googlies, thrashing over suitably ad lib answers with their spontaneous flow of statistics, even little jokes. Question Time is therefore a protective mechanism as well as an investigative one. Nevertheless it does provide a built-in security system alerting Ministers and departments to difficult problems and areas of misunderstanding or inefficiency. When it does unveil problems ministerial reactions have to be concealed, for the real art of reply is to be bland and non-committal: the bland leading the blind – astray. The formula is to offer no exposed points where grappling irons might grip: offer as little information as possible, it may be taken down and used against you. Thus, the standard joke of Minister and Permanent Secretary lost on the way to a meeting. Spotting a local, they ask 'Where are we?' The answer: 'In a car.' A perfect answer to a parliamentary question: true, pithy, giving nothing away. As one Under Secretary dealing with parliamentary questions put it: 'One must tell the truth in answering a parliamentary question, but one mustn't necessarily conduct a public striptease.' Nor of course must one make news, unless favourable, or announce anything controversial, because that is throwing bones to wolves. Written answers are best for bad news, not being exposed to questioning. Hence the flow of monstrous revelations, particularly from the Department of the Environment, in the form of innocuous written answers to stooge questions. So overused was this device that fears once grew that Mrs Thatcher might be tempted to declare war and announce it by written answer.

Care, control, stonewall. John Nott: 'I have not yet revised my estimate of the £5 billion cost of Trident.'

Ten days later he told Tory backbenchers it would be six billion. Before the end of the year it was up to £8 billion (ONO). It is still climbing. No Minister has ever broken down and confessed at Question Time. The most effective ministerial technique is a simple one of returning kick for kick, tit for tat without any compunction to answer half heard and quarter understood questions.

Each Question Time attracts its due quota of specialists anxious to establish a reputation. They are joined by headline seekers, passing muggers and those with nothing else to do. The regular quizzers are a kind of club: despite tight restrictions on the numbers of oral questions, ten MPs got in more than fifty oral questions in the

1979–80 session, the winner being Dennis Canavan with ninety-five. Most try for the Prime Minister because the form of her questions demands no thought, simply a desire to know what she is doing today or if she will go to Heckmondwike, because more specific questions are passed to the Minister responsible. Winning the draw to take a potshot at the PM means maximum publicity. The occasion fills the House. Yet few of those attending think much of the exercise. 'A monumental sham . . . but good for the tourist trade,' is Julian Critchley's description. David Marquand is more pedantic:

> This is supposed to be the House of Commons, collectively scrutinizing the executive, and it's ceased really to be anything of the kind. It's become a kind of mini party yah-boo slanging match. One of the reasons for this is that the opposition frontbench intervenes more and more in Question Time, so that if a backbencher gets up and asks a probing question of the government, the Shadow Minister feels he's got to leap up and make a party point. Immediately then of course all the government backbenchers have to leap up and fend it off and ask the Minister, 'Is my honourable Friend not aware that he's doing an absolutely, splendid job and the whole country thinks he's marvellous?' He says, surprise, surprise, 'Yes, I do think that,' and so the opposition backbenchers then play the same game. It's really become corrupted.

The behaviour which so shocks radio listeners is, like vandalism, a result of boredom. MPs know all the arguments. They have heard all the answers a thousand times. So they have fun. They barrack. They try to undermine confidence, hoping to destroy. Question Time is a combination of cockpit and the House of Commons at play. Every four weeks those interested in a particular subject gather to tease each other, put party points, show off their individual knowledge, and generate factoids to be scattered into the public debate. Because the press is so lazy, a quip at Question Time is more likely to get coverage than the most brilliant speech. Twice a week the whole House gathers for a more compressed, and therefore more crude, version of the same thing. Members clamour for attention, grovel for jobs, and rehash facts from that day's newspapers – with some deterioration in the style and the grammar.

The public is bemused. One interviewee in an opinion survey gave an audience researcher a view of Prime Minister's Question Time: 'Most of the questions seem pretty stupid and irrelevant to me . . . like "What have you been doing this morning?" Well, I should say, "Mind your own flaming business." . . . I mean, why take up valuable time answering silly questions like that?'[1] Prime Ministerial replies, all carefully rehearsed by meetings beforehand, reveal more character than facts. This is government by quip: Jim Callaghan, bland and avuncular; Margaret Thatcher, alternating between a deft knee to the groin and a self-satisfied simper. She has little alternative, given the calibre of the questions:

MR FOOT: How does the Rt Hon. Lady think that her colleagues in Europe can understand a policy which the Rt Hon. Member for Sidcup describes as 'incomprehensible'? Does not the Prime Minister understand that she must answer to this House? What does she think of the Rt Hon. Gentleman's statement? Following what the Rt Hon. Gentleman and others have said on this subject, do the Government intend to proceed later this year with further public expenditure cuts which will lead to further unemployment, further racial hatred and further crime?[2]

Some prefer a gentle tickling with a feather duster:

MR HUGH DYKES: Does my Rt Hon. Friend agree that the parliamentary rabble opposite have no recipes for Britain's economic revival? However, bearing in mind that we have an unprecedentedly large margin of spare capacity in men and material generally, and especially in the construction industry, is it not now possible to consider certain non-inflationary measures to revive the economy that would not lead to an increase in inflation?[3]

Others grovel:

MR MAXWELL HYSLOP: Is my Right Hon. Friend aware, and will she tell the House, of the great achievement of our Rt Hon. Friend the Secretary of State for Trade, who last month secured an enormous Brazilian agreement for British industry to refurbish Brazilian coal mines, power stations, and the transport media?[4]

Cruder spirits go for shock:

MR DALYELL: Will the Prime Minister accept the ghoulish truth, of which I gave her office details eleven days ago, that about a year ago to the day, thirty Russian technical officers were forced to eat their own testicles?

[1] Hansard Society Research by Kathryn Rowan.
[2] *Hansard*, 2 July 1981, Col. 1003.
[3] *Hansard*, 2 July 1981, Col. 1004.
[4] *Hansard*, 30 April 1981, Col. 904.

While some just bungle it, a disaster which can even happen to stooge questions:

MR CLARK: Has my Right Hon. Friend had time today to read a report in the *Morning Star* – not a paper usually noted for its support of the government, to the effect that redundancy payments are being used to set up new businesses on an unprecedented scale?

THE PRIME MINISTER: I am not a regular reader of the *Morning Star*. I have, however, read the *Daily Star*, which had a double-page presentation – entitled, I think: 'Adventure' giving details of people who have used their redundancy payments very successfully to set up businesses.[1]

Written questions are a more profitable and effective way of fulfilling the real purpose of the exercise, eliciting information. They are also more used: only 129 questions were asked in 1847. In 1980–1 there were 30,863 questions, 8,175 oral and 22,698 written, a steadily growing number because of the rationing of oral questions and the lower likelihood of getting drawn to ask it. Asking questions of either type becomes a virility symbol and dimmer MPs expect to impress their constituents, not having heard the story of the MP telling his electors, 'I have asked more questions than any other MP,' and getting the answer, 'Ignorant bugger.' Competition is encouraged by annual league tables. These are often topped by Arthur Lewis who poses as a professional ignoramus. This gives some idea of the intellectual calibre, while Michael Brown, ever eager for knowledge about anything, is coming up on the inside. The 1979–80 top ten are:

1.	Renée Short	1,360
2.	Austin Mitchell	922
3.	Tony Marlow	812
4.	Michael Brown	748
5.	Ernie Ross	719
6.	Robert Kilroy Silk	676
7.	Dafydd Wigley	669
8.	Arthur Lewis	651
9.	Frank Field	634
10.	T. H. Skeet	575
	TOTAL	7,766

[1] *Hansard*, 24 November 1981, Col. 749.

The table applies only to those questions ruled admissible. Perhaps one in five is rejected or has to be rewritten to come within the quite specific rules the table office enforces. Clearly, no Member can have that much he really wants to know. Some misuse researchers to devise questions or imitate those put by others. Some repeat questions in yearly or even monthly cycles to build up the total. Others make themselves available to pressure groups, to party research departments or even to those researching for books. Thus a legitimate device for unearthing information, for examining the assumptions and the facts on which government policies are based, and for providing facts to a hungry world, can be brought down to the level of Michael Brotherton, who asks the rate of VAT on lawnmowers. An average cost in 1981 of £50 per oral and £30 per written to answer each question makes the 1979–80 top ten worth £232,980, or about double the total annual wages of the Members who asked them. This rising tide of parliamentary questions even creates the remote possibility of using the power of Parliament to burst the cash limits. Though lazier Members complain, departments become unco-operative if burdened with more than they feel fair, and though the flow is becoming too great to be coped with, even by *Hansard*, nothing can be done about it. Nor should it be.

The House spends most of its time on routine gamesmanship, starting with the use of time. This is the Opposition's main weapon but a blunt one, for the ability to delay is limited by the techniques developed against the nineteenth-century Irish Nationalists and now mobilised against Her Majesty's Loyal Opposition: guillotines cutting short debate in the House, timetable motions in committee, strict government control of business. This leaves the Opposition only twenty-nine supply days devoted to its subjects: usually generalised denunciations, more like a gas attack than precision bombing, or regional debates, which hand major issues to local dullards to rehash for the local papers.

The real parliamentary gamesmanship centres on specialised techniques. A glossary:

The Ambush

Members pretend to go home, then hide in offices or houses round Westminster. When the government is lulled into a sense of security all converge on the House in the early hours of the morning hoping to defeat it. Used by the Tories against a tired Labour Government from 1950–1 and by Labour MPs organised by George Wigg to retaliate effectively from 1951–55. It was also used by the Conservatives in 1965 but not much since. The opportunity is now ripe for revival though in theory, Conservatives should do it better. They have more houses round Westminster and a greater sense of public school 'fun'. A more common variation is to keep a few Opposition MPs on as nightwatchmen to keep talking going through the night, while the rest go home. Thus government has to keep large numbers of troops around and tire them out. As a third variety of this art form there is the manoeuvre worked by Labour's Chief Whip, Michael Cocks, on 3 December 1981 when, at the last minute, he withdrew his name as one of six sponsors of two Opposition motions, leaving both with insufficient names to be discussed, and the government with a gaping void in business which the Opposition could then fill, after some government delaying tactics, by debating Social Security changes.

The Delegate to Deputy System

Nothing to do with the Coal Board but a simple commonsense system whereby senior Ministers announce everything good, leaving deputies to announce everything doubtful or disastrous. In extreme cases, interest rates can be allowed to go up and crises to develop in the autumn when the House is not sitting and senior Ministers are away, so obviously no one at all is responsible.

The Early Day Motion

Registering views without the risk of having to act on them by putting down motions which are not debated and collecting signatures which carry little commitment. Labour likes attaching itself to every available cause as do the ideologues on the other side. So both play a numbers game unless there is all party support, in which case it is played against the government. To be acceptable, a motion must not be ironic. Vivian Bendall put down a vital motion condemning powered skateboards. An amendment restricting this censure to skateboards over 250cc was rejected when handed in with a smile. It was accepted by another clerk when delivered straight-faced. It then received fifteen signatures, not bad for such a high-powered motion.

Without any such irony, the Early Day Motion is also a chance to display classical learning, a rare phenomenon in the House of Commons:

> MR ROBIN F. COOK: That this House notes with surprise the recent statement by the Prime Minister that 'Ulysses resisted the siren voices and came safely home to harbour'; recalls that on the way Ulysses suffered a shipwreck in which he lost his ship with all hands; notes that on reaching Ithaca he was unable to use the harbour because his palace was occupied by the hostile suitors of Penelope and that he was reduced to the loyalty of one herdsman and a dog; and wonders whether the Prime Minister's novel version of Homer anticipates the forthcoming wreck of British industry under Conservative steering or merely reflects the depressing decline in education standards following the cuts in public expenditure.

The Eight-Minute Quickie

The Speaker's Office keeps meticulous records of who speaks and for how long. Once when complaining that I had not been called, I was amazed to be told that, with seven speeches from November 1980 to May 1981, I had been called more frequently than 90 per cent of backbenchers – and then that I had added insult to injury by speaking for more than twenty minutes on six of the seven. In 1979, the average contribution was clocked at three ten-minute speeches per backbencher per session, making 0·03 seconds per constituent.

The Euro Get-Out

Faced with a decision in the EEC, the Minister proclaims his determination to fight for British rights, whips the House into a frenzy of xenophobia, then comes back saying, 'Sorry. It was nine to one. We had to have an agreement. We can't wreck the Market on this.' Used by John Silkin and less expertly by Peter Walker on fishing, where the House is committed to demands for twelve miles exclusive, a dominant share of the catch up to fifty miles and the ability to impose its own conservation measures up to 200. It will get none of these things. It does not want to know that. MPs want to be able to go back to their constituents saying, 'We wuz robbed.' It discredits the system, but it is supposed to save seats.

The Filibuster

A 'talk in' to talk out or hold up a bill. In July 1980, Terry Davis filibustered on the Consolidated Fund Bill, by going through each estimate in detail. Scenting excitement the Cryers, Mikardos, *et al.*, converged on the Chamber to add their mite by prolonging debate beyond 2.00 pm at which point the coming day's business is lost. In 1981 Ian Mikardo pledged unilaterally to a Post Office Engineering Union meeting that the Telecom Bill would be fought tooth and nail. Everyone else then had to go along with this to stop the party looking silly, forcing a twenty-five-hour sitting on All Fools' Day which ended at 3.30 pm next day and thus lost a day's business despite an agreement by Labour whips to get the bill through. Nothing was gained in either case. The government always makes up the ground by piling more business into remaining time. Yet virility is displayed. Particularly by insomniacs.

The Full Opportunity for Debate Excuse

Members acquiesce in unpleasant decisions, provided they are allowed to talk about them afterwards. Both parties waste enormous sums of money on nuclear weapons which will never be fired, pollute the country with nuclear power stations it does not need, encourage the greedy to make Britain a dustbin for nuclear waste, or give away Britain's fish to the Common Market. Backbenchers allow all this so long as they are promised 'a full opportunity for debate'. The decisions are then confirmed, but everyone feels better about it. Except the public.

The Language Code

Presentation is a major part of politics: it is not what you say, it is the way you say it, so the language code becomes almost as important as the reality. Margaret Thatcher, as the Dr Goebels of economics, has a genius for putting what she does not understand into language everyone can follow by the simple trick of turning complex economic issues into simple moral ones: forget currency fluctuations or Keynesian multipliers; it is all a matter of working harder. For less. Harold Wilson was even more homely but he preferred to get his illustrations from football.

The same system prevails in the House of Commons when there is a standard language code to say what everyone knows without any risk of putting it down in print and having it held against yourself at a later date. Thus:

I will require notice of that question.
Translation: You're probably right. I'm not admitting it here.

We have this matter under review.
Translation: My God, you are right.

No final decision has been taken.
Translation: We're committed but it won't do to announce it yet.

I will write to the Honourable Member.
Translation: I have not got the foggiest idea.

Those of us with the responsibility of office must take a wider view.
Translation: I agree but I was overruled by the Prime Minister.

This is what the people voted for.
Translation: There must be some justification but it's not sensible to give the real one.

This matter does not come under my departmental responsibility.
Translation: Sir Keith Joseph did it.

Wasting time with debating points.
Translation: You're right but I can't say so.

The circumlocutions are as numerous as they are obvious. When the government acts, accuse it of gimmickry. If it doesn't, accuse it of complacency. If the Opposition are right they can be accused of talking differently from the way they acted in power. If they're half right, say they're divided. So it goes on. Space is provided on the inside cover of this book for your own examples. The code also applies within parties. Tories making damning indictments of their government's economic policies must always preface them with an expression of admiration for the Prime Minister's courage and with congratulations on her astonishing success in getting inflation back almost to the level it was at when they came in. Rebels must excuse their fault by a vigorous attack on the other side. Graduate Labour MPs sitting for industrial working-class constituencies must always speak on behalf of the working-class and if possible adopt left-wing politics as camouflage. Since parties are organised hypocrisy anyone who wishes to succeed must conform to the mores and the language. Indeed this code is the only way to communicate successfully. Harold Macmillan led the Tory Party left by talking right. Harold Wilson led Labour to the right by talking left and men like James Callaghan or Ted Heath, who talked and led in the same direction, get accused of brutality and insensitivity. All this is the language of politics. That of Parliament is more simple: circumlocution. Never refer to people by their proper names or directly. This is a non-you place, as Bob Litherland found on first arrival:

> One thing that happened to me coming from local government: I was talking to the Minister and I just referred to his last remark with a 'You have just said' and the chairman stands up and says, 'I haven't said anything,' and sits down . . . So you go on again and you say, 'You have just referred,' and the chairman stands up and says, 'I can tell the Honourable Member I haven't referred to anything,' and the whip then whispers to you, 'If you say "you" you're referring to the chairman.'

Objection

MPs can be very objectionable as a means of asserting an influence they do not otherwise have. Private bills are held up if one Member objects, giving MPs power to put pressure on sponsors for all kinds of reasons: on British Rail for service changes, or local government over particular disputes. Thus the Humberside Bill, a much-needed local measure filling in various gaps in local law and protecting the lug-worms on Cleethorpes beach was long held up, first by Hull members demanding better fire cover on the river, then, when the county changed hands and Labour took over, by Edmund Marshall over a school closure in Goole. Finally Kevin McNamara blocked it along with him to force the county to make a statement on a local arsonist. The bill fell a year behind an already slow schedule as a result. Finally it passed in March 1982 just before the lug-worms became extinct, with objections withdrawn but none of the things the objecting Members had aimed at conceded. Since any member can grind any axe it makes the whole process of private bills exposed and unpredictable. It also allows pressure on those organisations, from local government to British Rail, which need it.

The Politics is about Choice Syndrome

MPs justify the indefensible on the grounds that, disastrous as it may be, we should actually sympathise with them for choosing it. While Mrs Fenner, Tory MP for Rochester and Chatham, vigorously opposed the 1981 decision to close the dockyard, Michael Brown (MP for Scunthorpe) supported the closure of Normanby Park Steel Works on the grounds that it was for the greater good of British Steel and Scunthorpe itself, even if it lost thousands of jobs in the area.

This was, however, before the next Scunthorpe closure rumours in 1982. In the same way, three million unemployed can be defended as a necessary prelude to better things (say 2·5 million). Labour MPs voted for cuts in 1976 on the grounds that the alternative was the collapse of a Labour Government and the return of the Tories. Not true, but it makes the unacceptable more palatable.

Recirculation of Excuses

Each government, as it comes in, does what it wants for two years, then runs into the ritual crisis and responds with the traditional policies of incomes policies (such as that J. R. Tolkein character, the Tebbitt, or 4 per cent Norm), high interest rates, and announcements that the promised land is postponed (*vide* 1961, 1966, 1972, 1976, 1981). Thus the arguments can be recycled by civil servants trained in chop logic. When doing the obviously harmful, the argument is always shifted to courage and the need for it. When wasting public money, they invoke the need to care, help, protect, stimulate. When cutting spending, they are leaving money in the pockets of the people to exercise their freedom of choice. When chopping up nationalised industries, small is beautiful. When flogging them off in a bankrupt's progress, they are being transformed by a new incentive because the language tends to be 'private good; public bad'. When the economic situation is really bad Ministers discern light at the end of tunnels or shift ground to the mystical by seeing a change of spirit or an 'invisible miracle'. This is usually like the Vicar of Lilley, who announced that the world would end in 1697 and explained in 1698 that it had, only no one had noticed. Alternatively, they can bring out the Dunkirk grey. One coat covers any mess. The British like to think they are at their best with backs to the wall and this government is clearly determined to give them the chance to prove it. Always invoke the basic principle of chop logic: shift the argument on to another issue or another plane, so that people have to talk about that, not the messy case in point. Unless things are good. In which case, talk about them endlessly. British politicians may not need this latter part of the technique.

The Commons people have very uncertain egos. The old joke of the headmaster's report, 'Knows nothing but thinks he knows everything. Should go into politics,' is too cruel. Yet politicians are expected to radiate confidence even when they've no idea. They are supposed to have the answers when the sum total of their knowledge is that their own side is better than the other lot. Interviewers on television and questions in Parliament are constantly forcing them to nail themselves to every available cross in a way which was never necessary before. So it comes hard to them to admit that they are wrong, and when things do go awry they badly need instant excuses. This sense of infallibility *manqué* and the long list of hostages given to fortune make Ministers and MPs generally very dependent on two sets of individuals who provide the necessary balm. The party researchers supply a never ending stream of what the other side said. This can be used to prove that they got it even wronger, or, in Britain's recent economic mess, that they said or did the same thing and so can be incriminated in the blame. The civil servants have a more neutral job, that of providing excuses, justifications and defences of the indefensible. All three can be doled out in much the same form to successive governments since each is usually in the same mess, albeit for different reasons. After a time dependence on both sources becomes total, a process that takes the politicians further out of touch with a public which has heard it all before and is bored and fed up with the endless argument over 'You did this, they said that'. Admission of error would come as a shining light, yet the dynamics of the two-party system preclude it.

The Resignation Game

Resignation is a ritual. 'I am placing my office at your disposal' means 'I've been told to go'; 'Retaining every confidence' means 'I hate your guts'; 'Serve from the backbenches' means grinding knives there. The resigner makes a statement in the House which always falls flat. He then has a choice between the Marcus Fox approach of grovelling servility; the St John Stevas approach of feigning acceptance and loyalty while planting as many knives in as many backs as quietly as possible; or the Nye Bevan technique of a long and bitter attack on rivals (in this case Hugh Gaitskell) and a disclaimer of responsibility for his own acts, because no one is 'Mr Clean' in politics. Grapes as sour as these should be trodden privately if possible. There are too many Members too easily dismissed as chip-on-the-shoulder merchants; witness the would-be-vultures now hovering hopefully over the Thatcher Government and the reserve of Members on both sides who never quite made it and took refuge in malign sourness as a way of life. The basic rule of resignations therefore is get your lies in first, because those you have left and the cynics will quickly combine against you. It is a trifle humiliating to be forced to resign an office no one knows you have but when, on 17

March 1982, I submitted a non-voluntary resignation as a Labour whip after voting against the Prevention of Terrorism Continuance Order, the *Daily Telegraph* announced that I had apologised to Michael Foot and wanted to go; the *Guardian* that I had 'wandered into the wrong lobby by mistake'. Both managed these revelations without talking to me. It was both annoying and untrue, but all indicative of the need to take the gun you are handed, to go away quietly and shoot yourself like an officer and a gentleman, and use it to put bullets in as many other people as possible first of all – provided you use a silencer on them and remove it for yourself.

Ten Minute Rule Bill

A request for leave to introduce a bill which would then be put into the waste-paper bin and forgotten, were it not for the fact that the publicity it develops makes many think it has passed into law. Normally two are proposed a week and Members have to be prepared to sleep in a third-floor office all night so as to be the first in the Public Bill Office at 10.00 am to get one. They then speak for ten minutes in support. Any lunatic who wants to oppose can do so. Labour bothered over every one, treating them as issues of principle. The Conservative Government usually acts more sensibly by leaving anything it does not like alone. The House then votes. Useful mainly for drawing attention to any issue, from televising Parliament to safety of children, since the aim is publicity not action. It is also effective financially, since the sponsor usually gets a lot of press coverage and television and radio interviews which can, for a good subject, bring in as much as £100. Even a bad one generates a reputation: George Foulkes is now Parliament's – perhaps the universe's – expert on Space Invaders. Since the bills are usually meaningless they are better big, such as Anthony Steen's Unemployment (Abolition) Bill, or the Britain (Restoration of Greatness) Number One Bill.

The 'They Did It Too' Excuse

Most government decisions have previous parallels. Is unemployment three million? Labour put it up one million. Is the government's economic policy in a mess? Labour had to call in the IMF. *Ad infinitum*. All this raw material is quickly provided by teams of political archeologists pillaging every conceivable site and tomb.

For some years everything can be blamed on predecessors. Harold Wilson still talks of the 'record balance of payments deficit' of 1964.

If things are really bad, you can blame say, the previous three decades, as Mrs Thatcher is now doing. One of Speaker George Thomas's favourite stories is of the incoming Minister who was kindly left three envelopes by his outgoing predecessor, to be opened in each crisis which struck the department. On opening the first he read, 'Blame your predecessor.' At the second crisis the advice was, 'Say you are instituting an urgent reorganisation.' In the next crisis he opened the third and read, 'Take three envelopes . . .'

The Whinge-In

Government backbenchers make angry noises, show concern, air their feelings. Then collapse. On 15 July 1981, Anthony Grant moved an amendment to the Finance Bill to give hotels the same tax allowances as industrial buildings. A succession of Tories from seaside resorts, and one from Birmingham, poured into the almost deserted Chamber to praise hotels and attack their own government for its intransigence. Nigel Lawson abruptly rubbished the whole idea and threw them into confusion. Some accepted the insult, others called nervously for a division. They then bungled that by being unable to find any tellers; deliberately.

Such are the games. While the Chamber plays them life is transferring upstairs. To the committees, the House in miniature: same strengths, same weaknesses, both exaggerated. Like the Chamber, standing committees depend on a small proportion of Members. Only half the House make themselves available with any regularity and the actual work is done by a much smaller proportion, as the class register shows.

Committee Attendances
No. of MPs

	1978–9	1979–80
Not called	179 (28%)	68 (11%)
Appointed but did not attend	83 (13%)	36 (6%)
1–4 attendances	194 (31%)	127 (20%)
5–9 attendances	71 (11%)	63 (10%)
10–19 attendances	66 (10%)	95 (15%)
20–29 attendances	24 (4%)	73 (11%)
30–39 attendances	—	62 (10%)
40+ attendances	—	89 (14%)
Chairman	18 (3%)	22 (3%)

Most assiduous attender was John Mackay with ninety-one.

Appointment to committees is nominally by the Committee of Selection; in practice it is largely influenced by the whips. Some committees produce competition for places, normally from the Opposition Members. On most, whips find difficulty in assembling a team of regular attenders because demands can be heavy: forty-six sessions for a housing bill, forty-two for a local government bill, compared to only one for a statutory instrument. Government has the added problem that the role of their Members is total boredom: brute votes expected to attend and vote, but not to speak, and certainly not to vote independently. Mistakes do happen. Jeff Rooker and Audrey Wise (both Labour) were appointed to the 1977 Finance Bill after two Tribune MPs withdrew. They proceeded, with Tory support, to drive a huge hole through the Bill and immortalise themselves. Such slip-ups are rare.

A government has a built-in committee majority. Its proposals, late revisions, rethinks, modifications, will all be carried. The Opposition labours in vain. Its far more numerous amendments will be voted down, while the minority parties show their indifference by bad attendance, Liberals tending to insist on a ten o'clock bed time, SDP Members visiting Westminster only as they can fit it in to their busy schedules. A new set of eyes is useful, but cannot improve things much in relation to the scrutiny which has already gone on, so the role of the committee is not line-by-line review of legislation, but delay by debate. There were over a hundred government defeats in standing committee from 1974–9, but the balance of power was unusual in that period. Usually committees are argumentative rubber stamps. Some Opposition amendments are accepted: it would be an extraordinarily incompetent Opposition which could not find some flaw. But nothing of substance. The only real opportunity for an Opposition is to air its views. Its Members seize it. At length. Passage of time, reinforced by public debate, can produce reconsiderations, usually on inessentials, sometimes on substance: in the 1981 Finance Act, faced with storms outside, the government dropped a whole clause on agencies and recast its small business start up scheme. Yet such changes come only because the committee delay allows outside opinion to make an impact. The main committee business battle is always a foregone conclusion.

Committees are like a microcosm of the House: same faults, same procedures, all amplified. Except that mistakes are more private.

MR STRAW: Now that I come to look at the amendment I cannot for the life of me work out why I tabled it. It seeks to delete paragraph (a) of subsection (4), but as I read paragraph (a) it seems eminently reasonable and sound. I should be grateful if the Minister could tell me what he thinks I have in mind.

MR LAWSON: I wish that I knew. The sentence in front of me says 'This is probably a probing amendment', but we were not at all sure what the Hon. Gentleman was seeking to probe. I suggest that he might care to withdraw the amendment and buy another candle.

MR AUSTIN MITCHELL: Might it not be reasonable for my Hon. Friend to ask whoever selected the amendment [for discussion] what he had in mind in selecting it?

MR STRAW: I share the view of my Hon. Friend the Member for Grimsby (Mr Mitchell) because while we are allowed to make mistakes, I do not think that the clerks should be allowed to.

THE CHAIRMAN: Order. The committee is moving out of order and I think that the Opposition would be the first to complain if they were not given a proper opportunity to discuss what they had tabled.

MR STRAW: Indeed it would. I beg to ask leave to withdraw the amendment.

Amendment, by leave, withdrawn.[1]

As in the Commons itself, civil servants are present in a box behind the Speaker to advise a Minister by passing notes. In committees, this life support system is even more obvious because they sit at a table on the Minister's left.

MR HOMEWOOD: Is the Hon. Gentleman able to tell us the extent of the tariff?

MR PARKINSON: I do not know whether the Hon. Member for Kettering (Mr Homewood) has served on any of these committees before. If so, he will have noticed that, from time to time, the Minister rises, plays for time, and suddenly a piece of paper appears in his hand, as a result of which he is relaxed and happy. I am still waiting for the second piece of paper. That is why I am being helpful in explaining the procedure of committees.

MR DAVIS: I believe that the Hon. Gentleman was on the Companies Bill Committee in 1976 when just such a situation arose over the indecipherability of certain company documents at Companies House. My Hon. and Learned Friend the Member for Accrington (Mr Davidson), the then Minister, was presented with just such a situation. He had a note passed to him which unfortunately was indecipherable.

[1] *Standing Committee E: Finance Bill*, 9 June 1981, Cols 482–3.

I hope that the Hon. Gentleman will not be placed in that position. I may have saved him a little time.

MR PARKINSON: The Hon. Gentleman is being very helpful . . . I think that most questions that I may be asked are covered by typed answers, but the one answer that I cannot find is the rate of tariff to be imposed by the order. Therefore, I shall write to the Hon. Gentleman giving him that figure.[1]

Members are less than ecstatic about committee work. To Jo Richardson, it is disillusioning in Opposition:

You sometimes feel like sitting back and saying: I don't know why I'm bothering. Why am I beating my brains out sitting up there night after night on the Social Security Bill, for example, which some of us did, when we know we can't win. At the same time one has to remember, and it's a very important fact, that the fight has to go on, on every dot and comma of the legislation put forward by the opposite party . . . and in the end you come to accept that this is the way it is.

While to Mark Wolfson it is even more disillusioning as government fodder, for Ministers want bodies on their side, not minds:

I think it's very salutary for the backbencher to find that when he is on the government's side during the bill the pressure from a minister handling the bill through the whip is to ask the backbenchers to keep relatively quiet because, for every contribution the backbencher makes in committee, there is a further opportunity for the other side to take up more time and in the standing committee system there is no balance between an opposition speaker and a government speaker . . . I would like to see two things happen in the standing committee area. One, a balance of speakers, and secondly, the involvement of experts . . . So that the standing committee ceases to be something of a charade.

Select committees are different. They are the most hopeful procedural change of recent years. Yet their long and painful gestation illustrates just how slow a very conservative institution can be. Select committees are nothing new. They were used in the nineteenth century, sometimes for complex and lengthy enquiries. The post-war period began with domestic select committees like Privileges and Services, and three standing committees: Public Accounts, which still functions to audit government spending with the help of the Comptroller and Auditor General and a staff of six

[1] *First Standing Committee on Statutory Instruments etc.*, 7 November 1979, Col. 8.

hundred beavers, the Estimates Committee; and the Committee on Statutory Instruments.

In the 1950s a Committee on Nationalised Industries was added with some initial success but later disappointment, and by the 1960s parliamentary reformers, encouraged by American experience, came to see such select committees as a way of allowing Parliament to scrutinise the Executive more effectively. This argument had considerable appeal to the crop of highly educated Members brought in in Labour's pedant revolution of 1964 and 1966. They found themselves with nothing to do but support a government with a huge majority, and saw committees as a useful way out. More importantly, the idea found favour with Richard Crossman. As leader of the House he established two select committees on Agriculture, and Science and Technology. The first failed, because it quickly ran into difficulties with the department. The second was more harmless and therefore more successful. So the precedent was followed by Education and Science, Overseas Development, Race Relations, Scottish Affairs, and a committee to which the Parliamentary Commissioner reported. Then came a less happy change, the Expenditure Committee with six sub-committees, all beavering away with minimal resources and staff and almost no response on the part of House or government.

Not until 1978 was a more rational pattern imposed. Then the Select Committee on Procedure proposed the establishment of twelve select committees, each related to the work of one Department of State. Robert Rhodes James objected to this division of responsibilities:

> I cannot think of any subject which is of any importance which is dealt with by only one department. That was the strength of the subject approach which took a subject, whether it was the aviation industry or prisons. I was on the Select Committee on Prisons, and prisons isn't just the Home Office, nor is it just the Prisons Department in the Home Office; it's a whole number of people including obviously the Treasury and the Department of Health and Social Security, and so on. So the moment you take just a departmental approach, you miss out the whole strength of the previous arrangement. But I'm a heretic on this. My voice was virtually solitary.

Others objected to the whole system. That nineteenth-century traditionalist Michael Foot saw it as weakening the Chamber. Normally, this would have impaled the proposal on the Catch 22 of parliamentary reform: to be acceptable to the government a proposal has to pose no threat, but if it poses no threat it is unacceptable to the band of parliamentary reformers in the House. However, backbench reformers were sufficiently dangerous under a minority government to force a reconsideration of the government's own position and the Conservatives, ever eager to embarrass, committed themselves to such an extent that Norman St John Stevas, an enthusiast for the new system, was able to push the proposal through the incoming Cabinet. Twelve select committees were established, plus others for Scottish and Welsh affairs, though a mandatory requirement for eight days to be set aside to debate their reports was dropped. They were not given all the powers they needed. Their chairmen were not paid. They were not allowed to compel ministerial attendance. The Civil Service Department told officials not to disclose advice given to Ministers or information on inter-departmental exchanges. Yet it was an important new start.

The new committees threw themselves into their work with enthusiasm. Each chose its own subjects for investigation and its own staff, usually part-timers. Specialist advisers who cost only £27,092 in the 1978–9 financial year cost £126,937 in 1980–1. Up to 31 May 1981, committees had had 549 formal evidence sessions, examined 575 officials on 913 occasions, received 421 memoranda from departments and paid twenty-eight visits abroad and ninety-three within the UK, at a total cost of £172,337. The strain fell on only a minority of Members, as only 277 MPs are on all the select committees, domestic and subject, but on the departmental committees the attendance record averaged 75 per cent, high for this dilatory institution. The result, up to summer recess 1981, was a total of eighty reports issued by the committees, mostly high quality – all with the supporting evidence. The Treasury and Civil Service Committee has been the most successful because of the happy accident of a government with curious economic policies and a chairman of stature, Edward Du Cann, who was also chairman of the 1922 Committee and a Chancellor of Exchequer much *manqué*. Its reports have provided a devastating critique of the government's economic policies. Similarly, the Environment Committee's review of government housing policies and calculations has knocked away much of whatever intellectual basis Michael Heseltine's policies had.

The experiment has its faults. Terms of reference are too vague: policy, administration, expenditure and 'associated bodies' came under their purview so they find difficulty in focussing their minds and attention. Because so much of the ability on the government side is drained into office, the government numbers on the committees are not always up to the intellectual calibre required. They embark on *ad hoc* policy forays not the hard grind. Their attention is too easily distracted. Senior government backbenchers as chairmen have proved a leaden weight for some, and Industry and Trade and Home Affairs both seem to have been ineffectual. They have had to refight many of the old battles and they have lost. The Defence Committee, for example, was refused six documents which had already been leaked to the Press Association and received extensive publicity. Several other committees have complained about inadequate release of information. Perhaps those are teething troubles. The collective achievement is far greater than the cynical view that 'they keep a lot of lunatics off the streets' or act as an expensive form of adult education for some recalcitrant raw material. The experiment is still developing, and at the very least it is casting light on areas previously obscure. It forces government to justify policies. It examines their intellectual basis. It provides raw material for informed opinion. In a world where information is power it provides more, and, as it settles down to the longer term, more basic, enquiries it can become even more effective. The counter argument, that the committees merely pile up mountains of facts which then impede the activities of Members, is one of no account. It assumes that ignorance is bliss. The government can ignore the reports. It usually does. Yet facts, arguments and explanations are all accumulating in a body of evidence which one day may be used against it. Only one test is still to come. The going has yet to get rough. When it did in the Nationalised Industry Committee's 1978 clash with the British Steel Corporation, party loyalty pulled the committee back into line. Labour Members spoke against their own report in the House. Two who refused to soft pedal were dropped from the Committee. The same could well happen again, which is why the committees are well advised to move forward gingerly.

As the Commons enters the 1980s it does not live up to the aspirations of the parliamentary reformers of the 1960s. The House is not at the centre of national life. Even though government is preoccupied with the Commons, it still does not control the Executive. The House does not prepare and inform opinion adequately. Nevertheless, it is more powerful and effective than at any stage since the nineteenth century. Its Members are more professional, better backed and more independently minded. They have a more effective machinery for developing a critique of government. The ultimate power has actually been used. As Parliament loses respect it has actually got better at doing its job.

The result has been to create two classes of Members. A devoted, hard-working Member suffering from political *retinitis pigmentosa* has always been able to make a name and an impact: Sir Gerald Nabarro and his Clean Air Act, Sir Bernard Braine and his campaigns to defend Canvey Island against pollution, to protect the rights of Commonwealth citizens, or reject the Maplin Development; Tam Dalyell and George Cunningham with their struggle against devolution; Jack Ashley and Alf Morris and their campaigns for the disabled. Yet the numbers have been small, the specialisation obsessive. We are now developing a broader spectrum of Members prepared to put in a substantial work and time commitment to the select committees and, thus, to build up a specialised expertise. Professionalism has not arrived. Yet it is on its way and there is no going back. Information and influence become addictive. Backbenchers who have learned the habit of dissent will not fall meekly back into line. Specialisation is the only way to make an impression on issues or governments and the House is gradually providing the wherewithal to develop and pursue it. It has to. In a complex modern society there is no function for MPs who merely represent the collective ignorance of a fairly ignorant community.

Unfortunately there is no clear and obvious way of going forward either. The public, to which members are usually so sensitive, gives no lead. If they think of parliamentary reform at all, people outside the House think of insane hours or all-night sittings. They are irrelevant. The House cannot sit in the mornings. It needs that time for committees and correspondence; Ministers need it for departmental duties. Most Members come from outside London and are in exile in the capital. Since they have little else to do, there is no harm in working them to the maximum. Another criticism over the waste of time involved in divisions also means little. It would be unreasonable for absent Members to vote and the lobbies do provide an intermittent reshuffling of the pack, putting leaders and led cheek by jowl. The complex procedures of the Commons are often lampooned. They certainly give power to the priesthood of clerks and make Members unduly defensive because no one really understands them, not even the Speaker. Yet to George Cunningham they are still a tool, not a master:

The procedural rules of the House are quite grotesquely complex to such

> an extent that we have to have these very highly intelligent clerks to understand them. But in the end, so long as the Member realises that if he's got a procedural problem, the best thing he can do is not ask another Member but go to one of the clerks, then the procedure will not stand in his way.

So the most widely discussed lines of reform turn out to be blind alleys. Indeed there is something to be gained by sitting even longer and spreading the session over the full year. The House of Commons should not be pushed into a drawer and forgotten for the summer, as if politics and problems ceased to exist through August, September and October, while the country is governed by an autocracy. A four-day working week spread through the year would make Parliament more relevant.

Yet if public opinion provides no leads the necessary reforms are clear. The House provides adequate supervision and control of neither delegated legislation nor the flow of regulations and dictates from Brussels. It needs a strengthened committee on statutory instruments, and much more powerful committees on EEC legislation. Both need power to reject, holding up disputed items until the House decides. On EEC matters particularly, the House has tied its own hands. It can scrutinise draft EEC regulations, then attempt to influence the British Government to get them changed, which usually makes both sides impotent, MPs because the government will not or Ministers because it is too late. Even the Lords provide better scrutiny. Yet to get effective control for the Commons requires changes in the European Committees Act of 1972 to give the House the positive powers it certainly needs to stop the succession of Euro-follies on noiseless lawnmowers or how to tell sheep from goats.

Because it is not adequate as a protector of the rights of the subject, the House needs a committee on rights and civil liberties, with both powers to investigate and report and the backing of a strengthened ombudsman working to it. Instead of taking the government's word and the bureaucracy's consultations on legislation, standing committees need power to investigate and enquire, to examine witnesses and to hold hearings before they settle down to the detailed consideration of a bill. This was tried briefly under the liberal St John Stevas leadership of the House. Then standing committees held hearings on deep sea mining, on education and on criminal attempts, but the government has not dared to repeat this procedure since, though it could be applied to the whole range of bills, and perhaps particularly to the Finance Bill. To do it and even to do their present job properly, standing committees too should have advisers available, since most Members are not well informed enough to deal with most bills, and the help which pressure groups can provide is limited. Why should Members be dependent on the self-interested efforts of pressure groups rather than the more sustained and useful efforts of official advisers?

The Chamber needs to be freed of some of the present clutter of report stages which could go upstairs to different and enlarged committees. Then the House would have more time for the major issues of the day, for select committee reports and for Private Members' legislation. Private Members' Bills do fill in loopholes, clear up minor problems and tackle matters for which government has neither time nor inclination. They also provide real satisfaction for Members. Robert Rhodes James was one of the very few actually to get such a measure through from the unlikely beginning of a Ten Minute Rule Bill:

> It all started with my first surgery in Cambridge when a couple came to see me with a very sad story. Their son and daughter-in-law had been killed in a car accident. There were two children of the marriage who were now under the guardianship of someone else, who had broken what was entirely an oral pledge to allow this couple to see their own grandchildren. They had consulted lawyers who had said, 'You have no legal rights at all,' and I thought this was an amazing thing . . . I mentioned this to a journalist who very kindly gave us some publicity, upon which I was absolutely snowed under with letters from all over the country . . . and that's how it all began . . . I discovered that I had entirely by accident lunged upon a major social problem . . . To be absolutely frank, I thought it was a fairly forlorn adventure but I was determined to do my best and push it as far as I could go. I was then enormously heartened by the number of colleagues on both sides who said that they would support it because they had come across similar cases themselves . . . I did it through what was called the Ten Minute Rule procedure and it's very unusual indeed for any bill introduced under that procedure to get anywhere. But I had a particularly good cause and strong support from the Labour Party and the Liberal Party as well as my own party. The only people who were resisting me were the government of the day.

Only the first six in the annual ballot stand a real chance. They get a guaranteed debate and £200 for drafting expenses. The others tread a harder road so the number of such bills is small. In 1979–80, ten Private Members' Bills passed the Commons (a quarter of the total in the Lords) taking up only 4 per cent of the House's time. The year after, there were fourteen, ranging from indecent displays to private zoos. To pass they must be innocuous, minor in scope, or restricted to subjects certain to get unanimous support. A Praise of Motherhood (No. 1) Bill would do well, but inadequate provision of time lays more controversial measures open to filibuster and delay of the type which has sunk recent ritual 'Abortion' bills (the conventional name for 'Anti-Abortion' bills) as well as attempts to open up government. Indeed bills can even be filibustered by proxy, as in 1981, when a bill of Laurie Pavitt's, to check tobacco advertising, was never reached because of ninety-four amendments, mostly from Bristol, to the bill on private zoos which preceded it.

Most of all, Parliament needs better backed MPs with a legislative and research staff like their American counterparts. This would allow them to keep more pans bubbling on the oven and do a better informed job more efficiently. Such is the logical extension of the reforms already made. The changes are as obvious as the difficulties attending them. Opposition to change is clearly old fashioned, centring as it does on outdated views of the Chamber as central and influential and of the Member as an unspecialised layman which do not correspond to modern realities. The real basis of the opposition is unspoken. It is the huge vested interest of those with second jobs and outside commitments, all of whom feel that the MP is overworked, overloaded with paper and pressures, because they are. Voluntarily. Yet reform does mean harder working MPs. It also means a fairer distribution of the work. A disproportionate burden now falls on the parliamentary workhorses. As measured by questions, voting and committee work in the 1979–80 session, these are:

MPs asking more than 10 oral (O) and more than 100 written (W) questions, with more than 300 divisions (D) and more than 50 attendances at Standing (Sg) and Select (St) Committees – 1979/80

	QUESTIONS			*COMMITTEES*	
	O	*W*	*D*	*Sg*	*St*
N. Baker (Dorset, North) Con	10	110	403	27	68
A. F. Bennett (Stockport N) Lab	30	155	397	72	33
K. L. Best (Anglesey) Con	21	243	415	42	27
G. R. Cryer (Keighley) Lab	57	548	438	21	83
T. Dalyell (West Lothian) Lab	76	196	337	32	31
J. Evans (Newton) Lab	51	150	365	57	–

	QUESTIONS			COMMITTEES	
	O	*W*	*D*	*Sg*	*St*
W. W. Hamilton (Fife C) Lab	42	194	370	57	48
B. J. Heddle (Lichfield & Tamworth) Con	12	305	395	51	–
F. O. Hooley (Sheffield, Heeley) Lab	65	517	329	11	58
A. McQuarrie (Aberdeenshire E) Con	23	488	336	41	29
N. J. Spearing (Newham S) Lab	31	212	351	67	99
I. M. Sproat (Aberdeen S) Con	12	352	322	45	31

These are the parliamentary activists, the people who keep the place going. Compared to their efforts, a much larger number of MPs either do a lot less or direct their activity into less public channels. In the same session, fifty-five Members (9 per cent of the House, but an even bigger proportion of the non-ministerial ranks) asked less than twenty questions and attended less than ten committees. Restricting this group to those who also voted in under 200 divisions out of the 500 total shows the following Members who, on these measures at least, had a quiet session.

MPs asking less than 20 questions, attending fewer than 10 committees and voting in under 200 Divisions, 1979/80

	QUESTIONS			COMMITTEES	
	O	*W*	*D*	*Sg*	*St*
Amery, H. J. (Brighton, Pav) Con	3	10	236	9	–
Bagier, G. A. T. (Sunderland S) Lab	3	10	190	1	–
Dunlop, J. (Mid-Ulster) UUUP	2	9	65	6	–
Edwards, R. (Wolverhampton SE) Lab	0	0	183	1	–
Fitch, E. A. (Wigan) Lab	0	17	172	1	–
Fletcher, R. (Ilkeston) Lab	0	0	122	0	–
Galbraith, Hon T. G. D. (Glasgow, Hillhead) Con	1	1	187	8	1
Heath, E. R. G. (Sidcup) Con	0	0	97	–	–
Mabon, Dr J. D. (Greenock and Port Glasgow) Lab	0	13	158	1	–
McMahon, A. (Glasgow, Govan) Lab	0	9	92	3	–
Macmillan, M. V. (Farnham) Con	0	0	164	1	–
Maguire, M. F. (Fermanagh & S. Tyrone) Ind. Rep.	0	3	18	0	–
Mulley, F. W. (Sheffield, Park) Lab	0	8	97	–	0

	QUESTIONS			*COMMIT-TEES*	
	O	*W*	*D*	*Sg*	*St*
Peyton, J. W. W. (Yeovil) Con	0	1	141	0	1
Roberts, A. (Normanton) Lab	0	14	188	0	–
Ryman, J. (Blyth) Lab	1	1	174	3	–
Urwin, T. W. (Houghton-le-Spring) Lab	0	6	178	1	–
Williams, Sir W. T. (Warrington) Lab	0	0	158	–	1
Wilson, Sir J. H. (Huyton) Lab	0	2	156	–	–

The list includes some major figures. They are not idle but that particular session they were clearly not attending many committees or asking many questions. The reasons can be numerous: bad health, laziness or simple exhaustion from a session spent bombarding Ministers with letters and working to the point of collapse at all the other parliamentary activities unrecorded in such simple measures. Yet it is nonetheless a fact that if some MPs worked a little harder, the House would clearly be capable of taking on considerably more work and playing a much greater and more effective role as an institution.

Government itself is the final obstacle to reform. The changes to date have all been authorised versions. Crossman, though no great politician himself and even incapable of finding his way to the Public Bill Office, still wanted a reputation as a reformer. Michael Foot, as a constitutional antiquarian, was actually opposed to most useful reforms but was part of a government which could be overruled. St John Stevas was positively enthusiastic, fortunately so because a majority of the Cabinet was not. Without similar government backing, further reforms are unlikely. Yet that backing will not be forthcoming in a climate in which many think reform has now gone far enough and others think that it must threaten government's credibility. These views must be heightened by the inevitable sensitivities of a government well into its term and therefore more defensive and suspicious than in the first careless rapture. Parliament needs the Executive's permission to make itself better at a job which makes the Executive's life more difficult. If, therefore, further reform is to come, it will probably come not because the public or the House want it, but because Parliament has to adjust to reflect changes in the wider community, or because the gap between it and a complex, difficult reality widens once again, as it will without reform.

LABOUR
TORY
COMMONS PLAYERS

6 The Nature of the Beast

Members of Parliament are male, middle-aged, and middle class. Norm Westminster is a 45-year-old dark-suited, university educated, professional sitting for a safe seat. He entered Parliament in his late thirties, has up to ten more years to serve. His psychological make-up is less easy to define. That has not stopped self-appointed experts rushing in. No section of society is more categorised, analysed and dissected than MPs. There are almost as many generalisations about them as there are Members. None is important, for politicians have become fair game and most generalisations tend to be highly coloured. Ex-Members tend to be rather jaundiced. David Marquand, who was an MP for eleven years, views those who stayed behind as different creatures from the kind of staid academics who get university chairs:

> Nearly all of them have a slight gambler's streak. I think that's almost a prerequisite for a political career. They are people who've taken a bit of a gamble with their own personal lives because it's not a safe career . . . so I think there's that sort of insecurity element. You have to like insecurity a bit or thrive on insecurity to be happy in the House of Commons. I think perhaps associated with that MPs are . . . in a way warmer than the population at large. If you're with a group of MPs the atmosphere is more emotional and, in a sense, warmer. It's a rather spurious warmth maybe, but they emote more easily than do the general population.

On the other hand, those who have not been in are more critical, while the Members themselves verge on the self-congratulationary, Martin Stevens particularly so:

> It's the most difficult job in the world, being an MP. You're taking all the sins of the world on your shoulders . . . You've got to have an affection for your fellow man and you've got to have this burning motivation which drives us all along, to want, in however modest a way, to play a part in the government of our country. Now the other side of it is that you are also a pompous windbag and ego-hunter whose

uncontrollable vanity leads one to take part in television interviews . . . Vanity obviously plays some part but I don't think it's part of my major motivation.

Outside speculation is slightly more cool in its appraisals. People very rarely volunteer compliments about politicians.

The most sustained and amusing psychological analysis is that of Leo Abse, a private Member. He has put a little Freud to a lot of use:

> Westminster is the power house transmitting socially sanctioned aggression. It inevitably becomes the Mecca for all those who wish, even as they did in their nurseries, but now without fear of disapproval, to scream with anger, spit at their enemies, bitingly attack opponents, boldly hit out at wrongs, real and imagined. Like moths around a flame, the aggressive flutter around Westminster. Outside Dartmoor and the armed forces, there are no more aggressive men than those sitting in our Parliament.[1]

Abse describes anti- and pro-marketeers as ocnophils and philobats. The one clings to objects and feels safe only in familiar surroundings. The other resents ties, is excited when journeying from place to place. So the speculation goes on, as endless as it is rootless. Thus Harold Wilson's long-winded optimism is put down by Abse to brusque weaning. The unbreast-fed Harold has been forced by an inconsiderate mum into that class who 'will never reconcile themselves to the reality that they have lost their pleasure sucking for ever: they deny the fact and fantasise that their mother's breast will flow for them for eternity.'[2]

According to Abse, ambitious MPs have little interest in genital sex, Tony Benn is working out his ambivalence to his own father by attacking paternalism in society, and most individualists can be explained in equally curious ways. Each man to his own DIY psychoanalysis kit. All that is needed is a little knowledge of MPs, rather less of psychology and there is all the material for many happy hours of speculation and casual character assassination.

The ready generalisations we are all too prone to make float on air. The remorseless American social science machine, ever eager for new worlds to process, has begun to analyse American legislators. Sadly no one in Britain has attempted the necessary psychological inventory. Almost certainly if they did MPs would angrily refuse to fill in the questionnaires or undergo the tests on the grounds that they were

[1] Leo Abse, *Private Member*, p. 53.
[2] Op. cit., p. 262.

'too busy' and already bombarded with questionnaires, which they are, though only to the tune of perhaps half a dozen a year. Some organisers take the precaution of offering a fee of £20 or of accompanying the questionnaire with an attractive lady interviewer. Either guarantees success but a mere psychoanalyst in a white coat might produce a slightly different response and without such detailed analysis collective descriptions are merely gossip.

The only straightforward analysis is in terms of observable characteristics. But which ones? Psychic researcher Joe Cooper maintains that Zodiac signs have bearing, not so much in the way the star charters of magazines use them, but as an indication of the way people orientate to each other. On this basis, the signs of those MPs misguided enough to publish their birthdates show the following pattern:

	Total Members	*Labour*	*Alliance*	*Conservative*
Aquarius 21 Jan–19 Feb	7·2% (43)	5·7%	2·6%	7·4%
Pisces 20 Feb–20 March	9·0% (54)	10·4%	13·1%	8·0%
Aries 21 March–20 April	10·2% (61)	9·4%	15·8%	9·2%
Taurus 21 April–21 May	7·7% (46)	7·5%	10·5%	7·7%
Gemini 22 May–21 June	10·7% (64)	9·9%	5·3%	12·3%
Cancer 22 June–23 July	11·7% (70)	13·7%	13·2%	10·7%
Leo 24 July–23 Aug	8·8% (53)	8·0%	15·8%	8·3%
Virgo 24 Aug–23 Sept	7·3% (44)	8·5%	2·6%	7·1%
Libra 24 Sept–23 Oct	7·5% (45)	7·5%	2·6%	8·0%
Scorpio 24 Oct–22 Nov	6·3% (38)	6·1%	5·3%	6·7%
Sagittarius 23 Nov–21 Dec	8·0% (48)	7·5%	10·5%	8·6%

	Total Members	*Labour*	*Alliance*	*Conservative*
Capricorn 22 Dec–20 Jan	5·6% (34)	5·7%	2·6%	6·1%
TOTALS	600	212	38	326

A fairly normal distribution but, with a few exceptions, Joe Cooper's analysis of the figures by comparing them with birth distributions in the total population indicates that the House of Commons has a significantly higher proportion of Geminians and Cancerians. The latter, strongly represented in the Labour Party, are conservative in instinct but caring, indeed like the crab sign itself, men of hard exterior and soft centre, caring deeply about the group rather than the individual. Gemini, much better represented in the Conservative Party, tend to be positive, quick thinking, adaptable, doughty fighters, particularly when it establishes their dominance, but like so many of the younger generation of Tories, men on the make. The high proportion from the Aries sign is also a significant deviation from the expected frequency. This is a domineering sign, representing a reforming zeal which was also very strongly represented in the 1945 post-war Parliament, and indeed embodied in Tony Benn, an archetypal Aries. Labour has more from Pisces, a water sign concerned with the well-being of others and with supporting the underdog, yet not averse to their own careerism, a combination of characteristics of which Sir Harold Wilson is a classic example. The Social Democrats, as distinct from the rest of the Alliance, show a significantly high proportion of Leos who, appropriately for a party of chiefs without Indians, are supposed to be of a domineering personality, people who like to lead and be bosses, who like to shine. The Liberals, with more from Aries, are much more inclined to dynamism and activity, the kind of people who like to get cracking and get things done, a trait common to Bismarck and David Steel and the best-cracked-pavement-pounder.

Such is Joe Cooper's diagnosis of the House horoscope. Members and the wider public will make of it what they will. As a poor Virgoan I can't help picking holes in the whole approach. Virgoans are far more academic and pedantic. Being a Labour version of the species my own inclination is to look at the social background of MPs as a far more rewarding field of study. It is, however, one characterised by a perennial tension between the elitist and the representational aspect, the diminishing dialogue between those who want the best men and women for the job, and those who prefer to have a House of 'folk like us'. The wider public are constantly ambivalent about whether they want Members they can look up to or blokes they can identify with and who they feel will know their problems and the realities of their lives. MPs are automatically an elite because they are picked out by being elected. Yet at the same time representatives cannot be too unrepresentative by being too far out of line with the mass of the people.

We are a class-ridden nation and the British tradition has always been elitist. Historically the Commons have drawn the bulk of their Members from the aristocracy and the upper middle class: public school men, Oxbridge chaps, a class born to lead and seeing politics as one way of doing so. New groups thrust their way in as they rose, first manufacturers, coming in mainly after the First Reform Bill, then manual workers, beginning with the miners, whose political power was always greatest because of geographical concentration. Yet, at the turn of the century, the Liberals were still overwhelmingly middle and upper class, attracting the new rising men, the journalists, the lawyers, businessmen. The Conservatives represented the landed interests, wealth, the military and the top professions, some industrialists and a few great cities, principally Birmingham and Liverpool.

The rise of Labour broke this pattern. It attracted old Liberals and groups who would have gravitated to the Liberals in their heyday; but Labour was essentially a working-class party, tied to the trade unions. The House thus came to reflect the dominant division in a class-divided society. Trade unionists confronted employers, miners confronted coal owners, the have nots confronted the haves. Each party was the essence of its interests. The clash of interests in the Chamber was essentially the same as that of the monolithic classes outside.

Today the House is more difficult to analyse. Some MPs are mavericks moving from job to job before moving into Parliament. Some are polymaths like the ever modest Nicholas Fairbairn (of Fardell but MP for Kinross and Perthshire), who gives his occupations in *Who's Who* as 'Author, painter, poet, TV and radio broadcaster, dress designer, landscape gardener, bon-viveur and wit', but whom I have classified as a mere lawyer. Yet classifying people by the occupations they held longest is enough to bring out the patterns. Each parliamentary party has become slightly more representative of the whole nation, moving to the middle and narrowing the social gap between them. Labour has become more middle class, more professional and less working class. The Conservatives have gone down-market as the public relations, advertising, asset stripping and money manipulating element make the party more raffish and less like the honourable ranks of dullards it was in days of yore. The professional element has grown. In Julian Critchley's view it has grown too far:

> (The Conservative Party has) become socially far less grand, although it still is pretty grand if you scratch about. There are not many Tory MPs living in semi-detached houses. In fact there are probably more of them living in great houses. But . . . it has become more middle class without any doubt whatever . . . I remember looking at the newly elected Conservative MPs after the May '79 election, and an eccentric Labour MP who was standing next to me turned to me and he said, 'My God. They all look like scrap dealers.' Which of course is unfair because Mr William Waldegrave doesn't look a bit like a scrap dealer. What I think he was trying to say is that they all wore in their buttonholes Rotary badges. But this is partially true too of the Labour Party, the horny-handed sons of toil are now to be found perhaps in the whips' office in the Labour Party. But the party has become full of school masters and lecturers and to almost the same extent the Conservative Party has become full of small businessmen, some journalists, some lecturers too. So it has become altogether more middle class.

Some of the victims of our various questionnaires echoed this view:

> The nature of the work is such that to be a candidate and then an MP, you have a better chance than most if you work in a profession which will take you back if you lose your seat. So we end up with too many from the talking professions: researchers, journalists, lawyers, and not enough doers, eg: scientists, architects, engineers, who regard the creation of wealth as more important than spending it.

As did David Penhaligon:

> It's always been said of the House of Commons that the most powerful party is not the Conservative Party nor the Labour Party but the Lawyers' Self-Preservation Party . . . they pass nonsense on Thursday and charge a lot of money in court on Monday for sorting it out.

The House is becoming more middle class. Those at the base of the social pyramid, the poor, the manual working class, the white collar workers, form a diminishing proportion of the Labour Party and a particularly low proportion of the House.

Parliament is less of a social elite: the very wealthy and the upper middle class no longer dominate its proceedings. Yet it is also better populated by ability, better educated, more achievement orientated. The battle between capital and labour, the tension between working and middle class, is still there outside the House, even if it is steadily fading. In the Commons it is both more bitter and more stylised because less natural. It is carried on by surrogates, acting on behalf of someone else. Class differences in the House itself are more subtle because each side is some rungs up the ladder from the mass of the voters.

The difference in background between the two parties is still clear enough. Of the 358 MPs who filled in our questionnaire, two thirds of the Labour Members had manual worker fathers but only 16 per cent of Conservatives were as plebian. A third of Conservatives, but only 16 per cent of Labour Members, had parents in the professions and Labour's professions were the less grand. Company director fathers sired a quarter of the Tories, and 6 per cent of Labour; while 15 per cent of Tories came from military families, 4 per cent of Labour. The land played a diminishing role; only 6 per cent of Tory parents were in agriculture, and politics provided a background for 4 per cent of Conservatives, 5 per cent of Labour Members. These Members are not now as solidly working-class or middle class as their parents were, but growing up must have conditioned them. So the battles of a generation ago are now being fought over by descendants who are themselves socially, but not emotionally, closer together, rather as if the Sealed Knot Society had taken it upon itself to restage this century's battles rather than those of the Civil War.

Labour is led by an upper-class public school man, the Tories by a self-made grammar school lass who worships her creator, though she is democratic enough to talk down to anyone. Yet the election of a social climber as Prime Minister hardly proves that the classless society has arrived. The real differences came out clearly in our survey. Public school chaps make up two-thirds of the Conservatives, a tenth of Labour. Three quarters of the Oxbridge graduates were Tory. But only 42 per cent of those who had been to other universities were Labour.

The Commons are substantially better educated than the total population. Their elite status is most obvious in this respect, for three fifths of MPs are graduates, over a third from Oxbridge, but under 4 per cent of the nation are graduates and under a tenth of graduates went through Oxbridge. The parties have drawn closer together in this respect: both are now elitist. Less than a fifth of Conservative MPs have been to grammar or modern school, but nearly three quarters to the public schools where the Tory jelly is moulded. Almost two thirds then went on to Oxford and Cambridge where the jelly sets. Thus Eton still supplies more MPs – (fifty-two in the current House; fifty of them Conservative, which is 15 per cent of the Party) – than any other single school. The next most popular public schools, Winchester and Harrow, provide only nine each and all the remaining public schools a total of 160 MPs, 138 of them Tory. By contrast, there are 207 ex-grammar school MPs and 130 modern school alumni, 112 of the latter Labour. Whatever the claims that we are one nation, the education system still contrives to produce two.

Common educational background has helped to maintain the cohesiveness of the Conservative Party in the period in which its class base has been shifting. That change is one away from the land, now only 7 per cent, and to a lesser degree from military careers, now a minute number, and towards business and the professions. The largest single category of Conservative MPs since the war has been company director, most of them substantial. Barristers and lawyers come second and have made up about a fifth of the party for most of the period, though over the years rather more teachers and journalists have crept in. The proportion of each has doubled to 4 per cent and 8 per cent respectively.

The days may be gone when the Tory backwoodsmen actually owned the woods. The Party is neither as upper class nor as respectable as it once was, for the solid wealth of the counties has gone and the new men of merchant banking, advertising, public relations and money manipulation are a generation on the make, not the offspring of the made. Yet the party remains overwhelmingly upper to middle class. Only one manual worker has found his way there since the war. The Conservative Party has merely reflected the changing nature of Britain's upper class as prestige has shifted from the aristocracy and land. Though the large business contingent, currently nearly half of Tory MPs, has grown, its members are drawn mainly from finance and commerce, not from the very different interest of industry. Those who manipulate money are well represented on the Tory benches, those who actually make things very badly. Management, too, is seriously under-represented, for Tory businessmen MPs are those who control their own fate or have a firm financial base, not people who have to work in hierarchies compromising the demands coming down with the pressures coming up, and hence knowing the hard realities of Britain's battered industry. Indeed, with Geoffrey Robinson, Terry Davis and John Garrett, management contributes as much to the Labour side as it does to the Tory. Thatchernomics, designed to improve moral attitudes in industry by an economic survival course, appeals to the lawyers who are so well represented on the Tory benches. Those actually engaged in industry would take a different view if there were enough of them in the House to have a voice.

Labour's transformation has been more dramatic. Half the 1945 party attended only elementary school. Now two-fifths have been to grammar school and over half are graduates. Indeed that proportion is still rising and getting on for two-thirds in 1979, including some ostentatious PhDs such as Dr Oonagh Macdonald, Dr Gavin Strang and Dr David Clark, as well as some closet ones such as Dr Denys Alan Reginald Race. Today the people's party has become the pedagogues', eclipsed by the generation who grew up under and benefited from the 1944 Education Act and the huge post-war expansion of the universities. The earlier generation succeeded at the University of Life; the present failed the practicals. This 'embourgeoisment' reflects progress up the social ladder as children of workers took advantage of widening opportunities in education and more generally. Since few who climb the educational ladder ever go back to being manual workers, the trend within the Labour party has been for the solid working-class element, currently only just one-fifth, even with the inclusion of the trade union officials, to be outweighed by the professions; particularly by teachers and lecturers, who now make up very nearly a fifth of the Parliamentary Labour Party, by journalists who have been around 8 per cent for much of the period since 1945, plus social workers and public sector employees. Genuine manual workers, nearly a third of the PLP in 1945, were only a tenth in the 1970s. With teachers the proportions are reversed. Thus Labour ends up more professional, in the occupational sense, than the Conservatives. Its professions are lower down the ladder of esteem, less well paid, but perhaps by these very tokens more assertive about their professional status, except when they are posing as working class for political purposes.

Labour is still a coalition between working and middle class. This makes it more divided than the Tories because it is inevitably less homogenous. The middle class element has grown to dominance but is divided between the pedagogues and the other professionals. The conditioned loyalist instincts, the deference to the leadership of a working class trade union core, which was content to bring Labour to power and then loyally to sustain it there on the basis of trade union solidarity, has been replaced by a more argumentative and more opinionated party as the better qualified, better educated professional contingent grows. Ideology, considered response from the mind, has been replacing instincts and bitter experience. There are more people who can tell you more clearly how the working classes think and what they want. There are fewer who know it for themselves, fewer still who have experienced real hardships.

This situation has not been changed in any fundamental respect by the breakaway of the Social Democratic Party. A mixed crew have embarked on that Noah's Ark. Yet they are on average more middle class and better educated (including more who have been to Oxbridge) than the Labour average with more professionals (27 per cent of SDP MPs) and in particular more lawyers (29 per cent of their MPs; only 9 per cent of Labour's), and fewer workers. The trade union core of the party has remained the most loyal. The SDP are also younger by two years at an average age of fifty-one, compared to Labour's 1981 figure of fifty-three years, for these are mainly the 'ministrables', people who see themselves as having a career and hence anxious, when one vehicle no longer serves it, to transfer to another. Just over a quarter of the PLP are over sixty. That machine, however rickety, will see their time out. The SDP has some in this category, such as David Ginsburg who was unlikely to have been reselected in Dewsbury, but it has more younger members, people like Tom McNally, whose career could have been nipped in the bud prematurely by reselection problems had they not taken avoiding action. The only other distinguishing characteristic is Catholicism, for though only 17 per cent of the party are known to be Roman Catholic, this is a higher proportion than even the party which was hitherto the most Catholic, Labour. It is not enough to make them a British version of the strongly Catholic Democratic Labour Party which kept the Australian Labour Party out of power for so long, yet it is enough to indicate that the same kind of political consequence of Roman Catholics moving up the social scale might well make an impact in Britain.

A nos moutons. Class conflict is preserved in the Commons as it fades (or rather, pre-Thatcher, faded) in the country. So the Commons battle is artificial, the battles of generations long ago re-enacted by descendants and carried out the more strenuously and noisily because the less real. The Conservatives are substantially wealthier than Labour; ranging from the millionaires, or nearly so, who make up nearly half the Cabinet, men like Willie Whitelaw, Peter Walker, Michael Heseltine, Sir Keith Joseph, George Younger of the brewing ilk, Francis Pym, Lord Carrington (RIP), richest of them all, plus probably a millionaire by marriage in Mrs Thatcher. They also include one-man multinationals such as Keith Wickenden (who feels no conflict of interest in bidding to take over state ferry services), wealthy professionals and landowners, right down to those described as 'small' businessmen, which does not necessarily mean persons of restricted income growth. On the Labour side, average incomes are substantially lower. Private wealth is hardly a factor, except the occasional man of wealth like Tony Benn, who inherited some and married more, or, formerly, Harold Lever, who is said to have once told the House, 'Most of my constituents are poor and humble though I am neither.' There are also a limited number of those whose steady savings, astute investments and outside jobs over a long career in politics have made them reasonably wealthy: Jim Callaghan's 200-acre farm was worth £300,000; Denis Healey's Hampstead house £75,000. Yet on the whole few on the Labour side started with anything and only a minority of the cunning or the ultra-cautious finish up with much more. Even these gains are frowned on both inside and outside the party and those with either background or money have to spend much of their time living them down. The best example of this whole process is Tony Benn's biography in *Who's Who* where contributors more or less write their own. In 1960 it was twenty-seven lines, by 1968 forty-three, but by 1975 it was down to thirty-eight, with the public school background replaced by 'Education: still in progress'. Then it got down to formal statement of job. Finally it disappeared.

The press loves to highlight a Labour MP with a big house and money, as if either was a crime and as if the ethics of Labour should be of those of St Francis of Assisi when he is in fact the Prime Minister's patron saint. Yet Labour MPs with business interests do have a more difficult time locally. Jack Dunnett in Nottingham Central has faced party pressures because of his business and property interests. So has Harold Lever, while in October 1974 William Baxter from Stirlingshire West had to step down because of his business affairs. Labour MPs with a business background, or wealth, are well advised to take the protective cover of left-wing politics and speak loudly about them to distract attention from present inequalities. Particularly their own.

The division into two armies, however modified, is still the most striking characteristic of the House. It may even be a difference in intelligence: Parliament, like the pedagogic professions, is a natural place for those from a working class background who aspire to rise. Minorities gravitate to show biz, rising classes to teaching or Parliament. It is less attractive to those whose ability will allow them to make money or exploit power they have anyway. So on the status quo side of politics those who can, do. The less able and less intelligent from this camp drift into Parliament. Defending the interests of wealth is not as intellectually demanding as making it. Nor does it demand the same intelligence and acumen as rising in the world, for to struggle up from the working class to Parliament is harder and more demanding than to gravitate down into it. This is pure speculation though nicely calculated to provide solace to the self-raising flowers. Yet it is not unrelated to the 'feel' of the Commons and the tone of the two parties, particularly the 'stupid' party which works more by instinct than by the applied intelligence which has reduced Labour to such chaos.

As social differences between the parties have narrowed, they have become more keenly felt. Being an MP imposes common patterns of behaviour, even similar suits. The smart joke is that they all look the same from the back, large, except the minority, like Joe Ashton, who dress sharply because their wives pick their clothes. Each party still lives a largely different lifestyle – which it feels obliged to maintain. Differences are worn like a badge of identity, the more assertively so because class and party differences in the community are easing as society becomes more pluralistic. Uncertain MPs feel it necessary to cling more anxiously to what they know. People outside have a more uniform classless lifestyle but MPs are constantly looking over their shoulders to see whence they came, clinging to basics as a form of reassurance. The parties fight on like Japanese soldiers marooned on some remote atoll long after 1945, not knowing the war is over – or at least different in that it is being fought with chips and computers, not guns.

The minor parties could provide a buffer. They fail to do so. Until the Labour Party invented the continuous creation of the SDP, the minor parties were just not big enough in numbers, 6 per cent of the last House and, despite the emergence of the SDP, only double that in the present. They are not big enough to make their own social waves so they tag along behind the big ships: like bum-boats. The Social Democrats are like Labour's right wing. The Liberals are hardly unique. David Steel has much in common with the Social Democratic generation of '66. Cyril Smith is a Labour rose by any other name. Richard Wainwright and Stephen Ross hold their seats from Tories. The Liberals are a party of business, small this time, and of public schools, also lesser. If the two major parties had not become more intolerant and exclusive most Liberals could be absorbed into one or the other without anyone noticing, while Jo Grimond floated benignly above. Indeed the trend in the 1960s was for the men of the middle to gravitate to one side or the other as the only way to get real influence. Now the traffic is the other way, typified by the Social Democrats in the House and by a more marked trend in the country. Celtic nationalism has always been difficult to fit into the hard and fast categories of the mass parties. It will remain *sui generis*. Even so, the SNP in Parliament, rather than looking unique, gave every appearance of being a combination of Conservatives together with people who would otherwise have gone to the Labour Party. They were a mixture of small businessmen and graduates, particularly yap, demonstrating their nationalism more by their devotion to their native beverage than by any other peculiarity. The Ulster Unionists in their various sorts are Conservatives in less attractive guise, combining the same (but earthier) mixture of landowners, small businessmen and clergy. In fact Ulster Unionists pioneered the Tory voyage down-market.

This failure of the buffer zone to keep the parties apart leaves the House of Commons divided into two camps, each gazing at the other in mutual incomprehension and some distaste. There are contacts across the lines. It would be amazing if there were not. Yet they are exceptional, tenuous and frowned on by the activists: Eddie Griffiths' visits to Ernle Money's family home were one of the charges against him when he was thrown out by the Brightside Labour Party before the '74 election. Party in the House means social apartheid: separate lives, self-contained worlds, a situation accepted half-heartedly by Alan Clark, viewing the social world from his own castle but the political from a much lower viewpoint:

> I have the advantage that I sit on the front bench below the gangway so I sit opposite a lot of very active, cheerful, vociferous and hard-working Socialists who are in there every day and really doing their job as an Opposition. And naturally as we're constantly exchanging insults and comments across the gangway, I get a kind of acquaintance with them.

> I think if you only come in late at night, and you sit way back on the fourth or fifth row, and you're not really interested in the House of Commons, which I am, you probably don't have much cultural or social exchange with the other party and you probably don't really get to know them. I suppose you may meet them on foreign trips and things, but I've never done any of those. I admire a lot of them. I enjoy the way they perform and I respect them as individuals. [But] there is a limit to the extent to which you can let your hair down with a member of the opposite party and you've got to be careful. But you could well say, and I think it's true of many people on both sides, that they probably have more enemies in their own parties than they do opposite. Friends? I don't know.

Julian Critchley observes the same facts with more cynicism but also a touch of envy:

> A great difficulty is the divide between the parties, a sort of apartheid, gastronomic apartheid which is practised in the House of Commons because in the dining-room, which is large, at one end sits the Conservative Party in their jackets even when the temperature is nearly eighty, eating raw beef, red beef at least, and eggs in aspic. Half way down you get a small table on which the Liberal Party sits, wearing their jackets and probably eating stew, and then at the end – all with their jackets off, quite sensibly – sit the members of the Parliamentary Labour Party, eating black pudding and drinking beer. And nobody ever actually meets. The only person whom I ever saw actually sitting down together and mixing with the parties was Humphry Berkeley, who used on occasion to have dinner with Barbara Castle. They would drink champagne out of pewter mugs, and all the old things at both ends of the room would be absolutely enraged. It is rather ridiculous, this sort of apartheid that goes on. It's not as if there's any hostility between the parties as such. In fact you can make friends with people on the other side, but only if you go abroad with them . . . It's created more by the party system itself because clearly one of the topics of conversation, if not the only topic of conversation, is how well or how badly your government, your party, happens to be doing at this present time. And I suppose this is a conversation that could be more easily sustained amongst people of the same persuasion.

Homo sapiens divides by gender, *Homo Westminsteriensis* by party. Yet those parties are changing, less monolithic, more like holding companies or a collective umbrella for a series of different and diverse groups sheltering beneath. The evolution is inevitable. Society is more pluralistic. The common conditioning is weakening. The politics of decline mean harder choices, more divisive issues, placing parties under an increasing strain. The easy assumption that principles, party and personal ambition all advance together is no longer relevant, if party leaders lead their followers into a cul-de-sac from which there is no easy escape, as the Tories have done, or if organisational changes weaken the party and force Members to choose between personal survival and a bandwaggon which is no longer rolling anywhere but downhill. All this is now happening to both parties. Thus the old, easily accepted bonds of habit, life-style, conditioning and living together in the House have proved inadequate to prevent a major breakaway in the Labour Party. Because of the common class conditioning these factors have been stronger in the Conservatives. Yet they are still there in both parties and the bonds of 'life-style' will continue, if not to form a binding glue, at least to offset the strains to which parties will be exposed in the 1980s.

They will probably be effective in holding together those whom the politics of decline might put assunder, provided the reins of party are held more lightly and loosely. Party, and in all probability class-based parties, will remain the dominant pattern. This is inevitable in the House of Commons itself for, at the end of the day, people will always go into one of two lobbies for or against the government and its measures. Perhaps it is also inevitable outside. Most legislatures in the advanced countries are still characterised by a broad division, not so much between working and middle class, but between the have-mores (who are not always, but often, the have-*mores*) and the have-lesses; those with a bigger stake in the status quo and those with a broader identification with the mass. Where there are no marked divisions among religious, ideological or tribal lines, there is little alternative to such a broad divergence of self-interest. The badges may not be as boldly displayed, the talk may be more of economic calculus rather than the circumlocutions of encouraging enterprise or free collective bargaining in which class interest is now disguised. Yet the gaps will be there. As long as they are they will be represented in the House of Commons.

H.M. BACK-BENCH PRISON
CHAIN-GANG WORK SCHEDULE
WHIP

7 Party Man

MPs have to be schizophrenics: party men and parliamentarians, exponents of a sectional interest, defenders of the whole; bringing independent judgement to bear on the issues of the day, yet committed to a one-eyed approach. They have to criticise and control the Executive, yet vote for it if it's their party. Some see themselves as the spokesmen of the local party, far more as the voice of their electorate, a few like George Cunningham, cut adrift from Labour to end up SDP, give pre-eminence to none:

> The Member of Parliament shouldn't only feel responsive to his local party, he should be looking over his shoulder all the time. Every MP should have a crick in his neck but he should not just be looking at one thing, he should be looking to his local party, to his national party, to the totality of his electorate, to organisations in his constituency and so on . . . He has to be the fulcrum upon which all those different pressures come to bear.

These dilemmas are always there but usually evaded by the classic neurotic symptom of taking refuge in a mythical persona: Member of Parliament. Man of Judgement.

For most Members, party is basic. It is implicit rather than explicit. Parties have a dual nature. They are bodies of people dedicated to the same objectives. Yet they are also a concentrated focus of intense hatreds and mutual dislikes: those to whom we are closest we react to most intensely, and at times most disparagingly. Just one Labour example. The miners' MPs are the salt of the earth. Yet they have an in-built disposition to pull down their own over-mighty, from Roy Mason to Arthur Scargill. The group has in the past been full of malevolent innuendo about which miner MP did not have coal fired central heating (Tom Swain), which miner had the coal fire removed from his office in Northern Ireland (Roy Mason). The best example is the doubtless apocryphal story of Tom Swain and Dennis Skinner, each anxious in February 1972 to be in the House on Friday to react to the expected Wilberforce Report, yet each also anxious that his rival should not be. All Thursday they fenced for position, eventually reaching a truce. They would go north together so each could keep an eye on the other. Swain's wife met them at Chesterfield and kindly ran Skinner home. Next day, Skinner awoke to find that Swain had indeed reacted to the report and was in London. He had driven back to Chesterfield and got the next train back.

A good party does contain some pretty objectionable and curious aberrations from the norm, as well as such lovable characters as Reg Race on the Labour side or Harvey Proctor among the Tories, or those who turn being objectionable into a show-biz gimmick, Dennis Skinner and his Tory equivalent, Norman Tebbitt, the 'semi-housetrained pole-cat' currently trying to be a semi-housetrained statesman. Reactions and feelings are the more powerful because they build up. Parties have not evolved a useful role to dissipate them and ventilate either the likes or the dislikes. Our parties are just not up to the job which a modern democracy imposes on them. Like amphibians which have crawled onto land but never learned to walk, they have not evolved to suit the changed environment of modern politics. The parties in Parliament have developed much less than their role requires. They have a machinery of management and discipline. Yet they have no effective system for consulting Members, involving them in policy, or taking decisions collectively. Instead MPs hand over power, and hence their futures, to Cabinet and Shadow Cabinet, and seek solace not in sharing power but in carping at its exercise. They also seek escape in the traditional role of MP, much as others sublimate frustrations at work by stamp collecting or grumbling to the wife.

Party in Parliament is a convenience, not a control. The Labour Party has all the trappings of democracy, Conservatives rely more on personal channels and contacts. Yet the reality is similar. MPs are brought together behind a policy they have little influence on. This is a situation which does not occur in the same way in any other country.

Britain has not pursued to a logical outcome the evolution through which other legislatures have gone. Perhaps we are too attached to myths and too squeamish to accept the reduction of the Mother of Parliaments to a sham almost as opaque as Communist legislatures. Countries with less awe and more practical flair have recognised the logic of evolution by turning political parties into instruments of government. In Australia, New Zealand, Canada and South Africa, party 'caucuses' act as continuous checks on Cabinet. Their parliamentary parties are a prior-parliament where proposals are changed and tinkered with before they go on to the *de facto* second chamber: Parliament itself. In continental systems multiple parties and the processes of coalition government achieve a similar result. Party caucuses and the continuous process of negotiation and interaction give backbenchers a more useful role. The electorate, rather than being a chooser of governments and Prime Ministers, is a court of appeal called in only when the legislature cannot produce a government.

Britain has followed such trends only in the more highly developed but smaller parties in local government. There, group meetings of the majority party are usually the effective council. Our parliamentary parties are too large to have the same natural cohesion and internal discipline and from the Second World War until the 1980s we have managed to avoid a multi-party system. So despite the mythology the House has no real influence on policy, the governing party little enough. MPs in that party do have an influence on its Cabinet and leadership, but that influence is indefinable, diffused not properly articulated, negative rather than positive. The main and overwhelming influence works the other way: down from the top, pulling the backbenchers willy-nilly the way leaders decide to go. The backbencher finds himself suspended between the two worlds, not an effective MP because he cannot control the Executive, yet without scope to be effective in his party either. He is in limbo, not power.

After a long period of attempting to pretend that he was designated by God, the Conservatives now elect their leader. Once installed he controls the levers of power; Cabinet appointments, Central Office, the propaganda machine, whips. A series of safety valves are left to the backbenchers: the 1922 Committee; the twenty-three party subject committees and half a dozen regional committees, or the eight sub-committees, all of them functioning on a gentleman and players basis and attended by whips as 'observers'. The players play. The gentlemen meet, usually without them, to discuss their performance. The elected executive of the 1922 then relays their views to the captain.

Labour's system is in the process of what some view as evolution, others as destabilisation. Once upon a time, the Parliamentary Labour Party elected its leader annually. By a haphazard series of blunders that power has now been handed to an electoral college to conduct in the way calculated to be most damaging and divisive to the party. The PLP has no nerve for taking it back and the power struggle outside is now too deadlocked for it to be organised sensibly. So if a leader died in the eighteen months before a general election Labour would do better to invoke taxidermy than its new election procedures. The PLP still retains *pro tem* the power to draw up the manifesto in consultation with the NEC, and to elect its Parliamentary Committee of fifteen. In opposition this is the Shadow Cabinet, supplemented on the front benches by the leader's own appointments. In power the party merely elects a liaison committee to consult with the Cabinet. Proposals to elect the Cabinet itself, a standard practice in Australian and New Zealand Labour Parties, have been rejected by the PLP itself. The right is happy for the Prime Minister to appoint until the ides of Benn. The left knows it stands to get more people in Cabinet by a choice which has to balance factions than by an election the right could swamp. So the party elects only the officers of the sixteen subject and nine regional groups, all of which are serviced by the two clerks and two secretaries attached to the PLP. Members can choose to be attached to any six groups, although they can attend all. Officers are elected each session, a meeting which is usually the only one with any attendance as flying caucuses of left and right tour the committee rooms. The right usually sweeps the board.

The Conservatives, party of leadership, are better at listening than Labour, party of democracy. Because Labour is a party of factions, policies become battle grounds, divisions hard and sharp. The Conservatives are a party of tendencies rather than organised bodies of opinion, so sounding is easier. Perhaps too their leadership is more amenable than a usually embattled Labour leadership. Certainly admirers like John Stokes are full of enthusiasm for their present leader's personal charm and sensitivity:

> Mr Heath has great gifts but I wouldn't say that being a leader is one of them. Now Margaret Thatcher will speak to anybody, will say good morning to everybody, and she takes greater care of her backbenchers . . . I think it's because she's that sort of person first of all . . . but secondly of course because the backbenchers put her in and we now see her in the Cabinet surrounded by those who probably voted for Mr Heath.

Mothers have to be sensitive to their children and this one is assiduously so. Jim Callaghan made only rare lugubrious appearances in the Members' dining-room, and Ted Heath had to be positively pushed into the smoking room, but Margaret Thatcher makes regular, almost consciously brave, appearances to face the food and clutch at the company in the canteen. Backbenchers are invited along, almost on rota, to chat – or rather listen to – her over dinner. As Martin Stevens points out, for an Iron Lady she can be pliable:

> This is why Margaret Thatcher is such a good leader. Half a dozen times she's unaccountably backed down with something because she's realised you can't do that. Leadership is a two-way thing. She doesn't ask us to do things that her very sensitive antennae tell her we're not going to wear. Equally, it's up to us to give her the maximum support because we have very great confidence in her and her government . . . Now if you have both those processes working, the number of occasions when backbenchers have trouble with their consciences is going to be relatively few.

Those who ask when backbenchers will revolt against Thatcherism mistake Tory realities. Some will, more as the election gets nearer and nerves grow frayed, but most backbenchers believe in the policies. Thatcher is their leader. The real doubts come in Cabinet from those tainted by the practicalities of power. The higher up the Tory ladder, the greater the lean to the centre.

The Labour Party have their tribes: Tribune, Manifesto and Labour First. The Tories, on the other hand, are a tribe so there are no such internal blocks. There are, however, kinship groups, opinion-forming bodies which organise those of similar views in dining clubs rather than Labour's sub-parties. First for dinner came One Nation, formed by Enoch Powell and Iain Macleod after the war, and now consisting of just over a score of ageing Wets presided over by Maurice Macmillan, bringing in a few younger liberals and such returning prodigals as Sir Ian Gilmour, Norman St John Stevas, Angus Maude and Mark Carlisle. Younger Members have also formed their own such as the Blue Chip dining club, dining fortnightly, *chez* Tristan Garel-Jones or such other long-suffering wives as will take them. Blue Chip includes the brightest flowers of the crop of '79 (a crop particularly well seeded otherwise with dandelions and pansies), and it has produced *Changing Gear*, a wringing wet critique of their own government's policies. The Chipmunks in turn overlap with the less intellectual Guy Fawkes group who bring the marginal seat moderates together. Finally, there is the much more selective Ninety-Two Club, with such egregious luminaries as Major Sir Patrick Wall, who was so pro-Smith he looked at one time like the Member for

Mashonaland East, and George Gardiner, MP for Reigate and the *Sunday Express*. Described by wets as the 'Moronic Tendency', these are the shock troops of Thatcherism. These and the dozen other dining clubs are groups of like-minded friends rather than campaigning organisations, their bonds social to a degree not found on the Labour side. As a result, discontent as it develops is a mood, not an organised campaign. Tories intuit rather than articulate, eat rather than argue.

On the Labour side opinion has always been more organised. First came the Tribune Group which increased from forty-seven in 1973 to seventy-nine in 1975 and seventy in 1982. Tribune has not been a happy place for some years. It had its brave days, such as the 1976 fight against cuts, but for much of the time Labour was in power it was in the doldrums because of the close coalition between Cabinet and the trade unions. Then before it could enter into its own in opposition it became the focal point of Labour's basic and bitter argument. The divisions between the traditional and Bennite left are at their most acute there. The two sides are an old left – what *Militant* calls the 'verbal left' – which knows what it is against but not what it is for, and a new one, which knows both all too well from its more ideological view, but is politically far more naive than the hardened old pros and trade union hacks on the other side. This disunity has been heightened by the decision of many Tribune members to abstain against Tony Benn in the 1981 deputy leadership election. This made meetings divisive and unpleasant. It also forced Members back to basics: what is left? who is more left? a defensiveness which palsies action, disrupts and divides. To be on the left today is a constant process of definition, an incessant watching of positions so that one is not outflanked. It has more in common with theology than party politics. In practice it always had some of these characteristics, now they are obsessive. The left has never been about an instinctive radicalism, as Maureen Colquhoun found after her spectacular conversion to lesbianism as a way of life. She was shabbily shuffled off by the Tribune Group as an embarrassment (which, to be fair, she could be). Yet now a body of what were mates in arms, however fractious, is sharply divided. Trust is largely absent for the new left and the old, the new ideological and the old instinctive 'oppositionist' mentality, those who have a plan and those who work by reaction, might as well come from different planets, particularly since some of the old left feel their constituency parties (and reselections) threatened by the activity of the New Model Army men, mobilised by the new left. The left has always had uncomradely tendencies but nothing like this has happened before and not even the peace which passeth all understanding, as blessed by the Bishop of Stortford in January 1982, can disguise the divisions.

Tribune's opposite pole, the Manifesto Group, was formed in the 1974 Parliament. It was numerically stronger than Tribune but now, because of desertions to the SDP, is slightly smaller with just over sixty members. Lacking Tribune's bitterness and backbiting, it also lacks its drive and its conviction. Keeping Labour fit for nice chaps to live in is less compelling than building a new heaven and a new earth. In any case since the shedding of the SDP, most of whom came from Manifesto ranks, the group is more of a wistful backwater, thinking of days and people long gone, and wondering who might be next. The right is out of fashion and as dedicated followers they know it. Labour First, a centre group grouping of Labour's grey men, has not risen above forty adherents and has never become more than a discussion group. The rest of the party steer clear of organised groups, some on principle, some out of indolence or love of a quieter life than is possible in a polarised PLP.

Party structure is a system of participation, not worker control. If party groups did not exist, it would be necessary to invent them to organise the party, circulate information, convey moods and build up speaking teams. Yet all this makes them a necessary tool of management, not what they should be, a framework for backbench influence, a useful forum of activity for Members frustrated elsewhere. This failure does not stop Members like Alan Clark finding them useful:

> In the Conservative Party, every subject that has a Secretary of State also has a party committee. It meets every week and discusses the evolution of party policy in that field. The Secretary of State comes to it quite often and explains what he's going to do and what he wants to do. Behind the scenes there's quite a lot done through the vehicle of that committee to moderate or alter in a slight way, I don't think in major ways, what the Secretary of State wants to do.

Relationships vary. Jim Prior as Employment Secretary met the officers of the backbench employment group every week. John Silkin as Labour Minister of Agriculture kept closely in touch with his backbench group and carried it with him. Denis Healey was less assiduous; Michael Heseltine brought his Environment Committee in on his proposals to castrate local government too late to prevent a rebellion. In opposition, Roy Hattersley and his assistant David Hall did a lot of work with the Labour Home Affairs Group on the Nationality Bill, developing policy which the party subsequently accepted. Other Shadow spokesmen are less energetic: Labour's Economic and Finance Group has been more of a discussion club than a useful team builder for the budget battle. In general, Ministers and Shadows attend intermittently. They are questioned. Alternative views are put. Yet sounding boards are a different thing to real influence. Concessions, when they are made, which is rarely enough, are in terms of presentation or trimmings rather than substance, something which Julian Critchley finds particularly infuriating in defence:

> Nobody in the Tory Party who takes an interest in defence is ever told a thing. I have to get what information I use either from foreign academics or British journalists . . . Under our system we are obliged to accept the [Trident] decision once made. Under a different system we would be debating all the options before the Government actually made up its mind. But then this is all part of our frustration.

Bob Litherland, facing a similar situation in the Labour Party, finds it sadly wanting in contrast with what went on in Manchester Town Hall:

> I always compare this with my local government background and there we always moved as a group of people, took decisions as a group and you went in there as a unified body and that was the policy . . . down here it's so individualistic that you don't really feel as though you're part of the machine. The Parliamentary Labour Party is not run the same as in a local group and I find this very difficult.

In Australian and New Zealand caucus systems Ministers can be overruled by parliamentary party groups. Here Ministers get more out of it than the groups, assessing moods, charting the shoals between which they must navigate, and using the groups to rally the troops. All the groups get in return is a feeling of involvement, a few crumbs from the table of power.

Parliamentary party meetings are equally toothless. With Labour in power the 'payroll vote' of Ministers and even Paarliamentary Private Secretaries, all of whom are expected to toe the line in the party meeting, is enough to carry the day. On the Conservative side, deference and a feeling that confrontation is in bad taste do the same. We do not have party democracy. Too few backbenchers really want it. They would rather get on personally with Ministers, trying to influence and persuade them individually than use the power of party. Ideally, the party groups should parallel and supplement the specialised select committees by an overlapping membership. This would build up a concentration of expertise and give it two channels of influence, each supplementing the other, for in the last analysis the only way backbenchers can now turn growing expertise into influence is through their own party in a system of government by party. Until they grasp the potential of party power, the influence of backbenchers will be minimal, the last resort pistol-to-the-head technique of making trouble. Conform and tramp dutifully through the division lobbies, and backbenchers will be taken for granted. Show more independence, and they must be counted. Organise themselves, and they can make influence continuous.

The whips and Parliamentary Private Secretaries provide a more traditional and direct structure of communication totally independent of the committee structure by relaying party moods and views to Ministers and Cabinet. They either go out and take soundings, doing their job as perambulating ears or the views come to them, perhaps in the rotund shape of Martin Stevens:

> I go to the Chief Whip or to the Minister and I say 'Look, we're not going to be able to support you on this particular thing.' Over the Housing Bill I voted against the government four times but not until we'd had two almost all night clashes with John Stanley and Geoffrey Finsberg and they had made a great number of concessions which, from the point of view of Inner London MPs, improved the bill; but it didn't go quite as far as we thought it should have done . . . So it is in private meetings of Ministers that you get changes made and of course they've got to trust you. They've got to know that you won't come and leak it all, like I've just leaked to you . . . if you gain a good reputation, Ministers will always see you and always listen to you.

The nature of the informal consultations is difficult to know. Yet its effectiveness is open to doubt because it has to have the ultimate backing of the threat of revolt to change ministerial minds. These are still exceptional. The Conservative Government has withdrawn a series of proposals in the face of such threats. On Members' pay in 1979, Mrs Thatcher's first mean instincts were overwhelmed by impecunious backbenchers: an amazing development for the Conservative Party, for, in the 1950s when Labour backbenchers were anxious for more money, and the Conservative Cabinet was half disposed to give it to them, it was Tory backbenchers, particularly the knights of the shire, who stopped it on the grounds that it would completely change the nature of the job: they were there to serve, it was Labour members who wanted money for what should be done out of duty, and to give it to them might encourage them. Now the newer, money-sharp breed of Tories were not only holding their hands out but positively grabbing the money. Less sordid was the opposition to the proposed reduction in the BBC's External Services, which was stopped by backbench revolt, as were charges for eye tests, retrospective sanctions against Iran, 1980 immigration rules and the duty on derv.

Mrs Thatcher gave way in every case. Labour's leadership can be more wilful, at least until things become extreme, as in Barbara Castle's *In Place of Strife* (1969). Yet the disposition for tactical withdrawal, whatever the stage it comes at, has to be there as long as backbenchers show themselves prepared to abstain or even vote against their government. They are now much more prepared to do this than ever in the past. In the 1960s they abstained; now they go into the other lobby. An increasing proportion are coming to believe that a dog is allowed two bites, even three, provided, as John Stokes argues, the wounds are inflicted in moderation:

> Obviously you can't rebel against your party all the time, but if you feel very strongly you can. I'll give you an example. The other day in the House Mr Ridley came back from the Falkland Islands and gave the impression that the Foreign Office wanted to give them up. Now the House of Commons is absolutely opposed to that and the government will not be able to get it through. So there are certain issues where you can dig your feet in. It's more a power of veto, more a negative power than a positive power.

The Conservatives have a tradition of allowing rebellion, or at least paying lip-service to its virtues, provided it does not help the other side, as Julian Critchley points out:

> It's very much more convenient in the Conservative Party that if you wish to revolt you must in fact revolt over the right of the political spectrum, in which case you get the support of the bulk of your constituents . . . but if you revolt way over to the left of the Conservative Party spectrum, which is into the middle of politics itself, then you are more likely to get into trouble with your constituents . . . What happens to the Tory rebel? Nothing very much happens to him here . . . I think that we do have some admiration for people who stand up and say what they think . . . It doesn't help, I think, with the Whips' Office to some extent, because you are not likely to be rewarded and your career is unlikely to be furthered if you make a habit of revolting. Macmillan once gave advice

to the newly elected in 1959. He said, 'Revolt by all means but only on one subject at a time. To do more than that is to confuse the whips.'

Exactly the same is true in the Labour Party. Rebellion to the left is acceptable, a sign of virility, a delight to the constituency parties, even if it means helping the other side, for instance in December 1978 by throwing out the last vestiges of incomes policy. Revolt to the centre is ideological betrayal and class collaboration.

The slow transformation of MPs from lobby fodder to creatures whose foibles have to be calculated is really a feature of the 1970s. Then eunuchs grew balls and suddenly discovered that the old fear that a defeated government should resign was wrong. The governmental bluff was called. From 1945 to 1970 governments suffered only eleven defeats, none because supporters voted against them. Indeed, in the forty years up to 1972, there were only forty government defeats. Backbenchers became more restive in the 1960s, largely because there were so many able new men with little useful to do. Then, new issues produced new divisions: the Common Market created cross pressures and taught new habits of dissent; and the more abrasive leadership of Ted Heath, combined with the fact that governments were both less successful and facing more difficult decisions, to put more strain on loyalty. Backbenchers let down their own governments and even voted with the Opposition. Ted Heath suffered six defeats, three on three-line whips, such as the immigration rules of 1972.

The Labour Government had even more problems. They started predictably. From February to October 1974 it was a minority government, suffering seventeen defeats because opposition parties combined against it. The October 1974 election gave it a majority – just. At that point its problems began. Contrary to the assumption that a bare majority would inspire greater loyalty, the natives were restive, and frustrated. The government suffered nineteen defeats because of the opposition parties combining, but twenty-three because some of its own members combined with them, an unprecedented total. Income tax was lowered, sanctions on private firms scrapped in December 1978, a vote which effectively abolished the tatters of incomes policy, the Dock Work Regulation Bill was emasculated, the first Devolution Bill was beaten and the second had a Trojan horse built into it. The same thing happened in committees, only more frequently. The famous amendment for index-linked tax allowances, proposed by Jeff Rooker and Audrey Wise against their own government's Finance Bill in 1977 and eagerly carried by the Tories, was the most spectacular blow and the most expensive, tearing a great hole in the budget strategy. Yet it was only the tip of an iceberg. There were seventy-four defeats in committee from 1974 to 1978, most inflicted by the government's own supporters.

Backbenchers saw themselves as forced to do or die for a government which took all too little notice of them. Less imaginative counterparts in the 1940s and 1950s had accepted this as their lot. The more independent breed of the 1970s had constituency parties to answer to, and were even beginning to evaluate their own fate independently of the government, the most dangerous symptom of all in backbenchers. They were also frustrated because they were not being listened to. A personal illustration of this latter point indicates the nature of the process. As a Labour candidate in the 1977 Grimsby by-election, I had made the entire ITV and commercial radio coverage of the contest illegal, being then a director of a commercial radio station and forbidden by the IBA Act to appear on either medium on matters of controversy. Once elected, I told Merlyn Rees, as Home Secretary, of the anomaly. He undertook to look at it. In 1978 the chance came, a new IBA Bill, one clause of which was to allow such directors to be broadcast, provided they were speaking in parliamentary debates. This could easily have been extended. The Minister in charge of the bill, Brynmor John, declined to do so. I warned him that I might vote against it. Still no change. In committee I therefore struck out the entire clause as a protest. Being supported by Phillip Whitehead and Tories anxious to make trouble, I carried the day, instantly halving a two-clause bill. The government was then driven to using that Labour long-stop, the Lords, to put the clause back. The Conservatives, ever more mindful of the rights of directors, promptly cleared up the anomaly when they came in.

Conservative victory in 1979 restored an adequate majority and took away the pistol-to-the-head aspect of backbench rebellion under Labour. Yet the example had been set. Once tasted, independence can be addictive. Tory backbenchers were soon abstaining and voting against their own government on petrol tax, immigration and new taxes in the 1981 budget. In November and December 1981, rebelliousness reached a crescendo when the government was humiliated four times. The Heseltine proposal to require referenda on rate increases had to be dropped after a rebellion, making a large hole in the legislative programme and leaving the House with little to do but such useful and important bills as the Coinage Bill, dropping the 'new' from penny and allowing backbenchers to trundle out old jokes about 'Two P or not to Pee. That is the question.' Fourteen Tories abstained on the Chancellor's public spending package. They then forced withdrawal of the 2 per cent cut in unemployment benefit. Eleven voted against heavy lorries, forcing the Minister of Transport to 'review' his plans. The culmination was less public. At the end of 1981 twenty-six Tory MPs, including Sir Ian Gilmour, signed a letter to the Conservative Chief Whip, Michael Jopling, calling for an end to the government's draconian economic policy, though in practice few Tory wets agreed on what scale of reflation would be desirable.

These rebellions, many of them by people maltreated by the Prime Minister, others by younger backbenchers less than gruntled, were a symptom both of a less manageable Tory Party and of worse to come. As the life of the parliament runs down government's power wains, and backbenchers inevitably think more and more in terms of their own electoral future and begin to edge away from an incompetent government and an unpopular prime minister. The interesting thing in the Thatcher administration was not that this had happened but that it had come so late, and that for two years the government had been able to carry through policies so different from post-war norms with so little protest. The real test remained success and since it is intrinsically unlikely, short of a miracle turn-around in the economy, Margaret Thatcher must be driven to more and more concessions, such as the extensive and unprecedented consultations on the 1982 budget. These did not actually change anything but they did force the government to resort to conjuring tricks to get what was in fact a deflationary budget through. The scene was well prepared by leaks that the government wanted to be generous but suddenly found it could not be, because the oil price unexpectedly fell, reducing tax revenues. The few concessions made were presented as expansionary when they were countered by indirect tax increases and hardly enough to allow for inflation. So by sleight of hand a bemused party was kept in line. However, the Prime Minister's time was rapidly running out. She will certainly be less capable of using even the hint of dissolution as a means of discipline. To do so would be suicide, or suttee. Naturally, she prefers to bend with the wind and generously to allow Sir Geoffrey Howe to bear the burden of humiliation.

Yet if parties are becoming less effective as instruments of government, this indicates neither that they are breaking up nor that the independent Member of old is on his way back. George Cunningham has a dream of recreating nineteenth-century independence:

> I find the phrase 'The government's power over the House of Commons' deeply offensive. If a government has power over a legislature then you haven't got a democracy. It's the House of Commons which should be controlling the government . . . They all give lip-service to this and so do Ministers. They say, 'I am answerable to the House' but they don't really believe it in their hearts and it's only when the governments are defeated, and defeated quite regularly (once a month, on a major issue, would be a good pattern) that the place is working. It's only when governments get accustomed to being defeated that the Ministers start to pay attention to what Members think so that the Members are influential . . . I'm not suggesting that every Member should make up his mind on every issue simply according to his own conscience. You have to compromise with each other; you have to stand on a party basis or else the electorate has got no choice between rival ideologies and ways of running the economy and so on. All I'm suggesting is a modification of what we do now, so that more often Members say, 'Look, I don't agree with that. And therefore I'm not going to vote that way.' I would say that there are between fifty and a hundred Members who are perfectly prepared to listen to arguments of that kind and to use their votes accordingly . . . If that attitude of mind becomes more common then the place will work a great deal better. Government proposals, government legislation, will be much more carefully prepared because they will know that if they put forward bad legislation it really will be picked over properly and bits of it neglected.

It will not be realised. Members still agree with their party on most issues. They also take its view on trust on many others where they are not particularly bothered and are thus prepared to allow others to formulate a position for them. Some ideologues will be pinpricking continuously in order to demonstrate a purity of principle which is more important to them than party, but they are exceptional. Most rebels on both sides will fine-focus their differences, swallowing, as the backbench Tories did, ten pence extra on petrol to strain better at the ten pence on DERV, compensating for one revolt by strenuous attacks on the Opposition and more fervent loyalty on other issues. Party may be weakening. Yet it is still the only available instrument of government, the only way to turn party views into flesh and blood legislation, the only way to gratify most ambitions: the greatest grab of the greatest number. The small step for backbenchers is not a huge step backwards into the grave for parties.

Managing political parties is the job of the whips. Whether they are up to it is an open question, for they are mechanics, not graduate engineers. In theory, the Whips' Office is where conflicting upward and downward pressures meet. Whips serve the party leadership, see that the army marches, in step if possible, but at least in some facsimile of unity in the direction the leadership decides. Yet they are also the servants of the party, holding it together, seeing that it is not tested to destruction, warning of discontents and difficulties, sounding opinion and relaying it upward. In our executive-based government system, the first role predominates over the second. Information is gathered and mobilised to give the driver a better idea of what his machine will stand, rather than to make him change route. This is a more mundane role than the legends of whips controlling a machinery of correction and domination worthy of *Bondage Illustrated*. The Whips' Office is really a combination of the gossip exchange and the boiler room of the House of Commons. There, day and night, a disgruntled body of mechanics, bearing little resemblance to either the brutal domineering image of outsiders or the praetorian guard image they themselves prefer, tinker with the machinery, carry messages and trade character assassination of their flocks.

The Chief Whip alone lives up to the legends. It is impossible not to. Appointed by the leader in the Conservative Party, elected in the Labour Party, his is a position of authority, backed by a machinery for exerting it. The careers of Ted Heath ('Once a Chief Whip, always a Chief Whip,' according to Enoch Powell), Willie Whitelaw and Francis Pym, in the Conservative Party, indicate the boost it gives to prospects and, even in the Labour Party, John Silkin and Bob Mellish are not exactly low achievers. A Chief Whip is wicked uncle, capable of the most excruciating bawlings out, and kindly uncle, father confessor, shoulder to cry on, adviser. He is the friend of all and none. He needs the talents of an actor to play his roles convincingly, combining gregariousness with the conversational propensities of a Trappist monk. He also needs the dirtiest of minds to know all the dimensions of human activity his flock can – and do – get up to. Most Chief Whips have duly obliged. Just in case they are deficient in this respect, their subordinates keep them well informed.

Below the Chief comes the Deputy Chief Whip, symbolising the characteristics of the party: beery, backslapping on the Labour side, staid enough to be a prospective Speaker on the Tory. Then the Pairing Whip, the man who keeps the whole system going. He has the most direct power over the lives and loves of backbenchers, by refusing, or giving, leave to go. Below him come the fourteen whips, each taking responsibility for a region, each in close touch with its MPs. They are the workforce of the boiler room.

Conservatives regard their whips as a *corps d'élite*. It used to be a career in itself, parallel to the ministerial ladder. Now it is a training ground for those on the way up. Nineteen Ministers in Mrs Thatcher's first list had been in the Whips' Office. Even the more mundane whips can gravitate upwards, though often by way of reward rather than destiny; they have shown willing to devote themselves full-time to the party rather than the other distractions which can be so beguiling for Tories. On the Labour side, the office also has its quota of self-raising flowers: Anne Taylor, Terry Davis, Ted Graham, Peter Snape, all passed through it to the present front bench. Seven members of the last government had done so. Yet the older trade unionists set the tone, as the last resting place for sound party men with no further to go.

Whipping is a way of life. A daily meeting reviews business for the day ahead, a daily roster allocates an hour's bench duty each to see that the Chamber plods its weary way without (or in the Opposition's case, with) upset. Whips make Westminster work, deciding business, clearing up cock-ups, stage-managing everything from party clash to Speakers' decisions. All is decided through the 'usual channels' of direct negotiation between Chief Whips and House Leaders on both sides. The other whips bask in the reflected glow. Information is power, and they know what is going on. Just what influence this confers is clear after every division as the Lobby throngs with puzzled Members asking each other, 'What now?' 'Can we go home?' 'Is it two lines or three from now?' 'How long before the next division?' Whips like to enhance their authority by playing cards close to chest but on occasions like this they spread such enlightenment as suits them.

They also keep the record of yesterday's divisions, chase up the laggards, get explanations, keep up the pressure on those with the 'ten o'clock closing' syndrome – off home after the ten o'clock vote, in some cases without telling the whips or registering a pair. They check the condition of the ill and the location of the absent. Each whip has a shrewd idea of the foibles of his flock: who's so frequently on overseas trips that his nose bursts if he comes below 20,000 feet, whose preoccupation with firm pairs has nothing to do with whipping, who regards voting as a distraction from his real interest in specie, who is using reselection or deceasing mothers to absent himself, whose wife will know where he is, and whose will want to. This too is power. In theory they are the channel for communicating this essential information up the ladder. In practice they use their discretion in passing on information about which secretary has tried to bump herself off at which Minister's home. In any case the wise Prime Minister has his own channels of communication. Harold Wilson had George Wigg to fuel his paranoia, James Callaghan had James Wellbeloved to stir things and the Blessed Margaret has 'Supergrass', her PPS, Ian Gow. Perhaps Ted Heath's problems came from the fact that he had no one to feed him tit-bits and less interest in them.

In power, Whips' Offices are all bustle and activity: Members pleading for pairs, telephones busy, the daily gossip exchange in operation. Minute majorities heighten the activity to the frenzy vividly portrayed in Joe Ashton's play *A Majority of One*, as the sick, the drunk and the dying are gathered in, some to be brought, as Leslie Spriggs was after a heart attack, to the courtyard on life support mechanisms in ambulances. Others have been known to come stretcher-borne for the benefit of film crews, even though the whips had told them they were not needed, so keen are they to serve their party. This is the Office's finest hour. Its denizens will tell you so. At length. Whips keep tabs on Ministers, tracking down the absent, bringing home those overseas, arranging police escorts for the dilatory, check that no one is locked in the lavatory (the 'bog-trotter's' job), or asleep in his office, and generally do what they can to ensure the survival of the government by running round in ever-decreasing circles. Tension builds with each recalculation, and counter report, towards a tense decision, a defeat, or even on one occasion an allegation that a whip was told to break his pair and vote to give Labour a majority of one. Politics then is a matter of luck, life and death. That swearing, sweating, reality is an occasional fever. With a two-score Tory majority, life is an easy routine. The only drama comes from the government's own backbenchers and the inability of a Chief Whip under the present Prime Minister to decide anything for himself. In Opposition, the office is a backwater, the mechanics' tea room, where they sit round and complain about the management, each other, their members, the world in general.

To outsiders, and Liberals, whips are fearsome ogres pulling puppets on strings. To the new Parliamentary breed, 'the mavericks', they are hardly the respected figures they might like to be. Their biggest fan is George Cunningham:

> I always say the first time the first whip hits the water will be a great step forward for British parliamentary democracy. There's no harm in Chief Whips demanding things from Members. They just mustn't get it, that's all.

Such views misjudge whips. They are messenger boys, not masters, as a former whip, John Ellis, testifies:

> As much as saying, 'This is what the government is to do,' to the lads it's a whip's job to go through the Whips' Office to get the Chief Whip to go to Ministers and say, 'The boys are unhappy. You'd better get over to the House of Commons, you'd better have some meetings with them, this policy will not go.' It's a two-way business . . . I always used to say to them, 'Look, it's my job to try and help you if I can but I want to know. If you're unhappy with a policy, for God's sake tell me . . . If you vote against the government I won't be cross about that, but I shall be cross about it if you suddenly do it at five to ten at night . . . Whatever you're doing I want to know.' On that basis never threaten anybody or be cross with them for voting against the government. But for some stupid things – that's a different matter altogether.

As well as such exemplary patience, Whips have patronage. Overseas trips are effectively on their nomination and approbation. They vet proposals though such trips usually come as a reward for service rather than a means of discipline and they influence behaviour less than the day to day decisions of the Pairing Whip. Similarly, appointments to committees are nominally made by the Committee of Selection, but largely determined by the Whips' Office. Select committee posts can be used as something of a lure for that minority of the House keen on playing an active part. Standing committees cannot. Oppositions want to put up a good fight, but not all that many are keen to attend and whips on the committees can often be faced with the 'I didn't want to be on this committee in the first place' brand of defiance. Mercifully, every Parliament has its naive new boys. The week I arrived I was persuaded that to sit as a government backbencher on the Finance Bill Committee was an honour. I endured the honour for eight weeks and found it did not include speaking.

More direct means of discipline are lashing with broken reeds. A bawling out, differently phrased and conducted for each party, can be used for those easily awed, though, as Julian Critchley indicates, neither side understands the other's language:

> The language of the Conservative Party's Whips' Office is very different from the bad language practised by the Labour Party Whips' Office. I've heard one Labour whip actually rebuke a Labour Member of Parliament in such a way that if it happened in the Tory Party I would never have spoken to that whip ever again. Our rebukes are understated. They are the rebukes of a good regiment. They used to be the rebukes of a brigade of guards; now it's just a good regiment of the line.

Some of the survivors have written their own memoirs. Brian Sedgemore, former Labour PPS, describes interviews with Chief Whip Michael Cocks, who was asking for his resignation:

> Michael told me that politics was a 'filthy business'. I concurred. He then hit me below the belt with a reference to how I had caused him personal suffering. I felt a tear welling up . . . The Chief Whip rose from his chair and surveyed the room. There were three doors off it – one into the large Whips' Office, one into his adviser's, and one into the corridor to get out. He then secured all three doors. Looking around I could see that the only means of escape was to throw myself out of the window behind his chair into the courtyard below. 'You are playing with dynamite. You'll have to watch it,' he said gravely. 'Oh yes, and who will detonate the dynamite, me or you Michael?' I replied, and then left, unlocking one of the doors.[1]

Beyond that, nothing. The structure is founded on bluff.

Those who call the bluff might not get away early at the end of the session, or visit overseas, but they have little else to fear. One of the earlier sensations caused by Geoffrey Dickens was his announcement that he was going to a party, despite a three-line whip. Called before assembled whips for a dressing-down in the best public school tradition, he waffled, listened to tear-jerking stories of people called back from overseas or mother's funerals, to vote for their government, and went off to his party. On the Labour side, Dennis Skinner voted against his own government in a tenth of the divisions from 1974–9, a qualification for the NEC rather than any other form of punishment. Andy McMahon 'concentrates on his constituency' at home in Glasgow, while whips fume impotently. Defiance is easy and habit forming.

An MP who keeps his own constituency party on his side has little

[1] Brian Sedgemore, *The Secret Constitution*, pp. 222–4.

to fear from the whips. Even a report to the constituency party in cases of persistent non-conformity can be taken as high praise. Where the office does not go to such lengths, the Member can often win support by using the terrifying public image of the whips to portray himself as an independent spirit being bullied, though the office can get revenge by publishing his voting record in the local paper. Absentees do not like their electorates to know it. Withdrawal of the Whip is a sanction rarely used in the Labour Party, never in the Conservative. Neither party will use it now, if only because to do so would be to provide new recruits for the SDP. So whips are toothless watchdogs. People tramp through the lobbies, sit through the night, fight on through committees, and generally devote themselves to a life of futility, because they want to, not because they are made to.

Though MPs are party men, it is surprising how small a part the national extra-parliamentary structure of their political party plays in their lives. The party machine looms largest at election times but otherwise it is the source of a lot of largely unread research material and the reference point for a lot of inefficiently answered questions. In theory, MPs are the standard bearers of party, its spearhead in Parliament. In fact the larger party is a background noise which some listen to, some ignore, but which intrudes only if allowed. The generalisation applies to both parties, though in the Conservatives, the party is the leader's arm and shield. With Labour the machine is notoriously inefficient and, these days, impotent, since party reform turned out to have more in common with partycide than any process of organisational improvement. At a mandatory PLP contribution of £65 a year it is also a real burden. However, others see it as the sure sword of socialism and democracy, because their side controls it (*pro tem*). Instead of containing the endemic argument within the Labour Party the machine has become part of it, controlled for much of the time by the left to counterbalance the right's control of the PLP. That control is now so evenly divided as to be deadlocked, decisions being determined mainly by Michael Foot forcing questions of confidence.

The National Executive is an alternative power base. Some of the finest minds in the party, Dennis Skinner, Eric Heffer, Joan Maynard, Frank Allaun, Les Huckfield, Renee Short, have climbed the party pyramid to compensate for the inconsiderate failure of fellow MPs to recognise their true worth. This gives them an important source of influence as well as a chance to get their own back by invoking the arcane mysteries of the party. Like the medieval papacy, Labour has two popes, one in conference, hibernating in Walworth Road between seaside enthronements, one resident in Parliament Square. Labour MPs have to pay at least lip service to both, and the adherents of each pope direct their efforts to preventing the other taking any decisions, let alone purporting to speak ex-cathedra.

With that exception, MPs of both parties stand in a similar relationship to their outside machine. They sit on its committees, particularly those involved in policy formulation: the National Executive's numerous sub-committees on different aspects of policy, the more discreet bodies through which the Tory Party in opposition thrashes out its proposals. MPs also attend conference, unenthusiastically on the Tory side, despairingly on Labour's, for they have to sit there as if in the dock at some combination of Stalinist show trial and Nuremberg Rally. Despite this, naive souls like Alan Clark still find it exciting:

> You have to go to the conference. It's the great annual rally of the party. To exchange views, to hear what people are saying and thinking, to go to fringe meetings. I think the debates are a bit of a charade compared with the Labour Party, but there's a tremendous amount that's done behind the scenes. I wouldn't miss it for anything.

Conference is a chance for the elect to meet those rare creatures, ordinary people. Even if they are not. There is also the chance in the Labour Party to win attention or take part in the policy debate, for Labour still subscribes to the myth that conference is important even if it is not properly organised to be so, while most Conservatives know that it is a stage-managed sham. There is, however, one thing both sides have in common. The more realistic MPs stay away in droves or put in a brief appearance to see and be seen. The more gullible endure four or five days by the autumnal seaside where a drunken haze rolls out to sea from the bars. This is the grand jamboree of politics, with drink, sex and even more gossip, as optional extras.

The critics of party caricature it by portraying it as a machinery of tyranny. It is far more a matter of class background, class socialisation, and group conformity than of dictatorship and discipline. Party is weakening precisely because it is these basic social bonds which are being undermined by social change and by the new stresses and strains: the Common Market, the more sectional roles of the unions, and the gaps between professions and business, all combine to strain party and all are characteristics of a society in decline. The problem is clearest in the Labour Party. There conference and machine are more argumentative, less manageable, partly because the unions are less manageable, less able to deliver votes partly because the constituency delegates are much more middle class, public sector employees and yap professions predominating over the more loyal instincts of genuine workers. All this has then been compounded by a struggle for power carried on in the name of policy. Trends of opinion in a broad church are therefore taking on the appearance of sects struggling to control the chapel. The differences are now as real, if not as embittering, in the Conservative Party. Ted Heath forced hard choices, economic decline eliminated the possibility of holding classes together by distributing the products of affluence. Margaret Thatcher steered the party towards a collection of prejudices which collectively constituted an ideology very different to the easy-going Whigism, or even the organic conservatism, of earlier days. Conference too was changing, no longer as solid, the middle class doing its duty. It began to look a little more like the Conservative Party in Parliament: modern man on the make. Yet unlike Labour's it has never had the presumption of power, so it remains a rally, and its attitudes make it Margaret Thatcher's rally. But even the usual careful stage-management cannot conceal the rising dismay of industry and the small business sector hit by the depression, the doubts and hesitations over where to go next.

Each party is becoming more difficult to manage. Internal cohesion is fraying. The change is irreversible, much as ideologues on both sides might want to roll it back. The firm discipline, the ideological purity and the common purpose they seek are attainable only in sects, not mass parties. Each step towards them weakens the easy on-going bonds and unexamined assumptions, and makes the party more embittered, less united and probably less electorally attractive. Parties are becoming holding companies, umbrellas for many diverse groups and trends, rather than the monoliths they once used to be. They have little alternative. They must change with the trends, or atrophy into a sect, like the pure and useless French Communist Party.

The party system, like Parliament itself, is in transition. It will never be as strong again as it was from 1946 to 1970. Yet neither will it degenerate into the looser grouping of the nineteenth century.

Mass democracy cannot work without parties to give coherence to choice. So parties will keep on struggling for power and trying to keep their Members marching in some reasonable approximation of step, as the only way of getting it and holding it. The problem is how many parties there will be to participate in that struggle and what will be their nature. Will they remain, as now, broad parties of the similar-minded, coming together on a lowest common denominator programme, or will a genuine multi-party system be born out of present stresses and strains, so that the divisions within parties are formalised as new groupings while governments become overt coalitions rather than the same thing disguised as one party?

Parliament itself will have very little influence on this evolution. It will be determined by social trends and the reactions of the electorate to the multi-party system now in the process of creation. Parliament's job is to respond to changes forced on it from outside, adjusting to and accepting whatever system evolves, whatever kind of parties the electorate decide to send it. It has always done this. It will again and at the end of the day in the House there will still be two sides, still 'ins' and still 'outs'. Whether these two sides are two parties, or coalitions of parties, or even collections of individuals, has always been a matter of supreme indifference to Parliament. The Fun Factory functions whatever happens.

THREE LINE WHIP
CONSTITUENCY
REDUNDANCY
SURGERY TODAY

8 Constituency Man

Representing a constituency makes the House of Commons almost bearable. Constituencies vary. Some are identifiable units with an identity of their own. Others are unnatural slices of cities or bucolic blocks lumped together to create the necessary numbers. Yet all are people, the bottom line of politics. The pressure groups who campaign nationally have their roots there. Hostile words about estate agents or lawyers in the House get relayed down the grapevine to produce local pressures. The laws and regulations so learnedly discussed in committee are people queueing in the surgery. The moods measured by the polls are people looking you in the eye in the street or giggling behind your back. Crazy economic decisions in the House are a factory closed.

Constituents are the key to survival, the root of everything, the only reality in a mad uncertain world. They are valued as they value themselves by being 'safe' and discountable or marginal and demanding, yet for any responsible MP they are a joy, one of the few. They impose an overwhelming sense of responsibility. Yet they are also a curse for they can never be properly or fully served. They would not know if they were. MPs can never live up to their constituency. Or down to it. Yet constituents are their only source of strength. They give roots to reactions, patterns to feelings, and form the one point of certainty in a fickle confusing world. They are also the base from which governments, parties and the machine can be tackled and to which all feel obliged to respond. They are not the abstract, the ordered, the reason of state or the convenience of party, but people. When you cut them they bleed. In a democracy constituencies are listened to, and MPs are too because they represent them; people in the convenient jumbo-size 67,000 pack.

MPs are ambassadors accredited to Westminster. The similarities between representing Uruguay at the Palace of St James or Scunthorpe at another Palace are striking. Ambassadorial life can be totally absorbing. So can life at the Fun Factory. Ambassadors can use their power of mediation to strengthen their own position. So can MPs. An ambassador works to a regime back home and can be dismissed by it. The MP depends on his local party. He, too, can be booted out, though when this happens he must turn for political asylum not to the host nation but the SDP. Which is where the resemblance ends. MPs have to work harder. They must visit constituencies more. They don't get CD plates for their cars. And they serve two masters: the people and the local party, where ambassadors are Bennite, working only to the regime.

Britain is one of the world's most centralised societies. London contains a higher proportion of the population than comparable capitals. A highly centralised media focuses on it. Career ladders climb there. Government runs from there. Sensible countries have federal structures or a *de facto* federalism of competing centres. Britain's great wen swamps everything, turning regionalism into the politics of the parasite periphery. All of which is reflected in politics. In the nineteenth century, MPs were local notables. Now the distinctive local politics of Manchester, Birmingham or Leeds have gone, eclipsed by national politics articulated on class lines. The notables have shrunk, replaced by candidates brought in from outside.

MPs have become creatures of the centre rather than the constituencies. It became convenient for them to live in London. They pursued their careers there. They spoke to their constituents through the centralised media. Their constituents, at least the middle-class element, expected them to be there. London was the fount from which all flowed: laws, grants, benefits, aid. The nature of our political system strengthened this focus. Our Parliament was elected first for seven then for five years, long by most standards, making constituencies less demanding. Our party system was strong, and most seats were so safe that MPs could more safely ignore them, a marked contrast with the USA where frequent elections and weaker parties make the constituency all important, or New Zealand where smaller seats make the MP more important, and more noticeable, in his constituency. Our MPs were better at representing classes than constituencies.

This situation reached its apogee in the 1940s when the two mass parties had crushed all opposition. Since then the whole pattern of development has been the other way, making class less important, the localities more important. Local politics still lacked the vigour of decentralised systems, but became more demanding. In the 1950s it was possible to have an exciting political life in London. Gaitskell, Crosland, Crossman, the intellectual Labour Party, congregated there. The Conservatives were kept there more reluctantly by being in power. Now, the focus has shifted. MPs are much more likely to be transients in London. Political life has widened. The constituencies are playing a much more important part. A Labour newcomer in 1945 told of his first visit to the constituency after the election. A top-hatted station master met him to ask whether he would be following the previous Member in paying his annual visit at that time of year. A. V. Alexander hardly ever visited his Sheffield constituency during or after the war, producing such disgruntlement that his successor George Darling was selected on a radical promise of quarterly visits. When he was later appointed PPS to Arthur Bottomley, the constituency wrote to absolve him even from that promise 'in the light of his heavy duties'. Today the feeling that MPs should live in the constituency is becoming widespread. Members are finding that the growing demands of their constituents compel them to do so. Just over a third of MPs in our survey had their family homes in the constituency and rather more within twenty miles. A tenth lived between twenty and a hundred miles from the constituency, leaving the rest – a fifth of the whole – further away, some in perverse directions like James Lamond, MP for Oldham, living conveniently in Aberdeen. Distances impose strain. Tom Bradley, MP for Leicester East, lives in Kettering, going home every night; two of Coventry's four MPs, go home, trains permitting, and David Stoddart, MP for Swindon, is settled in Reading, equidistant between London and Swindon. All are long hauls after a late division. Nor does the pressure ease at weekends. Those living outside their constituencies compensate by visiting constantly. Some three quarters of our MPs claimed to spend forty or more weekends a year in their constituencies, a sixth, thirty to forty, and only 4 per cent less than twenty.

In most cases, distance from the seat is accidental: the MP has not moved his wife and family. For Joe Ashton and others it is quite deliberate. In the constituency life becomes a replay of *No Hiding Place*:

> There is stress from the party as well as from the public and the press. There are always people after an MP's job and eager to backstab or put in the poison. The press do not realise the effect personal abuse has on a man's wife, kids and family relatives, who have to defend him in the shops and factories. Most of us live outside our constituencies because of

> the endless stream of callers, most of whom are nutters. We get heavy breathers on the phone and idiots ringing after midnight when we are away in London. It all has an effect on wives . . . mind you, it's better than working down the pit.

MPs are forced into a double life, with double homes: nearly a third had their family home in London, the same proportion had bought a second home there, and the same number again lived out their exile in rented accommodation, none of it quite as bad as the 'smelly sock brigade' of John Concannon, Kevin McNamara and (up to 1979) John Ellis, who slept three to a room rented from an MP's widow. This leaves a tenth who could afford a hotel or club, the County, near Euston, being popular with Labour MPs. Though for others 'hotel' might be a misnomer; one stayed at the Salvation Army. Only a small number, mostly Tories, but also including Roy Hattersley, have been able to afford houses in the 'division bell area', that elastic one-and-a-half-mile region round the palace where division bells can be installed in the houses of those who can reach the Commons in the necessary eight minutes. Flats in that area start at £50,000 on leases, freehold houses at £80,000. So it is hardly surprising that there are now only two score bells in private residences, half the figure in the 1960s. For the others distance from the House merely adds strains of commuting in London to all their other problems, while living in London adds strains in the constituency. As one questionnaire answer put it:

> The general public are not aware of the stress on MPs who have to journey a hundred miles every week before they do any work. The fact is that they have to survive in an establishment that is out of this world. I would favour accommodation being provided by the government as near the House of Commons as possible . . . I am concerned about the manner in which we work on the cheap. No other MPs in any other country work the way we do.

The Member of Parliament is no longer the 'Westminster Man' he was twenty years ago. Yet he is not the constituency man he was in the last century either. He straddles: A1, Heathrow or British Rail Man, a political Flying Dutchman doomed to perpetual peregrination. There is, as Mrs Thatcher might say, no alternative. The steady increase in the work generated by the constituencies, the growing feeling that MPs should be there more, have combined with the growing demands of Westminster to put the MP into a limbo in-between. There is a full-time job at either end, but each distracts him from the other.

In the 1950s, Hugh Gaitskell got some twenty letters a month from his Leeds constituency. Most now get that in a week; some in a couple of days. The 1972–3 study of Tony Benn's constituency mail showed a total of 5,011 letters in and out in one year relating to 1,106 separate cases; while a study of Humberside MPs indicated that if they are typical MPs must write between 3,000 and 16,000 letters a year to Ministers alone, omitting the huge numbers they sent to departments locally and to a whole series of government agencies. The Department of Health and Social Security Head office – working in the sector which generates most problems – was reported to be getting 2,000 letters a month, mostly from MPs in 1979–80 in the private offices of Ministers. In the month of July 1979 the Minister of State in the Home Office responsible for immigration received 1,243 letters from parliamentarians.

The sheer deluge of mail is best illustrated by the numbers written to and from Ministers in the different departments by MPs in the single month of January 1982.

	Letters To and From Ministers	
	To	From
Agriculture	216	311
Defence	424	332
Education	867	492
Employment	428	401
Energy	120	119
Environment	886	1,009
Foreign Office	442	634
Health and Social Security	Not available	1,950
Home Office	1,550	1,750
Industry	310	343
Northern Ireland	225	237
Prime Minister	70 approx	70 approx
Scottish Office	362	273
Trade	592	481
Transport	659	574
Treasury	818	947
Welsh Office	120	146

Borough constituencies, with all human life in one boundary, marginals, and middle-class retirement or commuter seats, where people have the leisure, education and sense of self-importance to write, generate the most mail. Tory rurals produce the least. Yet any seat with no town hall to take the burden of complaints focuses everything on the MP, as well as creating the problem of greater distances, a particular problem in the larger Labour seats like Joe Ashton's Bassetlaw, with seventy parish councils, or John Home Robertson's Berwick and East Lothian with four towns, eight hereditary peers, and only one set of traffic lights. Neither can compare in area with Joe Grimond's Orkneys, or Nationalist seats like the Western Isles, yet such rural seats offer one big advantage: the population is rooted, not constantly turning over. To help a constituent with a housing problem in London or Manchester often moves him over the very artificial constituency boundaries to express his gratitude elsewhere. Mobile populations build up no loyalty.

Constituency work is becoming the opium of the parliamentarian. It absorbs, satisfies and distracts from the real job. Alan Clark's patrician view is that it is all a matter of duty:

> It's a burden. It undoubtedly adds heavily to your workload. But it's very rewarding. Every MP should get twenty or thirty notches in his gun every year for people who he's helped . . . it certainly consumes time but it's just part of the democratic system . . . and I wouldn't discard it because I think that the contact you get with your constituents and the familiarity that you get, particularly for someone like myself who has had an absolutely privileged existence from birth are all vital . . . Because I'm an MP I'm constantly brought into contact with really hideous individual problems and I do my best to solve them. I think it's good for MPs to be aquainted with this kind of thing.

While Julian Critchley can adapt a more sardonic approach, looking out from Aldershot at the efforts of others:

> A lot depends on the kind of constituency. If you're lucky enough to have a safe seat in an area of nil unemployment, therefore of great local prosperity, and if, in the Conservative Party, your seat is safe, it's therefore very largely a middle-class seat, and most people can afford lawyers or solicitors if they get into trouble. So you are left with only a relatively small amount of constituency surgery work to do. Now if, on the other hand, you're a Labour MP or, indeed, if you're a Conservative or Labour MP in the marginal seat in which there is a lot of unemployment, then quite clearly all the pressures are very much greater.

The MP is the local ombudsman. Problems come to him because they are increasing and he is there. Some MPs take pains to help, others seem largely untraceable. Most are all too available. In a sample of twenty MPs telephoned at random, only one could not be contacted, the most distant date for an appointment was a fortnight away. Most seemed embarrassingly eager for customers. This may not last because the work is growing steadily. It comes in three ways. Most MPs have surgeries, some once a month, most once a fortnight, a few weekly. Some mining MPs do not bother; the old-fashioned ones used to argue that 'they always know where my back door is', but such a view is now rare. Some Tory MPs leave such mundane business to their party agents; but nearly everyone else feels it vital because, as Jo Richardson points out, surgery provides the personal touch:

> When I go to my advice bureau a lot of people come along and they start out by saying, 'I don't really know where to start my story.' I say, 'Start wherever you want and tell me and we'll see what happens.' And in the end it turns out it's about something I can't possibly help them with, perhaps a housing problem, because I'm not on the local authority, or perhaps a legal problem, perhaps a marital problem. I always feel very pleased when they get up, as they frequently do at the end, and say, 'Thanks very much, at least you listened.' . . . I think people feel better if they're able to go and talk sometimes to a stranger about their personal problems.

A 1967 survey showed that under 10 per cent of MPs did not hold regular surgeries. That proportion must now be even lower.

Surgeries are usually held in one place, but can also be alternated round the larger constituencies, or even, in the case of John Butcher's converted taxi surgery, transferred to a confessional on wheels, parked in designated places.

Then comes the steady flow to the MP's house in the constituency or to his party office. It also comes through the agent. Nearly half of our sample – mostly Tory – had a full-time agent, a quarter had one part-time; while a further sixth had a full-time secretary in the constituency and a third part-time. Finally, the unstoppable mail pours in. A 1960s study of Members' mail showed 13 per cent receiving less than twenty-five letters a week from their constituency, two-fifths from twenty-five to fifty, and the rest more, a hundred or more in the case of a tenth. The figures have certainly gone up since then.

MPs grumble at the growing load. In fact they love it. It gives them a sense of usefulness, a sense of purpose coming by recorded delivery. It puts them in touch with constituents. It accumulates Brownie points. So they take on everything: local government matters which should go elsewhere, and which some, like Enoch Powell, still sternly send back, personal problems, medical matters. The result for Lynda Chalker and for MPs generally is to generate more letters: mail breeds mail.

> I don't believe that anybody who writes to me should go without a reply, provided the jolly old Post Office actually deliver it. If I can help I will help; if I can't I say I can't. Now that, and particularly being a woman MP, means that you get a lot more post, I gather, than men in similar positions, because people write to you about things they wouldn't write to a male colleague about. It's a pretty tough job because, not only are you trying to deal with the representations made to you and pass these on to Ministers, you're trying to answer queries, and very often you have to do a lot of research . . . One letter in often means four or five letters out.

David Penhaligon estimates his output as 200 letters a week to constituents. This rains like confetti down on all, even lunatics. Margaret Jackson in Lincoln had a regular visit from a man suffering from death rays emitted by his television. She persuaded him of the benefits of watching in wellingtons. David Hunt, the Wirral MP, was given on election a list of cranks to ignore. He did, until five years later he got a heart-rending letter from one claiming unfair dismissal. Hunt asked for more details. A large suitcase arrived by post containing 3,000 documents and details of the dismissal which had been in 1937. A few MPs ignore the rising tide: one mining MP reckons that a letter only merits answering when it is a third repeat. Such rejection is rare. Former American Senator Stephen Young returned curious letters with a note, 'I think you should know that some lunatic has been writing to me and using your name.' One MP who used this in Britain found to her surprise that the stab in the dark was correct: the 'correspondent's' lodger had been writing.

We have not educated our people to the complexity of our systems of social management and administration. A substantial proportion, perhaps a fifth, are unable to cope with the machine. A publicly financed network of bureaux dispensing professional advice on social security matters, legal rights, consumer questions and administrative problems is the only answer. Until it is provided – and the Citizens' Advice Bureaux with their middle-class bromides come nowhere near

– the MP is the residuary legatee; known to enough people, assumed to be powerful, and available. He gets everything.

There are some who cannot be helped. Like others, John Stokes, influenced by another nineteenth-century moralist, Samuel Smiles, does not always try:

> You can help on tax cases . . . I would think that in five out of six income tax cases, the individual is right and the taxman is wrong; and we have the right to appeal direct to the Chancellor of the Exchequer and to get it put right . . . If people want a telephone I can always help and the pole goes up in the garden in a few days. But lots of other matters are beyond anyone's help. They're often casualties of life – they have asked everybody, the social services, the DHSS, the councillor and as a last resort they come to the Member. They don't like the neighbours, their children are unruly, they are separated or deserted wives. These cases are sad; it's right the MP should know about them, but you have to have the moral courage to say, 'I am very sorry indeed for you but there is nothing whatever that I as an MP can do.'

Perhaps the grievance merchant does not expect it: his personality might disintegrate with the problem. The inadequate can be helped, if only by pointing them in the right direction, and most successes are with this group, which is not too difficult given their propensity to endure brush-offs at the counter and their inability to put their case properly. With the rest, the rate of success depends on the subject: high on social security, where the pressure on the system leads to mistakes, middling on tax, low on immigration.

The MP has two strengths: he writes from a good address which gets his letter taken seriously, whatever the contents. He comes in at the top, relating directly to Ministers, departmental managers, whatever level he chooses. Anomalies arising at lower levels, particularly at the counter, that front line between the people and the machine, can thus be looked at anew by those better qualified, a safeguard which a sensible machinery of administration will welcome, whatever burden of work it imposes. Yet mainly the MP will fail. He starts with a partial point of view, for he cannot know the full complexity of each problem. He is a safety net, not a first recourse. The machinery is usually efficient and works by fair priorities. Ministers do not do political favours though they might try harder for their own side. MPs themselves have no innate powers. It would be disastrous for fair and efficient administration if they had. Yet, as one questionnaire answer put it, they do have some power:

> The effectiveness of MPs varies according to the field in which they are attempting to operate. Any backbencher who is not bone-idle can deploy a good deal of fire-power to relieve an individual problem of a constituent who had got himself in a tangle with a bureaucracy (wrong tax coding, pension book lost, driving licence swallowed by Swansea, etc, etc). In many cases, MPs are far more effective and quicker and have wider terms of reference than the ombudsman. I believe that this is largely due to the fact that the Civil Service is very apprehensive of Question Time. They pride themselves on giving a good 'crib' with the supplementary and if the Minister is made to look a fool, the kicks go all the way down the rank and file. Written questions and letters to Ministers about particular cases benefit from this too.

Failures do not always preclude gratitude. Constituents can be impressed by a personal explanation from Sir Geoffrey Howe of why they are out of a job to help their country or by a letter from the chairman of the Coal Board, signed in his own fair hand. It becomes a status symbol and a proof of effort, even if it only says 'Get knotted' politely.

In the campaign, would-be MPs compete to parade their constituency knowledge. They pronounce on its problems, proclaim their friendships. Once elected they are alone, ignorant, lost: their only friends ideologues with a local standing similar to lepers. They now have to 'learn' the constituency, putting it together like a jigsaw. Parliament is a voluntary activity. The constituency is mandatory, and the price of election is eternal availability. At first, both constituency and party are supportive. The party is relieved to have kept the seat, temporarily grateful to the person who did it. The constituency will give the Member a fair go, probably because most are not sure who won anyway. Both phases will pass, but this is a sheltered period during which the Member can get to know people, and build up the contacts to allow him to live on his reflexes later on when times turn hard and the going turns rough. It will.

There is a large amount of fantasy in all this. Surveys indicate that though most MPs claim to know their constituents personally by face, if not by name, and like to see themselves as local institutions, in fact under half the people in the average constituency know who their MP is. Almost certainly, then, even fewer would recognise him if he assaulted them in a dark alley. This can be both a blessing and a curse, for Members want to be recognised; it makes life easier, but not all the time. Yet the MP's nature is not ego – or not entirely so – and MPs need to be known in and to know their constituency. It is a condition of survival and a matter of duty. They set about the necessary task in different ways, some using notoriety, others hard work. Soon Members will follow the Americans and feed information into a computer. Already a few have card or word-processor indexes of key men, names of wives, key firms. Without such easy informality it is a long, wearing process of visiting factories and fondling the Chamber of Commerce, the Trades Council and all the other bodies which must be flattered, if not actually listened to. Some constituents expect their MP to be in the constituency: all Members have examples of punters demanding the MP and, on being told that he is in London, asking what he is doing there. The House of Commons expects a Member to take part in its proceedings. Both demands can be a terrible inconvenience and each becomes as clamorous as it is allowed to be. Constituency management, the art of being in two places at once without visiting either, alleviates the problem. A conspiratorial relationship with the lobby correspondent of the local newspaper is easy to establish. He is anxious to keep stories flowing into his paper and loath to give any indication that his job is as useful as any other gutter or fall pipe. So he is prepared to cover the flow of questions MPs leave behind to be fed in when they are tripping round the world hunting a diminishing supply of facts. The local newspaper does not like to overpay its photographers, so they take stills at ten functions crammed into one day, then publish them *seriatim* later. Visits to the constituency should be high-profile, with as much as possible crammed into as short a time as possible. Those with homes there should have drawbridges. Wives and families have to be managed too.

The MP is a middleman between his constituency and the centre. Politically, this means interpreting (or, in opposition, misinterpreting) government policy in the constituency, representing its view in the House and the party. He is also a gatekeeper, admitting constituents, pressure groups, businesses, organisations and local lunatics, to the centre of power. At its simplest level, this is a messenger boy function: writing letters on their behalf and sending on the 'Dear Fred' replies which indicate (usually inaccurately) that he is known personally to the Minister. At a higher level, it involves taking deputations to departments, public authorities, parliamentary committees. The function is hardly necessary. They could find their own way. Yet it flatters the MP's ego and perhaps takes them in at a higher level and earlier than otherwise.

Gatekeeping involves real effort only when it requires procedures an MP alone can invoke. There is a lingering attachment to having subjects discussed in the House. Faced with a problem such as a factory closure, flood damage, an epidemic of casual murder, the astute will seek to put it on television, realising correctly that the authorities are moved by fear of publicity because they know that the media reach the public. On the other hand, the dull and dutiful turn to Parliament, assuming that this gives not only dignity but action. It does not, but the House has provided for just this contingency. A Member can raise a question under Standing Order Number Nine providing for emergency debate. It will be refused but he has shown willing, particularly if he is Les Huckfield, who raised the same one, day after day. He can ask questions to generate publicity in the local newspaper. He can also apply for, and with persistence get, an adjournment debate. This will occur around midnight. Attendance will usually be two people, Member and Minister, usually one of nature's fall guys, a Junior Minister, who replies. No action will result: the Minister's brief is to show sympathy and concern but say nothing. Yet an awed public will assume that the problems of Drighlington have been debated by a packed Chamber. Something is being done. The eyes of the world are on them. The effectiveness of these little confidence tricks stems from a naive belief that Parliament runs the country and that there hovers above it some benign authority ready to act on its words. In fact it does not, there is not, and Parliament has influence only in the way television does, by appealing to public opinion and creating fear in responsible authorities. As a result, it has less influence because it is less good at both than the box.

The more astute, and less publicity conscious, MPs go directly to the heart of the problem. Faced with the threatened closure of Norvic Shoes in Norwich with 1,200 jobs, because the bank was demanding liquidation, John Garrett and David Ennals stiffened management, went to the bank, secured a loan and stopped the closure. Several months later trading conditions had deteriorated so sharply that the factory closed. Yet it might have survived. Had it done so, it would have been a far more effective intervention than the usual parliamentary effort. Such techniques can be successful, yet only in very exceptional cases, as David Penhaligon found in the days when the Labour Government depended on Liberal support:

> I had a tin mine in my constituency, employing a thousand people, going bankrupt . . . it was to be closed and all the jobs would have been

lost. Now it was admittedly in the middle of the Lib-Lab pact, so I was then in a particularly fortunate position and I used the power that I had to twist the tail of the system to get the government to pay for the pumping costs. The great secret of tin-mining is to keep them dry and safe. The company wanted to switch the pumps off, and I knew the moment they switched the pumps off it was the end of any possible saving of the mine. So I managed to blackmail the government into paying for the pumping costs and eventually, after a lot of negotiations and coming and going, the tin mines were reopened.

Insecure governments open the way to porkbarrel politics; strong governments restrict this to marginal seats, a tax centre for Shipley, development area status for Grimsby before the 1977 by-election, a Humber Bridge announced before the 1966 Hull North by-election. In both cases the scope is small and an MP's job is usually to take credit for developments over which he had no influence, control or probably knowledge. However, the more spectacular gestures might elicit gratitude. In the Hull North and Grimsby by-elections the turnout actually increased, a rare event in by-elections.

One thing an MP can do is secure honours, only for certain specified categories and only after strict scrutiny – for the Lloyd George days of cash-and-carry titles are gone – but for minor matters like OBEs (Other Buggers' Efforts), MBEs (My Bloody Efforts), and CBEs. MPs need not bother about KCMGs (Kindly Call Me God) or GCMG (God Calls Me God); they go to civil servants, or at least to nice, non-striking, ones. For all else, including life peerages, the MP is a transmission channel and can help applications on their way. Most therefore get several recommendations, often from potential honorifics themselves. Some even claim a 100 per cent success rate, others admit to one in ten. In each case the procedure is the same. As a new Member I asked what to do and was airily told by the Chief Whip, 'Ring Mabs at Number Twelve.' No telephone directory gave me any Ministerial Appointment Board or anything like. Shamefaced, I went back to ask what Mabs was. It was Mabel Dodd, secretary to the Government Whips' Office, who supplied the forms. 'With a name like that wouldn't you call yourself Mabs?' asked the Chief Whip.

The most basic part of constituency management is the local party. In theory, the constituency elects the MP. In fact, the party appoints. And can discard. The local party's power is not absolute, but those preferring a quiet life would be silly to test it. A parliamentary salary is better than a footnote in a textbook. Some parties are accommodating, others very demanding. Tory constituencies have been known to turn out the MP. So have Labour. The Conservatives here, as in leadership matters, prefer a knife in the back and a body in the river. Labour goes in for wars of attrition. Yet, for the most part, this exertion of discipline is rare. MPs can be ticked off, as Nigel Forman and other Tory malcontents have been for speaking unkindly about the Leaderine's economic policy. Yet Julian Critchley has it well weighed up. It is really appearances that count:

> What they do expect from their MP is that he should be a standard bearer for the party locally, that he should not bring the party into disrepute locally, that he should be polite and assiduous with them. If all these things happen then, even were his views to be largely different from the views of many of his supporters, they don't mind very much. But it may be very different in the Labour Party which is a completely different creature. The Labour Party is a movement and not a party. We are a party, but providing you are polite and do your job properly within the Conservative Party, you can in fact hold a range of opinions reasonably securely.

One basic pattern of post-war politics is the perpetual shrinking of political parties, membership dropping along with support in the country from a post-war high. Labour's fall has been the fastest, from 706,161 members in 1950 to 358,000 in 1980; even less today. A £6 subscription and meetings which alternate between total boredom and bitter argument are both carefully calculated to put normal people off and accelerate the slide into sectarian status. The Tories have also lost membership heavily, from 2,250,000 in 1950 to 650,000 in 1980, and again less today despite a minimum subscription of 12½p. The SDP claims 65,000 at £9 a time, the Liberals 200,000 at £1 a time. Some MPs from the major parties are perfectly happy with this decline. An American Democratic Congressman once told me that at the end of his term, 'I had become the Democratic Party in my district.' The same can happen here with MPs who are keen on a quiet life, content to woo the old lady vote and dance with it at socials, or prepared to channel some of their secretarial allowance into the party's own coffers as well as make substantial contributions out of their own pocket. Membership falls to the point where the party is really a self-preserving conspiracy between MPs, councillors and ageing party members. Yet the examples are rarer than left-wing rhetoric would indicate. The more usual situation is that the smaller parties, like Liverpool Edge Hill,

Bermondsey, Ladywood and Sowerby, are infiltrated by the left who are welcomed initially as symptoms of the youth revolution and later resented when they threaten the hegemony of age. The parties then become battle grounds, eventually reacting against the previous domination. Such a situation can now develop anywhere in the Labour Party because most parties are small. The price of mass membership is eternal vigilance; particularly over the Young Socialists, who are usually no more than the stage name for the Militant Tendency.

Ladywood had only just over a hundred Labour members in Brian Walden's heyday, perhaps 250 today when the new clique has seen fit to throw out his heir. Chester-le-Street has 300, Woolwich 5,100. The average constituency Labour Party probably has 400 members, the average Conservative over 1,000. Only exceptional parties running special lotteries like Southampton Test or having large Labour or Conservative clubs have more. In general the Conservative Club movement is more active and a better recruiting ground than Labour's, though their highest political endeavours are usually casual adultery and serious drinking.

By Prentice's law, rows are in inverse ratio to membership, down to about the 200 figure, at which point they die out for lack of combatants. They will therefore become more common in both parties as the membership shrinks. The best examples of the art of local party jungle warfare are to be found in London, where parties are both smaller and more intense than in the real world. There constant turnover saps stability. London MPs have an easier life in not having to face the travelling which so drains the energies of others. In compensation they have to keep a more careful watch on their own backs. Yet the long-term trend everywhere is for local parties to demand more from their MPs. They expect more service, are more insistent on his living in or frequently visiting the constituency, they put up more demands for more commitments. This will make the life of the MPs less easy and take us towards disposable Members in the way that we are now getting disposable Ministers. Reselection in the Labour Party is only the outward and visible symptom of this long-term underlying trend in both parties.

Friction and political clashes are not new developments. The Suez crisis, a major clash of principle, produced a rash of MP disposals. Four Tories and one Labour man were pushed out by their local parties for rebelling over the invasion. Most gave up rather than fight and most had obviously blotted their copy-books by earlier dissent from party line or conjugal bed. One, Nigel Nicolson in Bournemouth, attracted considerable opprobrium: as one local party member put it, 'Nicolson didn't want the blood of either Englishmen or Arabs. What's a Tory MP for?' He went down with guns blazing in a protracted row which made him the Reg Prentice of his day. Except that Nicolson stuck to both principles and party, unlike Reg, who let down everyone who backed him and did not hang around to go down with the ship. Sporadic friction has continued on other issues and up to the 1970s Conservatives had probably managed over the years to dispose of more sitting Members than Labour, because they had a more orderly and effective procedure for doing so. Labour, with its more rigid constitution, goes in for the wagon-train and Red Indian approach to getting rid of Members. Consequently, most local parties usually preferred not to bother. When they did, unpleasantness, bitterness, appeals and reversals characterised the process in both the Prentice affair (Newham 1, Prentice 0), and Maureen Colquhoun's loving relationship with her local party in Northampton (Northampton 0, Colquhoun 0, Tories 1). One technique could be used by both parties: informal persuasion. In all the pious platitudes, 'life-time of service', 'standing down through ill-health', 'desire to enjoy the years of retirement', it is not always clear which departures are the bum's rush and which are gold watch affairs.

Despite these trends, the most recent issue of principle, Common Market entry, had fewer immediate repercussions than Suez. Some MPs, such as Dick Leonard or Ivor Richard, might have found more difficulty in getting new seats in the musical chairs after the redistribution preceding the February 1974 election. Yet at that contest none of the threats made against those who deviated from their party line materialised, though the issue did lead to ill-will in certain areas. Thus the fact that both refusal of reselection and pressure to stand down appear to be becoming more common is more due to sporadic local rows and breakdowns of relationships than broad general issues. Jeffrey Archer stood down in Louth, nominally voluntarily, after the spectacular collapse of his first attempt to become a millionaire. Robert Cooke stood down in Bristol West at the age of forty-nine after a section of his constituency had expressed concern at the lack of vigour shown in twenty-two years as MP. Nicholas Scott hung on through a series of rows in Chelsea over ideological issues, supplemented by a divorce for adultery. On the Labour side, Reg Prentice gave up in Newham after a series of parliamentary colleagues had mortgaged their credibility for him and a couple of Oxford students had shown just how far determination, money and legal ability could go in making mayhem of Labour's creaking constitution. Sir Arthur Irvine neglected Liverpool Edge Hill abominably for years but it took a long time for the dilapidated constituency party to pluck up the courage to tell him to go. After denouncing them for their lack of consideration, he died before the end of the Parliament, handing the seat to the Liberals. At least two others went quietly. Frank Tomney, a sixty-nine-year-old right-winger in Hammersmith North, found himself in conflict with a left-wing party and agreed to call twenty-nine years a day. He remained loyal to a Labour Government which desperately needed his vote and which he could have seized every opportunity to wreck. So did Ernest Perry in Battersea South, though he may have wanted to serve on for pension purposes.

This developing situation was hardened into constitutional rigidities by Labour's decision to opt for a system of reselection, which is as mandatory as a national executive which has no power to overrule general management committees can make it. Both parties have been moving in the same direction. By Prentice's law, Labour, with the smallest membership, got there faster by staging the biggest rows. And as is usual with Labour's constitutional changes, it opted for defining the indefinable and doing it in such a way as to create the maximum degree of inefficiency and inconvenience.

Mandatory reselection introduces a new dimension. Once the dust has settled, immediate changes will be slight. Despite the folly of beginning it before another round of musical chairs begins with redistribution, the exercise has not gone too badly. Some of those who were rejected were dropped for understandable reasons. Nearly all MPs have been reselected, including some whom no party in its right – or even left – mind would keep. Yet it has provided SDP recruits, helped them to survive the birth, and what happens in the future, particularly if Labour is in government, is another question. With this machinery and the present mood in the constituencies no government could carry on. The way of preventing future betrayals will have been by preventing future Labour governments: abstinence as a political prophylactic. The process also legitimises divisions, even *putsches* within local parties. It puts the MP in an exposed situation. It gives open licence to mobilise against him; all these are dangerous developments in a party which is naturally divided anyway.

It denies a major political reality: ambition. The MP who can accept a rejection as a rational expression of a reasonable will would be more of a Benedictine than a normal Labour man. Most are skilled at turning personal issues into major questions of principle. They will also have the examples of Dick Taverne, Eddie Milne and S. O. Davies, all of whom stood against their local parties and won. For a time. Even the one who failed, Eddie Griffiths, mustered 10,000 votes in Brightside. As an extra incentive, the MPs and related trades union has so arranged things that defeated Members get a tax-free allowance of several months' salary, depending on length of service. Why spurn this by lying down and dying at the behest of a Labour Party which cannot even afford a burial grant, when to fight for the seat guarantees several months, even as much as a year, of tax-free pay? Contrast all this with that ruck of candidates struggling to get seats who helped push mandatory reselection through in the first place, and the potential for disaster is clear. The Conservatives must be heaving a sigh of relief that they have kept their selection differences within the bounds of reason by making them personal affairs, not issues of principle.

Those anxious to avoid such a fate have to manage their local party: the Arthur Lewis treatment of a few friendly insults invites the Arthur Lewis fate. One technique in safe seats is membership restriction. Yet in the Labour Party this is being threatened by *Militant* permeations which bring a change of guards: politically motivated cronies displace the oldies but remain just as exclusive, if only because now no one wants to join. In the Conservative Party cliques can become even more demanding than genuinely active parties. Another technique is 'absence makes the heart grow fonder'. An MP in the backyard can be an MP devalued. He has to go there, but should neither become obsessive or obstructive, nor start doing Labour councillors' jobs for them. A third, similar, approach, increasingly necessary in London, is to sit back in the hope that the different factions will exhaust themselves in internecine warfare and the endless recruitment of new members: it is all in the lap of the sods, illustrated by an extract from North Islington's minutes: 'Following constant interruptions and the candidate calling a section of the meeting "dirty slobs", the chairman closed the meeting.' This waiting technique is not always successful: Islington has succeeded in mislaying all three Labour seats. A fourth technique, perfected by Tony Benn, is the guide-dogs-for-the-blind approach: the Member goes where he wants to, but the party thinks it is taking him because he is sophisticated enough to ask them for their decisions on crucial issues: should he join the Cabinet, leave it, stand for the National Executive, stand for deputy leadership, or better? They won't know. They will almost certainly think that the MP is paid to make up his own mind. Yet they will be too polite to tell him and will therefore feel constrained to say what they think the Member himself wants. In this way a Member could, provided he is articulate enough, get a constituency to support EEC membership and to oppose it, to support a referendum on staying in but not one on coming out, to support incomes policies and oppose them, to accept an industrial policy based on mergers and one based on unscrambling, in short, to follow the Member through all the inevitable meanderings implicit in a long career. There is also the option of blaming the party at a later stage if things go wrong. Members will not become puppets. They will merely Vaseline themselves well.

Last comes the most effective technique of all: management by mail. Letters and documents should pour out of the friendly, personalised word processor and into the letter-boxes of party members who cannot be bothered to read them but get the impression something is happening. Treat Members as adults or, in the Conservative Party, as seriously as possible in the circumstances. Constituency parties will then appear threatening only to quaking constitutional theorists who spend most of their lives quaking professionally. Like neglected wives, local parties really want neither a divorce nor legal rights but a certain amount of physical contact, to be told that they are loved and what is going on. They want to feel involved in an adventure which, after all, they do share. These feelings are both natural and right. No arrogant assertion of Burkean principles of independence, and no parade of constitutional excuses for what is often personal convenience, can ignore them.

Persevere. Problems come and go. Trouble-makers move in and out. Constituency parties turn over steadily in membership. The executive or the management committee or the association MPs start out with will be changed in five years, out of all recognition in ten. The same will be going on in the constituency. The people MPs rely on for advice, help and information die, move on and, like a flower bed, need constant pruning. MPs must stay involved and on the ball. They must also recognise that the relationship is an interdependent one, particularly in the Labour Party where there are so few agents, and that parties come to depend on MPs, not only for leadership but also for office services, even money. The trend is not as marked in the Tory Party, which, since the Reform Bill, has been less sympathetic to rotten boroughs, but their local parties are much less vigorous than they were. So the MP looms larger there too.

Most breakdowns in relationship between Member and constituency or party, or both, come not because of ideological misunderstanding, or permeation by *Militant* or by small businessmen, or both. Nor do they come because of plots, London always excepted. They develop because a member has given up on his job, on life, on the constituency or on any combination though less these days on his wife. Roy Jenkins and Sir Arthur Irvine gave up on constituencies, John Stonehouse on Parliament, Tom MacMillan on life. Yet all chose their own time to go, and the Jeffrey Archer routine of doing the decent thing is not essential for constituencies. Brighouse stuck loyally by Colin Jackson, increasingly unfit and befuddled. Eventually however, all parties recognise the inevitable. At that point it is time to go. A higher burn-out rate should be an inevitable part of modern democracy. MPs are on a treadmill, moving faster as the years go by. Problems multiply, constituencies grow bigger, expectations rise, our ability to fulfil them shrinks. There is no time to stand and stare, or to claim the massive dignity of parliamentary predecessors. The requirement is to keep running until it is no longer possible, then either drop or give way. No one is irreplaceable and there will be plenty of others eager to take the seat. Their keenness shows their ignorance of realities. Yet it is no use telling them that.

MP OPENS BUS SHELTER

9 Member for ITV East

MPs are in the media business. Most have something to say, all have their own medium in which to say it. They live by reaching the people. They succeed or fail by a market test; all of which makes them like anyone writing for *The Times*, appearing on page three of the *Sun*, or pontificating from the box. It puts MPs and media men into a direct relationship, part competitor, part collaborator alternating between inter-dependence and the warmth of trench warfare.

Happier medians have the ears, eyes and the attention of their audience. Parliamentarians do not. The Commons may have gripped the smaller political nation in the nineteenth century, when every word was reported in the newspapers that nation read. In the twentieth, they have lost out to Bingo, breasts and *Crossroads*. Around 200,000 visitors to the gallery each year, the circulation of Hansard, only 2,000 an issue, and the few hundred who attend political meetings, under a million all told at any election, all this is a miniscule collection compared to the ten million watching *Nationwide* or the huge circulation of newspapers. For practical purposes Parliament has no direct access to the nation. MPs are dependent on the other media: no man cometh to the people except by them.

Each side needs the other. Media men need MPs to provide raw material. MPs generate news in the House and outside it. They can break stories, provide the colour, the character and the clash the media feed on. They say what the media cannot. They give stories pegs by asking questions, initiating action, demanding debates. Some of the press even take them seriously. Politicians need the media: to reach the people, to build reputations, to further their careers, to supplement their bank balances. They also need the media to blame. The right see the media as left-dominated. The left see them as establishment lackeys. The medians themselves assume that if both sides hate them they are being impartial. Finally, the media are a permanent built-in excuse. Has the government's economic policy produced disastrous decline? The message is not getting across: fire Angus Maude. Is Les Huckfield detected changing constituencies in mid-Parliament? Blame a dispute with the local paper for inhibiting explanation. Has Benn-phobia produced a disastrous by-election result? Blame the media. Even Social Democrats blame the media, more an indication of Oedipus complex than reality in their case.

The best media blamers live by the media. If Tony Benn did not exist, the media would have to invent him: right-wing media have always needed a left-wing bogeyman, from Bevan through Foot to the present inheritor (transmitted by the laying on of adjectives) of the diabolic succession. Yet he in turn must bite the hand that feeds him so generously. The media justify the left's paranoia. Their ideological policies are viewed with suspicion by the electorate. Yet the prophet cannot admit that the goods are unsalable. So he has to put his failure to stir the people to anything beyond uneasy hostility down to a media plot.

Members and media interact through the Commons gallery: Parliament's mouthpiece to the nation, the media's foothold in Parliament. A cramped appendage to the palace until Adolf Hitler thoughtfully provided more space by bombing, the gallery is now a crowded, congested slum which opens into the Chamber. It houses 300 journalists, national and provincial, printed and electronic, sketch writers and specialised correspondents, scribblers and thinkers. Every British institution needs its first and second class. The distinction here is between those who report the House and the 'lobby', reporting government.

The lobby is the elite. Just over 140 strong, and divided half and half between national and local correspondents, it gets its name from the fact that in 1888 the House gave accredited journalists the right to enter the Members' lobby. A 1968 survey found the lobby median was aged forty-two, with eight years' service in the lobby, having left school at the average age of seventeen. One third voted Conservative, one third Labour, and one third Liberals plus professional abstainers or those awaiting instructions from their editors. It is not an elite through innate superiority. The political columnists are better informed and carry more clout. The sketch writers are funnier and write better. Exclusivity makes the lobby. It is a Freemasonry, membership determined by the club collective, though in cases of dispute it will blame the sergeant at arms. Both *Private Eye* and the *New Statesman* have been kept out, and *The Spectator*'s representative was expelled when it published a piece critical of the lobby. The club atmosphere is reinforced by the fact that correspondents spend as much time talking to each other as to MPs, and by the lobby rules:

> Do not talk about lobby meetings before or after they are held. Stay to the end of meetings. This rule should always be observed . . . Do not 'see' anything in the Members' lobby nor in any of the private rooms or corridors . . . Do not run after a Minister or Private Member . . . Do not use a notebook, or as a rule make notes when in private conversation.
>
> Do not crowd together in the lobby so as to be conspicuous.
>
> Sometimes it may be right to protect your informant to the extent of not using a story at all.

The unspoken rule is the law of silence. Correspondents see nothing, particularly nothing discreditable to Members or the House. One described his debut:

> 'Now, let me introduce you to an MP,' said my colleague, showing me round Annie's Bar for the first time. He found one. We shook hands and were about to exchange civilities when something rather peculiar happened to the MP. He began to list – first sideways, then backwards, then sideways again. Then his bar stool proved inadequate and he fell slowly to the ground. It seemed to take him ages to fall . . . I thought to myself, 'I'm not seeing this. I must not "see" anything in the private rooms and corridors of the Palace of Westminster.' . . . 'I think we had better find someone else to talk to,' said my colleague.

The tone is Boy Scout, the basis confidentiality, the offer to politicians is say what you want and we won't say you said it. So Ministers have the enormous advantage of saying anything off the record, trying out any ideas or character assassination and yet not having it attributed to them. Correspondents must deny even that the meetings have taken place, though they can use the information. There are breakdowns: when Peter Jay was appointed ambassador to Washington in 1977, criticism of Sir Peter Rowbotham, the existing ambassador as 'fuddy duddy' was promptly traced back to Tom McCaffery, Jim Callaghan's press secretary and hence, therefore, presumably to the Prime Minister himself. The son-in-law also rises. Similarly, Martin Flannery MP claimed 'privilege' when James Fenton of the *New Statesman* reported a bar-room conversation:

> The other day I met an MP who had spent the morning at the Grunwick picket line. He told me that the scenes he had witnessed, the behaviour of the police, was the worst thing he had seen since seeing photographs

of the Brownshirts and the Jews in the 1930s. I suggested there was no comparison with the Brownshirts. At that point he accused me of being on the same side as George Ward. I objected. He grew exceedingly angry and a deep Chaucerian flush rose to his face. As the blood pumped its way to the tip of his nose I pointed out that it would be better to save the Brownshirts comparison for a time when a real movement like the Brownshirts was proving a similar menace. This advice reduced him to a mad, ranting, quivering condition.[1]

Flannery replied:

The relationship between MPs and journalists is based on mutual trust in order to ensure the free dissemination of news. If every conversation of a private nature were to be retailed in the manner used by Mr Fenton it would open the way to all kinds of abuse.[2]

Fenton rejoined:

I in no way apologise for what I wrote, or for any distress I may have caused Mr Flannery. Lobby rule X states simply: 'All insults are on the record' . . . Mr Flannery is abusing his position as an MP if he insists that his boorish behaviour be protected by rules designed for a quite different purpose.[3]

The surprising feature is the rarity of such *contretemps*, given the large numbers and the wide range of characters involved on both sides. Britain is adept at making secret societies work.

The lobby functions at various levels. Correspondents representing a group or a chain of local newspapers keep in touch with their local Members, chronicling questions and speeches, communicating their views, putting the questions their papers want answered. Together with their big brothers they hang around the corridors and the Members' lobby as if for an immoral purpose, accosting not deep throats, but ever open mouths, picking up information, keeping in touch with what is going on, using, being used.

At the top, lobby correspondents have fairly regular access to the Prime Minister and daily contacts with her mouthpiece, the press secretary. Joe Haines as Harold Wilson's press secretary even wanted to extend this so as to give off-the-record briefings after each Cabinet meeting but that proposal was stopped by Sir John Hunt. This prime ministerial pattern changes. Harold Wilson began with a closer relationship with the lobby than his own parliamentary party. He

[1] *New Statesman*, 18 November 1977.
[2] *New Statesman*, 25 November 1977.
[3] Ibid.

was not the first Prime Minister to realise the importance of presentation, but he turned it into an art form in the way no predecessor had. Indeed, when a senior civil servant once remarked to him, 'It's a question of presentation, Prime Minister,' the Pipe Smoker of the Year replied with heart-felt concurrence, 'It all is.' Pause. 'Except timing.' The excellent relationship this established began to sour only as the lobby began to realise that the Labour leader was airing his Walter Mitty complex by telling them what he wanted to happen, rather than what actually would. It cooled completely as Harold retreated into his bunker phase between 1967 and 1969. In the second Wilson Government, his press secretary Joe Haines formally withdrew from the daily meetings, announcing that everything he gave to the press would be on the record. Ted Heath, far less adept at handling the press and much more awkward with them, as with genuine human beings, quickly became dissatisfied. He did, however, toy with the shy man's intimacy in the idea of de Gaulle presidential-style press conferences at Lancaster House, stick mikes, television cameras and all, but this idea was dropped after the first attempt because the lobby didn't like competing with the telly boys. Margaret Thatcher is inclined to hector rather than confide, treating the press like a class of recalcitrant children. Such an objective assessment of the material she is working with has stopped the Prime Minister establishing any easy relationship. She slipped back to the Wilson precedent of a 'white Commonwealth' of favoured correspondents, and in January 1981 did a little freelance briefing of *The Times*, *Financial Times* and *Guardian*, who promptly blew the experiment up in her face by letting slip the fact of the meeting and practically announcing the contents of the next budget before Sir Geoffrey Howe had had the chance to write it down. The annoyed reaction ensured that the experiment was not pursued. Prime Ministers cannot track down other leaks when it becomes known that they are themselves the Head Leaker. They can, however, harass their colleagues through briefings in that species of guerrilla war which typifies the Thatcher Cabinet. They can even denounce them in public. Mrs Thatcher told a press audience in a lunch-time speech on 12 March 1981 that she wished her Cabinet colleagues had 'more guts' and added, 'What really gets me is that those who are the most critical of the extra taxes are those who are the most vociferous in demanding extra spending,' an outward and visible sign of an inward something that may not have been harmony.

The middle level of lobby activity is the weekly briefings by the

Leader of the House, sometimes with a Minister, after the Thursday business statement and immediately afterwards by the Leader of the Opposition. All are exposed to questioning by 120 reporters on any subject, including questions which would certainly not be answered if they came from MPs. Questions Ministers refuse comment on in the Chamber are freely dealt with up the spiral staircase. Ministers themselves also brief 'by invitation', meaning that a press office has squared it with the lobby. There they announce policy changes, legislation, or come simply to put over their point of view. Inevitably, such ministerial briefings become a weapon in Cabinet conflicts, particularly with a Prime Minister assiduously counter-briefing. Jim Callaghan described the constitutional position: 'Briefing is what I do. Leaking is what others do,' and Margaret Thatcher has turned Cabinet government into a briefings versus leakings battle. It matters not who won or lost but how you laid the blame. By October 1981 the battle between dry rot and rising damp in Cabinet had gone so far that the Wets were getting their press briefings about 'Treasury defeats' in Cabinet out before the Number Ten briefing. They were even assuming a right of reply to Number Ten's own efforts through the private and press secretaries. Some use the system well: James Prior could hardly get a bad press because he is liked. Sir Keith Joseph has treated it like any other aspect of his personal relations, badly, regarding press conferences as another venue for a nervous breakdown. Treasury began the new regime badly by announcing the contents of every budget in advance. Now they have refined their technique, trailing worse than actually happens so that people can heave a sigh of relief when things are not as bad as they have been led to expect. The only common factor is that the whole operation is now more important than the merely mundane business of putting the case to the Commons.

The club and its rules suit both sides. Ministers put their views without risk – politics on the pill. The press know what is going on without having to dig. They are fed titbits on pledges of confidentiality and even if Ministers then go on television and repeat the information to an audience of millions at least the press got it first. They can have 'on the record' interviews on request but they rarely ask for them. They prefer the system as it is because they know that it gives them a monopoly of news and an inside track to power, and that without this artificial advantage, television would get the news first, and probably exclusive anyway. Lobby correspondents would be demoted from messenger boys to note-takers from the television.

So if it turns watchdogs into poodles, the system has the advantage from the press point of view that it evens up the competition, not only with the dreaded electronic media, but with each other. If truth had to be unearthed, digging could become competitive, hence dirtier work.

The only group not suited is the public: kept from what is going on, fed with what suits those in power, unable to piece together the story. It takes a certain sophistication to know that anything which appears on Friday about the Opposition comes directly from its leader, that 'some Ministers are believed to disagree with the Prime Minister' means Pym thinks it is time Thatcher went, 'complaints voiced' means blazing row, and 'PM trounces critics' means that she lost but got her story in first. Easy headlines encourage the Walter Mitty complex latent in every Prime Minister. Margaret Thatcher's Janet Brown complex has also been amplified because someone never sure of her real persona has been enabled to play so many by having her own dramatic abilities fostered by a compliant media so that she – and her audience – are in danger of becoming totally disorientated. It is never very clear whether the nation is being addressed by Queen Elizabeth I, Florence Nightingale, Boadicea or Dennis Thatcher's missus.

Politicians are all too prone to make themselves cosier than they should be. The lobby is loft insulation and boiler lagging. The only benefit accruing to the public is that through it the newspapers are given an advantage against television coverage which is their real competition. The lobby strengthens the papers and also gives the nation an antidote to undiluted telly-politics. The press are insiders. The electronic media outsiders. They are therefore even more easily manipulated. They never refuse an offer of an interview with the Prime Minister. BBC can always be played off against ITV. So we end up with a television which is in fact as compliant as the French, while conning itself and the public by a vigorous assertion of its independence. The whole political coverage would be even more servile if a press side with much greater ability to speak out and say what is really going on were not given the inside track. British news is far too managed and manipulated anyway. Those who are obsessed with bias in the media miss the whole point of the problem, which is that news manipulation and the series of incestuous relationships journalists form with organisations, firms and government departments mean that, far from being told what is really going on, because the journalists have dug out pristine truth, they are being fed with what the organisations want them to know. In a closed society, without the open competition of the American political system, this means managed news, and it is wrong that Parliament should set the example and that the process of manipulation should work from the top down.

The lobby is for leaders. Individual MPs have to be their own lobby correspondents, though of course they can give press conferences to announce that they are leaving wives or parties. Formally a band of brothers, each Member is in fact competing against every other to put over his views, to further his career and his cause, which is usually himself. MPs have to be self-touting and self-pimping. Mutual back-scratching facilitates the process. Local papers need their Members to help fill aching voids or give a local angle to national stories. Local television and radio feel a duty to cover local politics and see coverage as putting MPs on the box. National papers need Members for an imprimatur. The Queen is shot at: an MP has to be found to demand a ban on replica gun sales. Many are called, few are chosen. A paedophiliac diplomat is named in *Private Eye*: diligent ringing round the rent-a-quote Members turns up Geoffrey Dickens, who cannot pronounce the word but will agonise about announcing a name everyone in the know knows. Michael Foot cracks mild jokes to amuse delayed passengers on a British Airways flight and one Conservative bad-tempered passenger immediately runs to the press, creating a useful incident for those papers determined to exploit every opportunity to make the leader of the Opposition look silly. Yet nothing still has to be turned into something, so Vivian Bendall, a Tory MP who has previously got publicity by dressing up as a gnome (for a gnome club, not gnome rule) builds the matter up to front-page dimensions by expressing his concern about a possible breach of safety regulations. Summer is dull, but those Members who never go on holiday lest they miss an opportunity to get in the papers are ever ready to demand the recall of Parliament. For whatever reason.

MPs are made much more publicity-conscious than they are already. Besides, it is all money in the bank. Fees, ranging from £12 to £50 from radio and the telly (not the press, which has its printers to support, or commercial radio, which is too mean) are now a regular part of the income of all but the irredeemably ugly or stupid. There is a constant incentive to speak out. Never have so few been so well rewarded for so much rubbish. A good issue is worth £40. A party row can mean a steady income over several months or even become a form of post-ministerial unemployment relief. One of the by-products of Labour's new system of disintegration as a lifestyle is that MPs get richer as the party rolls downhill, an incentive to continuous creation of controversy which the Conservatives do not have. Being wealthier, they can afford to keep their rows behind closed doors.

Most MPs dislike television, though they must do so instinctively, lacking time actually to watch it. The numbers in the Commons five TV rooms getting a little intellectual stimulation after a dull day in the House by watching *Crossroads* or, in the case of Labour Members, picking up tips by watching *The Borgias*, are usually minute, though far bigger for Wimbledon. Popular programmes are seen only by the few addicts or those eager for populist references to make themselves look like men of the people, ie gawping cretins. I was bringing Amy Turtle of *Crossroads* into my speeches as a folksy touch for ages before someone told me she had been fired two years before. Yet if they don't watch TV, all MPs – even those who would be better advised not to – are eager to appear at the drop of a cheque. One of the least fraternal parts of regional group meetings with the regional TV companies is the continuous chorus of complaint about those who are on too much from those who should not be on at all.

There is a proportion of Members for whom no headline is too small. A few become obsessive, approaching every question with an open mouth. Some MPs even go to the lengths of deluging all the local media from television to church magazines with press releases every time the Number 15 bus is late. They learn after a time. To the recipients it seems a long time. The Michael Brothertons are ever eager to volunteer views, voices and visages to an unworthy media. One MP was invited to appear by Yorkshire Television. He asked what the fee was, and was told. His cheque for £15 reached the station next day. Such folly devalues the MP. It also fosters that cheerful contempt in which media men regularly hold the scrabbling mass of parliamentarians clamouring at their doors. Yet even the rent-a-quote brigade are necessary to the media. They alone provide the pegs on which all kinds of non-stories can be hung. Through the efforts of Michael Brotherton (the Mouth from Louth), Geoffrey Dickens, Tom Torney or Martin Flannery some of the finest minds in the country are brought to bear on the problems of the day. Unfortunately those who figure most frequently in the press and whom the outsider might assume to be the most active and involved parliamentarians are often the least highly regarded in the House itself.

It is not necessary to mimic the efforts of these latter-day Demosthenes. Intelligent exploitation of status can yield the average MP all the publicity he needs. Local papers are usually ready to print whatever is offered them. Helen Hayman found her local press so biased that at one fete the picture of the event featured the wife of the chairman of the Conservative Association and everyone present, except the MP who had opened it. Yet such experiences are very exceptional. Local radio stations, particularly the BBC variety, have hours to fill and little money to fill them. They will put local Members on at the drop of a vowel sound. Even local television is easy game – and it pays. BBC local programmes are dominated by a public service ethos, this being the path to promotion back to London. ITV puts MPs on because companies need their benign neutrality and it earns Brownie points from an IBA ever anxious to please Parliament. Paying MPs to appear on programmes no one watches is better than offering straight bribes of a few hundred pounds a year since the latter would not be allowable against the levy. As for the Members themselves, getting on television is crucial. Electors are prone to measure activity by it. It's not all what you do, it's what you are seen to be doing. It is also the avenue to advancement. Television is a creative medium. What it mainly creates is personalities. By Day's Definition, to appear on television is to be somebody. Appear nationally talking about something you know nothing about, and the press gravitate to you like bees to a honeypot. People send you masses of information. You get in press contact books and card indexes. Whenever the subject of econometric predictive models of the Paraguayan growth pattern comes up again you are on. They are on to you. Even if your power house is a cloud of gas you are better regarded than someone who has devoted his entire career to specialising in the subject. Moreover, if you get trapped, you can always say you meant Uruguay.

The media are an MP's oyster. A few basic rules for opening:

Never overestimate their intelligence

Tell them what you are going to say. Say it. Tell them what you have said. Recap.

Truth is a national phenomenon

Any distortions can be peddled out locally and few will know. As whip on the 1981 Finance Bill, I approached the government whip about a clause which rail unions feared might tax their free travel. Our reading of the clause was that it did not. We asked for a government assurance that this was the case, threatening to keep troops in the House to vote against it at 3.00 am, unless the assurance was given. It was. A week later, Teddy Taylor, who had taken no part in the debate, claimed credit in his local paper for getting the clause 'withdrawn'.

Remember personal contacts

MPs can be the local editor's link with the wide and wonderful world, the hack journalist's contact with greatness, the reader's security that someone down there speaks for him, even if he does not understand what is being said. This personalisation programme can be taken to the extent of buying up the local papers, as Aberdeenshire's Albert McQuarrie did before he even stood, though of course with no intention of influencing the election result.

Television is a different problem. MPs have a love-hate relationship with television. They love it when they are on. They love the opportunity it provides to reach the people. They love the money. They hate the fact that it treats them with casual disrespect and that it monopolises the attention of their constituents in a way they never could. Every MP is a self-appointed expert on it even though they rarely get to watch it, having to work while others watch. Yet one rule is basic. All the bravado, all the criticism, all the complaints, cover only fear. Politicians fear the box, which is why the medium has to be carefully handled. Interviewees should observe certain basic rules. Never be awed by it. Harold Macmillan compared television interviews to 'going over the top' in the First World War – against marshmallows. Enjoy it. Use the medium for all its worth (about £30 a go).

Some MPs arrive at the studios thinking they are about to be interrogated by the beast from 20,000 fathoms, or worse still, by Robin Day. In fact they face a harassed individual who knows nothing about the subject, who is held in total contempt by the studio staff because he gets more money and girls, and is usually chosen for his looks, not his brains; his knowledge of sport, not politics. His fellow toilers love to see him humbled. You have the chance. Television is a game, as I realised watching Harold Wilson and Robin Day chatting after a 1972 interview reviewed as one of the hardest hitting for years.

'That was a very good second question, Robin,' said the Leader of the Opposition.

'Oh, do you think so, Harold? I thought you dealt with it very well.'

'No, you were very good.'

'Really?'

Fangs ain't what they used to be. So:

Always appear live

And on your own. Films can be edited, other politicians can shout you down. The public dislikes shouting and argument. Live, you control the situation. You can say what you want. Alone, you can appear reasonable. Even Keith Joseph and Tony Benn can.

Put the interviewer down

Beforehand he will try to relax you, not to be helpful but to find out what you intend to say. If it is the BBC he will also try to make you drunk. Work on his neuroses: 'Why aren't you on much these days?'; 'What's you're favourite book – and have you finished colouring it yet?' Reveal nothing. Ken Woolmer, then Labour leader in West Yorkshire County, was once called in to defend what the *Yorkshire Post* claimed was exclusion of the press from county business. Before the interview, Woolmer complimented the interviewer on his questions, and chatted amiably about other things. On camera, he answered each hard hitting question with a simple statement: the facts were wrong. Collapse of stout interviewer.

Develop your studio techniques

Simplest is the Callaghan Diversion. Answer the question you want, not the one asked. At moments of difficulty, announce 'People aren't interested in silly questions like that. What they want to know is . . .' Cue in party political.

Other suitable techniques are:

The Milligan Method

Knowing that your victim's list of questions (usually written by someone else) can only be so long, be taciturn, like Spike Milligan in his odder phases. Answer with a 'Yes', 'No' or a chatty 'Don't know'. He is getting through questions quicker than the Iranian Army through tanks. Soon he will be in such a panic trying to fill time that you will be free to talk about anything. A dissertation on Labour's plans for trade relations with Ulan-Bator will be received with pathetic gibbering gratitude.

The Time Tactic

Keep your victim in play until he gets his 'wind-up' signal from the floor manager – the figure waving two finger gestures in the corner of your eye. Then begin your harangue. Do not under any circumstances go gentle into that goodnight. Denounce television for never dealing with things at proper length, an accusation everyone agrees with until they see *Weekend World*. Mention promises made to you of longer time: in the chaos that calls itself a television organisation, no one will know you made these up. Denounce your victim for his intolerance. The spectacle of him torn between his desire to maintain his own image and the floor manager's frantic throat cutting will be more rewarding than fiddling the government's small business start-up scheme.

Attack One: Deprivation

The interviewer's job is to ask of people more interesting than himself (you) questions devised by people more intelligent than himself (the researcher). These questions are written on cards, or, if the interviewer is really important, on a clip board. Grab either. 'Can I have some paper to illustrate my point?' He can hardly admit that he is useless without his lines. He will demonstrate just that.

Attack Two: Physical

By keeping an eye on studio monitors this can be direct, physical, and brutal. Check that you are on camera, tight head, which means close up, unless you are Lord George Brown. Then lash out with your foot at some sensitive area which, since he is a television personality, will be below the waist. The camera crew will see it. So will the control room. Both have been longing to do it themselves for years, and on television nothing matters unless the audience sees it. They, however, will have no idea why your scintillating talk is being interrupted by animal grunts and low moans, nor of why the interviewer has apparently left the studio to go to the toilet while you are talking.

Attack Three: Verbal

Direct it against the two things a television personality holds sacred: his pay cheque and himself. Attacks on broadcasting will be well received by lunatics all over the country. If on an intellectual programme, broadly defined as anything on BBC 2 or after 10.30 pm, rehearse a litany of accusations of over-simplification and provision of baked beans for the mind. Talk of insulting the intelligence of the audience. They will not understand, but it will look as though you are on their side. Your victim will have to defend his meal ticket: at some length because it is such a big one. Alternatively, attack the interviewer for his own views, which you can safely identify with any current position of the SDP (if discoverable). Any questions you do not wish to answer should be denounced as 'hypothetical', 'disingenuous', or just ignored, while you spontaneously launch into your rehearsed answer.

To use these techniques is to run risks. Either you will never appear again or you will be offered a television job at double your parliamentary salary. Then you will know you are not nice. On the other hand, moderate sensible use will achieve mastery. So enjoy yourself. Do not take television seriously. Smile. Relax. Chat away and try to turn television politics into what it should be: a branch of the same showbiz which swamps the rest of the medium. Political television is a ghetto, attracting no viewer whose vote is not 110 per cent committed and generating only time-consuming mail from cranks and lunatics. As a branch of entertainment, which it will be when you are on, it can attract those viewers MPs really need to reach. It also helps to build you, not as a politician, because that is to reduce you to the same level as all the others, but as a reasonable, regular guy. Which, in these days of growing hostility to politicians, parties and politics, is a safer thing to be. Much better to be the Terry Wogan of politics than the Michael Foot or the Margaret Thatcher.

Government and Opposition put over their views, on their terms, through the lobby system. MPs do the same through their own self-promotion. Only the House itself is unable to reach the people on its own terms. It had this ability in the nineteenth century. Then comprehensive coverage of parliamentary debates in newspapers circulating to the political class made Parliament a genuine national forum, airing the preoccupations of the political nation. Since then, the franchise has become universal and Parliament has receded into a backwater. People now get most of their news and information from the television – the one medium from which Parliament excludes itself. In doing so it forces television to provide its own political circus on its own terms. Bad politics drives out good. At the same time Parliament makes itself less relevant. Providing a stage for the party battle is largely useless if the drama is enacted for the benefit of the actors alone.

Other legislatures have grasped the need to reach the people directly. New Zealand began continuous radio broadcasting of Parliament in 1936, Australia's Federal Parliament in 1946. Nine legislatures, starting with Denmark in 1951, agreed to admit television for all or part of their proceedings in the 1950s, six more in the 1960s, more still in the 1970s, culminating with Canada, which began continuous television coverage on cable, with edited extracts on news and current affairs programmes in 1977. The American House of Representatives has admitted television for over three years after allowing it regularly for committee meetings. These go out on cable with extracts on the news and Congressmen can buy clips of their performances for their local TV stations, a situation which has made Senators, who have no such advantage, increasingly restive about the advantage TV confers on the house.

As in so many other respects, Britain lags behind. The case for radio was first put in the 1930s, and for television in the 1950s. Yet the first attempt to allow either was in 1966. Radio was accepted in principle in 1971 but not admitted on a permanent basis until 1979. Even now most people hear the radio broadcasts on television rather than on radio. Television itself has been regularly rejected by 131 to 130 in 1966, 191 to 165 in 1972, 189 to 164 in 1974, and 275 to 263 in 1975. The principle was finally accepted with a majority of one on the casting vote of the chair in February 1980. Even then there was no possibility of action, because only government backing could bring the cameras in and that looked, and looks, unlikely. True to form the House wavered on a misguided motion in December 1981, rejecting it by the ritual score on a lower vote.

A sample of the arguments mobilised against televising Parliament gives an idea of their quality. John Stokes:

> TV is obsessed with irrelevant details. It will show Hon. Members' dress, behaviour, yawns, and the occasional nap. The dresses and hats of our lady Members will be featured as will be the sartorial eccentricities of our more flamboyant male colleagues.[1]

Sir H. Nicholls:

> If Parliament . . . were brought in to the sitting rooms of viewers with some of its Members looking dowdy and some not looking effective, it would interfere with some of the acceptance by the people of its decisions.[2]

J. T. Price:

> So long as I can express my views freely in this House without the beady eye of some mechanical device interposed between me and my constituents, that is good enough for me . . . This wonderful medium . . . has tended to demean and belittle some of the greatest achievements of which we are so proud. It has sullied the image of people who are trying to do honest work and has glamorised the trivial at the expense of the serious.[3]

Joe Ashton:

> I once saw a Hon. Member try to bring two chickens in a little cage into this Chamber for a debate on cruelty . . . He was refused permission . . . If the television cameras had been there we would have had more of that sort of thing taking place . . . There could be a show called *Row of the Day* . . . In ten years we shall have all the showbiz razamataz with the canned laughter and all that sort of thing.[4]

Sir Myer Galpern:

> The same standards will be applied by those who are to edit the proceedings as now are applied to the people who appear on current affairs programmes. They say, 'So and so is no use. His speeches are dull and he does not show sufficient anger. We should not use him but . . . somebody more flowery in style who has at his command the well-polished phrase or somebody who gets up and creates a scene.'[5]

Charles Pannell:

> While this Parliament belongs to the nation, the ethos of this place belongs to the Members. How we behave, how we conduct this place . . . are the things that really count here. We do not allow Her Majesty to

[1] *Hansard*, 30 January 1980.
[2] *Hansard*, 19 October 1972.
[3] Ibid.
[4] Ibid.
[5] Ibid.

come between this House and its voice and no one else should come between Mr Speaker and the conduct of this House.[1]

The real motive is never expressed. Members fear television. Most do not like it. Some are seeking revenge for all the indignities it has heaped on them, particularly that of making Parliament irrelevant by screening, more successfully, its own political circus. To say so is to air their own inadequacies as Members and people. So the real motive has to be concealed behind the argument that the nature of the Chamber would be changed. Apparently it would cease to be a debating forum in which Members persuade each other and become a studio filled with declamation. In fact the Chamber has not done that for a hundred years and its present nature would be largely unaffected. The Canadian system, which is the one Britain should adopt rather than throwing ourselves on to the mercies of the two broadcasting organisations, puts television under a parliamentary broadcasting unit controlled by the House. This provides feeds to outside organisations and controls the cameras which in Britain would be seven remote control cameras suspended from brackets, requiring no television crews stumbling over each other, no wires to trip on, and only minimal extra lighting in a house which can be unconscionably dim anyway.

The change which is feared would not happen. False alarms about make-up being *de rigueur* are unrealistic: those who wear it already will continue, the rest will not bother. Indeed it could be argued that radio brought more changes, particularly Margaret Thatcher's tendency to speak direct to the microphone so that every word goes out to the audience even though many of them are unheard in the House itself. When television comes the tricks of the television studio will be irrelevant. Members speaking would be shown midshot so the techniques applicable would be those of Chamber debating, not the intimate trickery of the studio or the gushing falseness of the Prime Minister's own TV technique. Canada reports no real change except sharper debates and brighter illumination. The 'Ottawa Shuffle' of MPs slipping in behind the current speaker quickly stopped. There was no attempt to use cutaways of Members asleep, picking their noses or indulging in all those other activities which go on in the Chamber – particularly absence. Most Canadian MPs who had opposed TV quickly accepted it. Audiences liked it, and watched it. Perhaps the British Parliament needs some inoculation

[1] *Hansard*, 19 October 1972.

such as coverage of committees or the budget debate to show just how irrelevant its fears are. Better still, perhaps the Lords should go ahead so that the Commons will have to follow jealously.

Radio, thought of initially as the prelude to television, has complicated the introduction of the big brother medium. The internal inconvenience of radio was slight: a commentary booth in the Chamber, some forty radio staff for BBC and IRN in that former parliamentary office at Number One Bridge Street, condemned as unsafe for habitation by MPs but considered adequate for radio broadcasters. The external inconvenience was substantial. Instead of using the real strength of radio for cheap, continuous, coverage, broadcasters went for edited extracts and what they conceived to be the highlight of the week – Prime Minister's Question Time. The deficiencies were immediately obvious. The House is then at its most crowded and rowdy; the format is bawling point-scoring; the microphones, being omni-directional, pick up all the extraneous rhubarb; the audience, instead of hearing the competent debate of which the House is capable, get feeding time at Whipsnade Zoo. The farce was quickly taken off as a regular feature. Yet the damage had been done. The public minded less than the politicians: the broadcasts were popular on the whole and polls indicated the public wanted more. Yet the MPs had been horrified: truth hurts. The counter-argument that television now had to be called in to redress the inadequacies of radio and show what was really happening was little heeded.

Television will come, eventually. The public want it. A 1980 MORI poll showed 56 per cent for; only 32 per cent thinking it a bad thing; the rest 'don't know'. Yet public opinion will not be the agency of change. Nor will conversion of the obdurate in Parliament: misguided views never die, they simply fade away as time brings in younger Members with more realistic attitudes. Change will come because without it Parliament is reduced to a backwater, full of interesting life forms, thronging with fascinating activities, yet largely irrelevant to the people of Britain or to the life of their nation.

SURGERY
SATURDAY
DEP.

10 Behind Every Good Man . . .

Constitutional monarchy is a *trompe-l'oeil*. The monarch appears to rule. Power rests with the Prime Minister, pulling the levers behind the constitutional façade. The House of Commons is a sexual version of the same thing. Males hold the seats, speak in the Chamber, rise to the top, sign the letters. Most of the real work is done by women. Secretaries effectively run many constituencies. The strain of the political life falls on the wives, an unthanked, unsung and largely unpaid source of sweated labour keeping parliamentary government going. Parliament has an upstairs and a downstairs. The denizens of the one largely male, of the other largely female. Without the exploitation of those downstairs, the system would disintegrate and the House degenerate into a gentlemen's club, sheltered from the world, preoccupied only with itself.

The secretaries keep the system going by shouldering burdens greater than their pay. Since they are the only employee of most MPs, they are forced to become researchers, social workers, mistresses of the complexities of social security and minders. They end up as perambulating citizens' advice bureaux. Only over-fussy or untrusting MPs need to intervene in most constituency problems. So the secretaries keep things running while the Members are overseas, away, preoccupied with parliamentary duties and debates or chasing a mistress across four continents. They could do so if an MP did a Stonehouse, and it would be months before anyone noticed. When there is a legitimate Stonehouse and an MP dies they have to carry on and clear up the disaster, unpaid. Their salary stops when their employer Member dies or when an election is called, but not their work.

Wives and families are the other exploited group. Most MPs have managed to acquire these struggling masses, many of them yearning to be free. More than eight out of ten of the MPs who responded to the *Westminster Man* survey were married, with 7 per cent single, and a similar percentage divorced, separated or widowed. There is a theory that barrenness drives people into politics. Unable to have children, they widen their love to the world as a surrogate family, a claim countered by the arguments either that only the childless have time for politics (or feel sufficient goodwill for it) or that politics is the real reason for the inability to produce children in the first place, since it allows no time to indulge in the lesser pleasures of conception and permits no rival passion. Sadly, our figures provide little support for any of these views. Only a seventh of the married MPs had no children, a proportion not much higher than the general population, and hardly an adequate base for such sweeping theories.

Wives are unpaid. A proportion get some or all of the secretarial allowance, but their only fringe benefit is fifteen return tickets a year from home or constituency to the wonderful world of Westminster. What they do have in abundance is sympathy. They get it from outsiders, who sense that there is little joy in living on a platform exposed to the gaze and the slings and arrows of outraged constituents, or from the more articulate wives. Joan Burnie, former wife of a former SNP MP, said:

> When the washing machine floods the kitchen and the car won't start and I have spoken to no one over the age of ten for twenty-four hours, I am not the helpful uncomplaining wife I used to be and to hell with the falling pound and the fate of the nation. I want my husband in the house and not in the House. And tell him so. After a recent somewhat publicised break up the wife in the case complained that marriage to a politician was not unlike being a one parent family. Most MPs' wives know what she means.

It comes too from MPs themselves, ever anxious to keep alive the image of the long-suffering family and of the hard-working wife keeping the home fires burning and so propagating to each other the kind of image retailed by Robert Rhodes James:

> Years ago, Humphrey Atkins . . . had a very marginal seat. Just before the declaration of the poll he told his wife and two daughters that he'd certainly lost and that they were to go out with their heads held high . . . Well, to his amazement they won, and his children burst into tears.

Most of the married Members know well what they are doing. And at whose expense. Like John Ellis, they spare more pats on the head than pats on the behind for 'the little woman' or as constituents (ever groping for her name) put it, 'your good lady':

> I think I am very blessed in my wife. She's always very forgiving about

being mixed up in politics. We've brought up four kids. If we've made a reasonable job it's more due to her than me. She thinks all this business about the sick walking down there and people dying in offices is all quite mad . . . and perhaps she's right about it as well. But as I said last time when it became apparent I was about to lose the seat . . . I looked at her and I said, 'It looks bad. It looks as though I've done it again. I'm without a job. Do you forgive me?' And she laughed and said, 'No I don't forgive you', but laughed all the same.

If the young Members often find that the bedroom becomes the front line of the battle of the sexes, some like Geoffrey Robinson are happy to accept a public truce, he to fight his by-election in Coventry in 1976, she to pursue her own career:

She said, 'You go ahead but it's your affair not mine. Don't expect me to sacrifice my life to what you want to do.' . . . I remember in that first by-election seeing the Tory wife bedraggled and rain soaked following him round trying to talk to babies . . . I don't see why it should be expected of her. A woman has got her own life.

Most of the bachelors exude sympathy for the downtrodden wives of their colleagues. Martin Stevens does not:

What about the wives and families of our friends climbing Mount Everest and rowing across the Atlantic Ocean and doing all these things? Anybody who is going to do anything worthwhile in their lives are going to put pressure on their wives and families. I mean, we're not kids, we're big boys now, and we're doing something quite serious and indeed in this Parliament we're doing something that many people think is impossible. If you say, 'Well I can't do it because I'd promised I'd go and bath Nigel tonight or take my wife to her mother-in-law's', then that's being unduly frivolous. People who do it have got to realise what they're letting themselves in for. It's easy for me sure but the wives do kick up a stink . . . Every night at quarter past six the telephone goes and you hear the wife's voice coming over the line jabbering on just like in *The Glums* and the wretched husband apologising, grovelling, and saying, 'I can't get out' . . . and it's a miracle that their marriages survive . . . But I just don't see any alternative. I don't think you can possibly say, 'You can all go home,' because that wouldn't be much of a government.

Who are the unsung heroines of the parliamentary system? Are they Stakhanovite dish washers, devoted wives suffering in silence that Britain might be better governed, happy housewives glad that the lump is out of the way in Westminster instead of under their feet, or militant liberationists fulfilling themselves in their own way while their husbands taste futility from the Westminster fountain?

Are they gracious ladies living in style or angry and embittered political widows? Little public information is available outside the divorce courts or the press uncoverage of Geoffrey Dickens, Britain's most loved politician, or the occasional stories of errant Members' indignant mistresses. Aside from what the MPs interviewed for *Westminster Man* told us, a postal questionnaire proved to be the best source of information about the feelings of the wives themselves. That they were anxious to speak was clearly indicated both by the substantial response and by the lengthy answers and extra comments they supplied.

Most wives are conscripts in their new role, not volunteers. A few had married their husband after his entry to politics; a few, some of them among Labour's front benchers, were second marriages, either the MP's or, more usually, the wife's. A very few, like Labour's John Sever, married women who came to the House in the first place to lobby rather than love them. Yet the overwhelming majority, two-thirds of the wives in our survey, married their husband before he first stood for Parliament, and eight out of ten had known him and were presumably on the way to marrying him before the cataclysm. Some may have been surprised by his sudden interest in Parliament; and two-fifths said that they did not know he had had ambitions for a parliamentary career before they married him, but most knew and decided to live with it, and whatever other faults spoiled the lad. Only a small proportion both knew and found his political ambition off-putting. Almost the same small number found it 'an added attraction', though whether as an aphrodisiac or as a bromide was not made clear from a mere questionnaire.

Wives married the man, not the career. Their reactions to his decision to stand for Parliament were overwhelmingly dutiful. Two-thirds of all wives, and even more among the Labour wives, regarded that decision favourably, nearly a third thought that it made no difference, though it was presumably better than a sudden desire to wear women's clothes, and only 6 per cent were unhappy with it. The wives' written comments all reinforced this note of duty. Most were of the 'A man's got to do what a man's got to do' or the 'If it makes him happy' variety, both of which could have excused any aberration from a desire to be chairman of ICI to twenty years of casual adultery. Yet wives had little alternative but to acquiesce, for they can in fact have little idea of exactly what their husbands were committing them to. They did, however, have a reasonable idea of how important or unimportant the job of MP's wife would actually be. A third had thought in advance that the job of MP's wife would be very important, with Labour wives more likely to feel so, half that it would be 'somewhat' important, while the rest thought it would not be important or totally unimportant. Reality did little to change these expectations. The proportion subsequently finding their own job 'very important' rose only very slightly while the proportion now regarding it as 'totally unimportant' had dwindled almost away.

The stoicism of the wives and their willingness to go along with their husband's commitments may well be explained not only by an oddly submissive view of women's role but also by a shared interest in politics. Politically divided households are very exceptional, but a proportion of the wives came from politically active and interested backgrounds themselves, usually of the same political complexion as the husband's: 'Born and bred in a briar patch', 'MP's daughter', 'Two great-grandfathers had been MPs. Having met various prospective candidates, my husband was better than most', even one who said, '. . . I was an MP myself, the daughter of an MP, and now have a son-in-law who is an MP.' Our political elite is not only becoming one whose membership is determined by heredity, as it has been in the case of current parliamentary representatives of such famous families as Churchill, Maxton, Lennox Boyd, Hogg, Butler or Foot, despite or perhaps because of Eysenck's theory of IQ regression to the norm. It is also becoming one determined by marriage, the best possible preparation for exactly what is involved.

There were some wives who either did not or had not seen eye to eye with their husbands politically. Two Liberal and three SDP wives, the latter for understandable reasons, had not always supported their husband's party. A tenth of the Labour wives and a seventh of the Conservatives had not either, and from time to time examples become public, such as Robin Squire, Tory MP for Hornchurch, whose wife Susan was an active member of the Hornchurch Labour Party, or Keith Hampson, Tory MP for Ripon whose second wife has 'not yet' voted Conservative. Yet in each case the overwhelming majority of wives in the survey subsequently conformed. They also tended to support it strongly, half very much so. A mere seventh admitted to doubts about their own commitment to their husband's party, and the doubts they specified were hardly major crises of conscience, just occasional disquiets or matters which could be resolved by discussion, though a very small number in each party admitted to concern at developments taking their party in a more extreme direction. Almost dutifully the wives kept up a high level of interest in politics. Over half the wives were very interested and a third somewhat, so leaving only a small minority with little or no interest. Labour wives were significantly more interested than the Tories, three-quarters being 'very interested' as against just under half. However, this measure was before their husband's entry into politics. Most had become more interested since then and most of these were Conservatives catching up. They had little choice. One wife expressed a more general reaction in commenting that, even when her husband was physically present, his mind was often elsewhere, obsessively thinking about politics. Another said that her own interest and her husband's were such that the children were driven potty by it at breakfast.

The parliamentary wives do not, in the main, pursue independent careers. Just over half of the wives did not have a paid job, indeed an almost equal proportion had not had one before their husband was elected to Parliament, indicating that they were not pursuing something interrupted by politics. The proportion who had had one before but not after, at a sixth of the sample, matched exactly those who had moved the other way. Of the remainder some, like Janey Buchan, a member of the European Assembly, are powers in their own right. Others are career women, television producers, writers, a situation which bespeaks careerist marriages, as distinct from the usual marriages of couples who find themselves in a new situation. Most are doing secretarial work, usually paid for by their husbands out of their secretarial allowance. The Conservatives are more inclined to be the identikit wife, gracious for the middle-aged, modish for the younger ones. They also have a higher proportion doing neither secretarial work nor any other paid work than Labour, a party where older wives are very much wifely but there is an increasing proportion of career women. The low proportion of wives with other jobs is perhaps one of the most surprising things about the survey. A job is an escape from the inevitable disappointments of a parliamentary marriage, where a husband is married to constituency, party and Commons as well as his wife. It is also an extra income. Personally I would have been in the bankruptcy courts long ago were it not for a working wife supplementing the parliamentary pittance. Lastly, in some cases wives are especially useful: Lisanne Radice wrote a Fabian pamphlet, putting a powerful case for the improvement of the facilities and working hours of MPs, and Linda McDougall produced a documentary highlighting their stress problems. Others are a useful conduit for leaks to the media. Greater love hath no woman.

Children are the main work inhibitors, since nearly three-quarters of our sample MPs had children at home and of those who gave the actual numbers, 20 per cent had one, 45 per cent two, 23 per cent three, 10 per cent four, and 1 per cent five children. In the light of such ties, how much the wives saw their husbands and how much work they had to do themselves depended on where the wife and family lived. So did the effect of the political career on the children. On the whole it was adverse: father was at home less, the main burden of raising the family fell on the mother. However, most children did not go to school in their father's constituency so the effects of his involvement in politics were less, as questionnaire comments testified: 'Not much, although they sometimes complain if we do things on Saturday afternoon and/or evening for the constituency. We always keep the Sunday for the family and the recess periods help as well.'

'I think indirectly I have been placed in the role of both father and mother. However, my husband spends all the holidays with our daughters and they care for him deeply. They are aware of pressures on him.'

On the other hand, nearly a fifth of MPs had their children at school in their constituency. They had rather more to put up with as the outward and visible offspring of an absentee and often not particularly popular father: 'The children have to take abuse at school, especially at election time, and they also feel that they have a standard of behaviour to keep up to.'

'They hate election time – they are embarrassed at seeing his posters in windows, and they are inclined to get either teased or picked on at school then. Most of the time it's ignored.'

'My youngest daughter . . . attended the comprehensive school in the constituency and at times both staff and pupils made it difficult for her.' The experience of my children confirms this, even to the extent of a daughter desperately trying to conceal what everyone knew, that she was a politician's daughter.

Asked about the whereabouts of the 'family home', meaning the main home for those with more than one, most said it was outside the constituency. Omitting London MPs, a third reported that their family home was in London, just under a third in the constituency, and a similar proportion near it and only a tenth elsewhere, with Labour wives slightly more likely to live in the constituency than their Tory counterparts. It did not always correspond to what they actually wanted. Each place of residence had its disadvantages and advantages which many of the wives enumerated at length. Living in London can be the loneliest crowd spectacular in the world. Yet some wives saw it as necessary if they were to be with their husbands and have any home life at all: 'The advantage is that I see my husband every night – however late. The disadvantage is I suppose the endless driving up and down the motorway. I'd much rather live in London where I have a lot of friends.'

'The children have had their father at hand, even when his hours make this presence invisible to them! And they – and I – enjoy a pleasant anonymity in London, which is not possible in the constituency.'

There is no real solution to the tensions of someone who has to be in two places. One wife put it very clearly: 'The disadvantages are that whether you live in London or elsewhere, an MP's job is in two places (Parliament and constituency), therefore families are bound to be separated wherever they live.'

Some tend to straddle the problem:

> We took on a London flat after the election . . . it's not easy running two homes – but you get into a routine and it becomes easier with experience. You really need to duplicate many possessions to avoid taking too much luggage, and that is costly.

Others opted for the alternative solution, a home in the constituency. Yet that seemed to those who had it to produce even more problems:

> One is always on call: people feel they can call with their problem while passing the front door, in spite of a surgery held by my husband *every* week – sometimes *two a week*. One's life is never private and is always open to comment as you go about your daily routine: no going out in curlers or having disagreements with shopkeepers. As a wife it is virtually impossible to have a really close friend to whom one can have a moan, as all are constituents and therefore voters.

However, a few saw advantages in it: 'It is a lonely life without your husband . . . But it enabled me to carry on with my work as a teacher and I was close to friends.' Those who were social workers *manqué* took pleasure in helping people or being an all-purpose busybody, view it how you will.

There was, however, an even worse alternative: to live well away from both London and the constituency. Those who did this had an uninterrupted family life, no need for new roots. Yet they grumbled more than any other group: 'We have lived until a month ago an hour's drive from Parliament, three hours' drive from the constituency – inconvenient at both ends.'

'Life is three-cornered, which adds to the wear and tear. We are midweek in London and weekends are divided between constituency and home – so my commitment to the constituency is superficial.'

The best solution therefore appeared to be that of a home near the constituency, convenient for it, yet not exposed to its pressures on a full-time basis. Most of those who did this felt it gave them something as near the best of all worlds as it was possible for political families to get: 'I think it is important for a politician's wife and children to have their own existence apart from that of "politician's wife /children".'

In the constituency a wife is almost a deputy for an absentee head of state. Yet neither work nor commitment are restricted to those wives living in the constituency. Most wives in the survey did a great deal to help their husbands: nearly half did secretarial work – mostly paid out of the allowance but not always so – and mostly part-time, less than a third being full-time. Labour wives were more likely to take on secretarial work than their Conservative counterparts. Nearly all dealt with the telephone in the husband's absence, though such a job could cover everything from simply answering it to taking on constituency cases, being woken in the night, even coping with political heavy breathers. With husbands away, the great majority of wives attended functions on their husband's behalf, though most did so only occasionally, heaving a sigh of relief that it was not more often. Conservative wives were much more involved in this kind of role than Labour wives. They may even have been more gracious in doing it, being better schooled in the etiquette of apprentice royal behaviour. Canvassing at election time is more or less inevitable, given the tendency to view the wife as an ornament or an outward and visible sign that the candidate is either as normal, or as miserable, as the rest. So all but a tenth canvassed; a third helped with surgery cases, a chore which Labour wives were more likely to take on than Tories; half helped by visiting people, Conservatives more so: the lady of the manor lives on.

The attraction of politics is the feeling, however unrealistic, of being at the centre. If they got this at all, wives had it at one remove. Yet they visit the House of Commons, Conservatives more than Labour wives, 14 per cent 'very often', over a third 'quite often', 46 per cent 'occasionally', leaving only 1 per cent who never went near it. Once there, they can of course eat with their husband in the appropriately named strangers' dining-room, which has all the splendour of a baronial dining-room in some long-closed railway hotel. Yet the only facilities provided are the family room, a hard-won reform which was one of the achievements of the 1964–6 crop of new Members, and now filled, according to one wife, with 'unhappy looking women whose husbands are always late'. The family room, said another, is 'too damned formal. The whole dump is too damned formal'. Surprisingly more than half thought the facilities 'adequate', with Conservatives' wives more contented than Labour counterparts. This did not stop many wives having a whole series of suggestions for improving the facility. These ranged from a suite of rooms for every MP through 'facilities for entertaining on behalf of my husband' to 'a games room for children. More social gatherings to which wives or families are specifically invited. A crèche for young children of MPs and their visiting wives'.

However, most suggestions were more directly practical, concentrating on accommodation: 'We need apartments within easy reach of Westminster, hairdressing facilities, fixed dates for sessions and recesses, car parking for wives, a strict adherence to the ten o'clock rule.'

'Bar, coffee and restaurant facilities, and bathrooms and changing rooms for families are badly needed.'

'Accommodation for MPs would mean a great deal. MPs do not have time *at all* to flat hunt and an accommodation officer would be of great assistance.'

More to the point were the obvious needs of those with young children marooned in London on their visits:

> No facilities for feeding young babies either at the bottle or breast . . . no cookers for heating food, drinks etc . . . in the dining-room no high-chairs or such so that it is impossible to have a meal in peace. If I come down to either visit or work, it means bringing in food, camping cot, and high-chair, so that the children can be fed and entertained all in my husband's office. The general attitude is totally to ignore any family an MP may have unless it is grown up and then it is merely 'suffered' as an encumbrance.

A minority dissented from the whole train of thought totally and vigorously: 'I think they are adequate – after all it is a place of work.'

'Is provision for wives made, at other husbands' places of work? The House seems to provide more than say a factory, an office or a surgery, or the services.'

One other way of helping the husband is keeping his feet on the ground. The great majority thought that they helped the MP to keep in touch with realities in his constituency, even though many of them did not live there. Mostly they felt they kept him in touch with the cost of living and with the news; they were the link between the Commons cocoon and the real world. Wives seem to think that they are in better touch with the people and politics than an MP sitting in the House of Commons: 'I do the shopping, talk to people on a more informal basis in the constituency than he can. He follows the news assiduously himself but I fill him in on the more human and personal aspects.'

'I think I provide him with grass roots feelings and attitudes from friends, shopkeepers etc, which can be useful especially if they don't know you're an MP's wife. Also TV and media trivia – eg: who J.R. is!'

However, they could also relay the news: 'By telling him of news events in the constituency, and bringing his attention to news items he may have missed in the press.' Both local news and national: 'I send him to the grocer's and show him my bank statement! . . . I hear long current affairs programmes which he is not at home to hear.'

The wives were, however, also fulfilling another useful function. They are letter-boxes:

> Talking to people, people using you to get messages to your husband, telling you things they feel he may not feel very important. By doing the shopping! By listening to radio and television more than he is able to.

They also become his party agent, running things which he could not:

> Sitting on committees in the constituency, eg: community health council, trade council secretary, shop steward in union, district manpower committee, school governor, constituency chairman, reading local newspapers, attending Labour Group meetings, etc, etc.

Only a few therefore discounted the role, most of them because their husbands were so smart they did not need it: 'He does not need any help to keep in touch with reality. It hits him all the time.' Or so dim: 'My husband has never been in touch with reality. They say it's part of his charm.'

Most wives thought they made a contribution to Parliament and to the MP's job. Presented with three different views of the wives' role, two-fifths saw themselves as a back-up for the Member of Parliament: 'As an unpaid personal assistant, office manager, social work welfare officer.' A slightly higher proportion elevated themselves to 'part of the team':

> I think it probably true to say that the wives of Conservative Members of Parliament are very often (particularly in rural areas) called upon (and may like) to carry out a lot of . . . 'ceremonial' ie: opening fêtes, attending coffee mornings, ladies' functions, etc. The wives of Labour Members are very rarely expected or asked to carry a very heavy burden of this sort of thing.

Only a seventh described themselves as 'independent' and free to pursue their own interests and jobs. However, Labour wives were much more likely than Conservatives to take such a liberated line: 'I believe it is essential to retain one's own identity and not be a shadow.' Not all these took independence to the extent of another job: 'Own interests are essential. "They only come home to bring their washing," as one wife put it. But a full-time job – no, except in running the home.'

The more realistic were the more philosophical. The job, as they saw it, was something or nothing. Exactly what they made of it.

> If on the other hand one wants to be political . . . there is now plenty of opportunity. One could travel around England talking about politics. Central Office would be only too pleased to keep up one's diary full, and the constituency would grab you up to be chairman of the WAC (Women's Advisory Committee). So in all I suspect it is up to the wife to decide her role, unless her husband is busy pushing her one way or another! I talked to an MP the other day, who shall be nameless, and he told me in a grand and eloquent sort of way that he had allowed his wife the whole of three months off to have a baby, but now of course she was back on the job. I thought poor girl, but he will probably go far. So – like most things – it is what you want to make of it . . .

Other political widows provided little balm for the loneliness. Nearly a third saw other wives of the same party regularly, two-thirds 'occasionally', and a tiny proportion never. They saw even less of the wives of MPs in other parties: a mere 3 per cent said they saw such wives regularly and a quarter never saw this life form at all. Labour wives were more isolated from Westminster life than the Conservatives, for only a fifth saw each other regularly compared to over a third of Conservative wives, indicating that Labour wives are allowed to come to London less, a kind of self- or husband-imposed political purdah. Yet it is not all a question of Tory gregariousness, for their party does more to provide solace then does Labour, which makes no effort at all. There is a Conservative Wives' Association which a number of the wives commented on, and valued:

> The wives of Conservative Members have a voluntary organisation which meets regularly, not just on a fund-raising basis, but a social one. I have found this of great value as one can meet other wives and share the problems and humours of our life. At first it was very reassuring to realise there's 310 other wives who are in the same boat as you and this helped to counter a strange alienation feeling I think is sometimes experienced.

However, those who lived out of town were acid about sherry parties in London at eleven in the morning. There are also other activities, but mainly Tory:

> There is a House of Commons Christian Association which meets weekly – and is of course inter-party . . . The Conservatives had two other groups, which I know of: (1) a general invitation to MPs' wives for coffee mornings, visits of interest, etc. from the Conservative Parliamentary Wives aimed at making social contact amongst wives, and (2) 'Contact' – a smaller group where the aim is to have regular meetings with a variety of speakers – not necessarily political.

Some wanted more to be done: 'More encouragement to wives to join in functions, ie: circular sent with the Whip giving details of extra activities should be sent to the wives as well as the husbands.' But most did not.

A defensive mood emerges over the financial side of the Commons family life. The wives were particularly defensive about their husbands, about the lack of public understanding of the job, about the public's failure to rise in glad hosannahs whenever they appear, and most particularly about the amount of money they get. Over half felt that parliamentary salaries were not high enough, a feeling common to Labour and Conservative wives. However, only 10 per cent felt that they themselves should be paid. Those who did were not demanding: 'Perhaps some expenses – not a regular salary. Something like the mayoresses' allowance.' These suggestions were mainly along the lines of tax allowances and some travel expenses: '. . . But it would be nice if all train journeys to the constituency were paid for – I'd never drive again. For people with older children I think that their fares should be paid as well.' Even though some thought their own expenses were substantial, they tended to agree with this sort of view: 'It costs my husband about £1,000 a year to fund what I do (if you don't count the car). It's hard that he should have to pay for it, but I don't see on what basis it could be paid for by the government.'

Thirteen of the fifteen who thought wives should be paid gave a specific comment, and six of these thought that payment should only be in the form of legitimate expenses. One said that it should only be for secretarial help given, one for those who 'carry a responsibility', one 'in kind by better facilities' and the remainder specified a wage of between £2,000 and £3,000 p.a., but far more, mostly on the Labour side, were scathing about the idea: 'Only if the chairman of ICI's wife gets paid. Don't be silly.' Or: 'Terrible suggestion. Secretarial wives are paid. Believe in payment for motherhood, but for *all* women.'

Parliamentary wives, although *hors de combat*, and hardly ecstatically happy, still appear to be reasonably content. Asked whether 'in their hearts' they would want their husband in some other job, only a fifth admitted to 'Yes', a tenth 'on balance', and a mere 7 per cent 'very much'.

> When he's very tired I'm sure he would be better off as a judge! Then I revert to the feeling that this is the job he wants and what would he do without it. But as he gets into the middle fifties I'm thinking about that judgeship more often.

The great majority didn't want him to, some for reasons of their own: 'Don't want a nine-to-five husband. Don't want to leave London. Want him to be happy. I enjoy it despite some grumbles.' However, a dutiful minority specified on this, as on so many other subjects, that they would 'leave it up to him'. Others were more practical, preferring him not to have another job because he could not be happy in anything else: 'Although I object to the relatively small salary and the appalling hours, I know he would not be happy doing anything else.' This could produce an unhappy relationship: 'I would rather see him happy in his job, and if that means being an MP, then that's fine with me.' Politics, the wives accepted, was a drug and their husbands were hooked: 'It is something he has always wanted and I knew that before I married him. Anyway, once bitten by politics you can never get away.'

'I think he's a good MP and enjoys being one. The country needs people like him.'

'Once one has gone through so much it would be mad to give in now. Nevertheless one is tempted.' Some had obviously had their patience tried and ventured sensible practical solutions to the problems of the political widow: 'Election to the House of Commons should be automatic grounds for divorce.'

One widely felt resentment was the general feeling that his views were theirs, that they were a shadow: 'Whatever loony causes he espouses you'll be expected to be out there in your wellingtons making like you believe.' Or, as another put it: 'Forget you ever had an opinion of your own. No one will ever want to hear it. All they ever want to know is what does *he* think about it.' Yet even those holding this view admitted that it was no good driving the husband into another job just to get rid of this pressure. In the main, the wives' pleasure in the job appeared mainly to reflect their husband's:

> I bathe in the reflected glory of the great respect he receives from his constituents. He is very active locally, it is a closely-knit (geographic) community and he seems to know everyone and they know him. He is a full-time MP. He gets things done!

They tried therefore to get what they could out of it. Which was usually a chance to escape from the home: 'The opportunity to meet people from all walks of life and to attend functions that one would not normally go to. I am soon to go on a delegation abroad for the second time in ten years, accompanying my husband at his expense.' There was also a vicarious satisfaction: 'I find it fascinating knowing about that which one reads in newspapers, meeting all sorts of unlikely people. Having good long breaks which I can fit in with my job.' As for the husbands the only real perks were higher up the tree:

> There are no advantages to being a backbench MP's wife – only toil, tiredness and expense. There are great advantages in being a Cabinet Minister's wife – POWER (oh yes!) chauffeur driven comfort and endless perks, eg: Royal Box at Wimbledon etc. – and a role to play in my particular case.

One, however, did rather ambiguously volunteer a further pleasure: 'Being the closest witness of the MP's delight.' The spectacle defies imagination.

Resentments had to be dredged for by a series of questions attempting to get wives to volunteer dissatisfactions by diverting them on to the aspects of the job they liked least and what they 'positively resented'. In some cases this line of questioning struck oil:

> Trying to make everyone realise how wrong the media pictures of MPs'

lives are. The idea that we live on a perpetual gravy-train with lots of perks, in particular, is so wrong.

The lonely evenings. The lack of good organisation for 'pairing' or voting so that we can never be sure of a weekday social life, ie: visits to the theatre etc, as a vote may make his presence impossible. The enormous demands made on him and the lack of adequate financial reward.

People constantly invading my private life. Having to wear MP's wifette outfits and behave how I'm not.

Being an MP caused our separation. I did not like being the other woman, and it is not funny catching your husband in Westminster Underground with his arm round a blonde secretary eating ice-cream, and receiving the comment: 'You should let me know when you are coming to London.' The wife at home, with young children, seems dull and uninteresting. I would have liked to have lived with him in London and to move the children's schooling, but couldn't afford to do so, and the constituency demands attention all of the weekend.

The final picture emerging from the survey and from talking to wives is one of sadness. They married a husband and ended up in an empty bed bringing up children alone. Maureen Cunningham, wife of John Cunningham, lives in Durham with her children. Her husband commutes between there, Westminster and his Whitehaven constituency:

I think it's a very lonely life. Not that it's boring, because there is too much to do, but one gets a bit bogged down with tension and when you don't have a husband coming home in the evening to relieve it, it can be quite exhausting. I think it's more difficult in the beginning when the children were very small. Now they are at school all day, I've got the day to myself. I can get out, for one thing, and do the things I like doing, and it's much more easy for me to go to London now occasionally than it used to be. I mostly miss the company – someone to help with the chores in the evening. And there are jobs around the house which tend not to get done because there are things that I can't do that have to wait until he can do them, which isn't always the following weekend. It might be weeks or months later. I know the feeling that one-parent families must have. I think you just have to become resigned to it. I think the first sort of reaction is 'How on earth can you be married to somebody who doesn't live in the house?' and then you just become accustomed to it and accept it in the end. I think it's very important to communicate even if it's only by telephone. You always keep in touch; otherwise you do tend to start living an existence that just involves yourself. Then you find that you have to adjust when they come home for the recess. Catherine, the eldest

> child, misses him particularly. She was a baby when he first went to Parliament and she missed him a lot. In fact she was very upset by it. The other two children have grown up with it because they have never known anything else, although they would still like him to be at home, like other people's daddies.

David Mellor's wife lives in his constituency of Putney, much nearer Westminster. She feels the same strain:

> Being the wife of an MP, especially one as conscientious as David, could be a very lonely life. He leaves the house at eight o'clock in the morning and he doesn't get home most days until about one. I find that we do miss out on a lot of things like music, which we used to go to and enjoy a lot together beforehand. Friends have to take second place. Family too. He doesn't see much of Anthony which I feel is a great pity. And he does too. He misses them. The fact that we're always on show is a problem as a family. Anthony probably can't behave as normally as another child might be able to. It's more difficult for him if he misbehaves. I find if I take him shopping in Putney and he sort of goes mad in the supermarket it's very embarrassing, where perhaps it wouldn't be quite so bad for an ordinary family. You lose touch and contact. You never have a normal conversation. When I see him if you are not careful it's just a question of a whole list of messages because, of course, people are ringing here all the time and you never have a chance to chat about normal everyday things. The worst aspect of being married to an MP is not seeing him. Unless one makes a very special effort to go to the Commons in the week time one doesn't see him at all. It leads to all sorts of rows and so on but you just have to try not to let it; otherwise in the few moments that you do have together you are just squabbling.

MPs are not really family men at all. In generalising their love to humanity they deprive mere specific objects like a wife and children of most of it. The wives care. The children suffer, and no one with any degree of choice in the matter should be the offspring of a politician. To be so is an automatic guarantee of a deprived childhood, an absentee father and of all sorts of problems which it is difficult to overcome in later life. Some indeed do not, witness a suicide rate among MPs' children which must be above the national average, and tragic deaths, such as those of the sons of R. H. S. Crosman, Richard Wainwright and Peter Shore, as well as brushes with the law by other parliamentary progeny which indicate that all is not well in many parliamentary homes.

It is hard to resist the conclusion that MPs themselves, much as they feign to care, much as they appeal for sympathy over their deprivation, are really too self-centred to feel more than a few pangs. They miss wives not so much as people but as general factotums, personal body servants who they need to have with them to keep their show on the road by providing all the backing services, from button sewing to shirt ironing, and talking them up when they are down. Even the thickest-skinned politician needs this consolation regularly for the life is bruising, moods are mercurial and confidence often hides a fragile persona. Phyllis Knighton was mistress-in-waiting to Reginald Eyre (currently Parliamentary Under Secretary for Trade) for seventeen years:

> I did all I could to build up his confidence in himself and had the joy of seeing him relax and become more sure of himself . . . I eventually gave up child-care work to become a psychiatric nurse and what I learned through my work further enabled me to understand him and boost his ego when he needed it. I know he worried sometimes about his looks (though goodness knows why!) and I'd take every chance to tell him how good looking he was . . . I told him repeatedly what a success he was, how I also needed and depended on the support he gave me.[1]

Pressures make MPs male chauvinists. Families and their inconvenient demands are all too often relegated to just another of that jostling mass of problems and pressures which so completely fills their lives.

Domestic strain is inevitable and the Commons people must suffer from it more than most groups. Yet myths complicate the issue of the marital break-ups which result and make things seem more exciting than they really are. The Ramsey MacDonald syndrome, still strong in the Labour Party, amounts to a dread of young MPs from provincial working-class backgrounds arriving in London unsophisticated and gullible, and 'selling out' because they are seduced by the metropolitan life-style. Economically they go for money, socially for sex, falling into the arms, then of the duchesses, now of the television researchers. Similarly, the *News of the World* syndrome equates sin with status. Every brothel raided has bishops, judges and MPs amongst its clientele, even if the latter usually turn out to be Irish. Every call-girl plies the Chamber. Goggle-eyed constituents assume that their Member is away living up the kind of London delights they see on 'Away Day' commercials back home in dirty old Slagtown. High status and an exciting life must go hand in hand. Else why bother getting there?

[1] 'The MP I Loved and Lost to Another Woman', *Woman*.

There is fire to produce the smoke. Yet the amount which billows out is disproportionate to the small flickering flames which generate it. Most MPs are the soul of discretion, yet occasionally a scandal breaks surface. John Profumo ('Life is better under the Conservatives – Don't let Labour ruin it') provided it in the 1960s, Lord Lambton in the seventies, Geoffrey Dickens is bidding fair to replace Mrs Khashoggi in the eighties. John Stonehouse too became a *cause célèbre* but he had to emigrate to find real fame. Stuffiness also finds its victims. Even Richard Marsh, with a relaxed and irreverent life-style, got pushed out of Cabinet.

One ex-backbencher's ex-wife has even published her own testimony of a non-surgery consultation with a Minister:

> He fell on me with the intensity of a lapsed vegetarian attacking a T-bone steak. All thoughts of Harold Wilson vanished as he caressed me expertly and entered me deftly, breathing compliments in my ear. I could not really believe that my anatomy was all that sensational but who was I to argue when I was being so efficiently manipulated . . . Awoken a few hours later . . . he brought me a cup of tea, looking spruce and satisfied in his dark suit and silk tie. 'Goodbye, my dear,' he said, 'I must leave you now to go to my Ministry.' . . . One MP I know is right now making fortnightly trips to a friend in Paris while his wife is still convinced he is dutifully toiling round a large constituency propping up the faithful. Another young Tory Member living in London with his wife and children religiously visits his constituency every weekend. Sunday's a good day for assessing the local mood, he insists. In fact he returns to London on Saturday evening to spend the night and the next day with his mistress and their child.[1]

Given the context in which it appeared – *Forum* – however, no one can be sure whether the account is fact or fiction. It is doubtful whether the opening of the Cabinet papers for that period will shed more light on the situation.

There is clear scope for high living. In what other job would long absences, late returns and coming home in the early hours smelling of drink be accepted as part of the job? Separation is the soil for infidelity. Peculiar hours and work habits are the opportunity. Some can convert the London allowance into a love nest in London; one has even put his bachelor friend on the payroll. Meanwhile, wives are left in the provinces keeping up the constituency work and the appearances.

[1] Jane Kenny (Jane McKerron, ex-wife of Brian Walden), 'Is Your MP Good in Bed?', *Forum*.

Yet it can also work the other way. Tom Litterick had to wear himself out travelling to Birmingham every day so that his wife, who had been threatened, would not be alone. When the strain told in a heart attack (and a kind invitation from Norman Tebbitt to have another) he moved in with another woman in London, only to have the wife come down and attempt to set the house on fire. Most MPs face a straight choice. Living in London is better for the marriage and the family. Living in the constituency is better for votes and for doing the job adequately. Personally I live out of the boot of a car on the A1 and get the worst of all worlds.

There is a class of political groupie, though more common on the Conservative side than on Labour, where most party activists are more likely to be dedicated emancipationists eager to slap down any advances and humiliate the author. Most of the groupies are in any case nearer forty than the willing teenagers who flock round the pop world. To portray MPs as having to beat off flocks of adoring women is the exact opposite of truth. There is, however, the chance to trade up the social scale: when I remarked once that most people saw life in the House as gin and tonic on the terrace with Mrs Khashoggi for dessert, one of her admirers told me I'd got it wrong. The lady was more a meal and a half. Lastly there are the ranks of secretary-researchers. Two MPs have recently married ladies from the library. Nicholas Fairbairn's liaison was well publicised and became the lever for bringing out another minor indiscretion by Michael Mates who, it was revealed, had mated. Pamela Collison, however – a devoted researcher – announced after working in Michael Heseltine's office and after occasional one-night stands with Bow Groupies and Conservative candidates, 'I never thought of MPs as a particularly desirable class.' Which is perhaps as well, for the MPs. Or at least the Tories since her activities stoppped short of labour.

Any group has its proportion of mavericks, homosexuals, casual adulterers, broken marriages, and the House of Commons must by the law of averages have its share of human frailty, all human life is there, and some less interesting forms as well. Yet perhaps it is better concealed than among the general population.

Politics is absorbing to the point of excluding personal life, and an MP's lifestyle is also limiting. Liaisons have to be nasty, brutish and short for MPs have time neither for silken dalliance nor for the waste of time involved in casual pick-ups. Even trips abroad are closely shepherded. So side dishes can only be partaken in the most unappetising circumstances, a quick sex provision similar to the cafeteria's contribution to the diet. They also tend to treat inconvenient things like people as if they were public meetings or government departments. After a long relationship Reginald Eyre took his mistress on what she described as a 'Parliamentary delegation' to China. When they came back he took her out to dinner. She later wrote, 'There was still nothing to warn me that after seventeen years these were the very last moments I would ever spend with him. At the end of the meal he said, "I'm sorry but I've got to go. I'm going to be fully occupied for the next twelve months." ' Such delicacy and tact are made inevitable by MPs' own insecurities for they are neither libertines nor bold non-conformists. People in fishbowls have to conform, particularly if they are not well off and cannot afford the secrecy of the kept woman. Most MPs are deeply cautious men, terrified of any taint of scandal. They are also boring. Politics is their life, their conversation, their obsession, and, so far as the opposite sex is concerned, this gives them all the attractive power of the poor unfortunate in the bad breath commercials. Finally, most are mean. MPs are the kind of men who argue constantly about shares of expenses. They keep their money in purses. They count it out slowly. They live as meanly as possible when they are not paid for. Mistresses – together with wives and families – bear the burden of that meanness.

The known liaisons are more sad than scandalous, a generalisation which even the glamour of Geoffrey Dickens and Thé Dansant have been unable to rebut. Parliamentary marriages tend to drift apart rather than being wrecked by debauch or promiscuity, a sad progress of middle age, not a youthful transport of delight. Maureen Henderson, ex-wife of Douglas Henderson (Scottish Nationalist MP, 1974–9), tells a not untypical story:

> We started off together working for his career. It was exciting and there was a lot I could do to help . . . But no one gets to Westminster just to be an MP – they all want to get on and my husband was no exception. He worked terrible hours, came home exhausted at weekends and then went out meeting the right people. We had no sex life at all. Except as a symbol, I was in the way. We just simply went our own ways.[1]

The ex-wife of Sir John Eden, MP for Bournemouth West since 1954, found her marriage running down in much the same way, until the final discovery that it was just not worth preserving:

> I was an MP's wife for sixteen years and had four children. We lived in

[1] *Daily Mail*, 3 January 1977.

London and my husband's constituency was Bournemouth. I enjoyed it when we didn't have children, but it became a sort of club for him to go to, so you were really shut off. Your husband's always in the House of Commons and it's like a club for the men, they don't like to miss anything. So they're there more often than they are home. They have long hours. You never know when they are going to come home. So they don't really help with the children very much and at weekends they're always in the constituency. So you don't have weekends and you lose your own friends who aren't in politics. When you're bringing up children and they're small you don't really have a lot of time. I had other things to do. But I found as the years went on we drifted apart, and I was doing my things and he was doing his things. We became different people, we had different lives. I liked different things and wasn't prepared to sit in the lobby of the House of Commons night after night. The final thing came when we were going on a holiday and I arrived in London with the four children to take them to Scotland. He told us that he couldn't come with us because he had been sent somewhere to meet somebody. As far as I was concerned, I thought, 'This is enough.'

Sadness not sex: falling apart, not flinging into frenzies, the slow death of dreams. MPs change subtly over time. The man who comes home at weekends is often not the man a saddened wife married. As one put it:

He used to have a sense of fun and humour. Now it's gone and he's just got more pompous and pedantic, constantly telling me and everyone else what to do and giving endless lectures. He used to admit when he was wrong. Now he knows it all and instead of comfort and understanding I just get lectures. It makes me want to scream. I dread to think what he'll be like with ten more years of this. Being listened to does terrible things to them.

Even worse is the strain of the job. Politics is the most demanding profession, not only in terms of hours but of interest, attention and involvement. The life-style and its separations often bring out a sad slow divergence, a dawning incompatibility. Service and constituents put themselves before the wife and the family:

Some constituency parties insist that they will only interview potential candidates if they promise beforehand that if elected they will move their 'main home' to the constituency. This forces a wife to either spoil her husband's chances of ever becoming an MP or to move to an area where she will have to live largely without him. This puts an appalling strain on family life.

Or they get put first by the husband, contrary to myth:

> The job is very intrusive. It is not too much of a strain for me, since I have all the advantages – I like politics, enjoy meeting people, knew before my marriage what my husband wanted to be, and most of all, my husband, the children and I have a very good family relationship. I have known parliamentary wives who don't have all this – the job then becomes the 'straw that breaks the camel's back'.

Separation is part of the life-style:

> I saw an MP's wife's role as being primarily family /domestic back up, not active politically. It means accepting what is basically a one parent family situation most of the time (except financially).

Paradoxically, the parliamentary divorce rate is probably lower than that for similar social groups comparable in age and class in the total population. However, the comparisons are difficult to make and the figures are rendered unreliable by the efforts of some MPs to conceal failed marriages and divorces – a caution which causes first wives to vanish from *Who's Who* or *Dod* and quickly to become non-persons. Reginald Eyre, for example, is on his second marriage, but *Dod* ignores this fact. Thus if the divorce rate appears higher for Ministers and those near the top on whom the main strain falls, this could also be because the possibilities for concealment are less.

Yet an apparently lower divorce rate does not mean that the marital breakdown rate is also lower than in the community at large. It is almost certainly higher. This does not emerge, because MPs are conformists. They are conventional men, nervous of popular reactions and adept at disguising unpalatable realities. Many a marriage is kept going for appearance's sake. Perhaps, indeed, MPs bring their political skills to their marriages, for the art of politics is that of stringing people along, of compromising, of spreading benefits to as many as possible, but as thinly as they will accept. Those arts are almost certainly applied to parliamentary marriages, pleasing some of the people some of the time. Thus when it comes to marriage breakdowns, sex on the side is usually a symptom, not a cause. The real problem is the strain of parliamentary marriage, the worst in the world for those who believe marriage is about togetherness. Long-distance truckers might have more difficulties, but MPs' marriages come high on the testing to destruction scale. Absence may be the saving of some marriages. For most it is corrosive. Comments provided adequate testimony:

> It's often hard to feel full of love and affection for a spouse who spends most evenings outside the home doing things which seem interesting,

sociable and commanding public recognition, when one is stuck at home coping with domestic responsibilities which are often tedious, usually unsociable . . . and always unacclaimed. It's especially hard to feel these things when one is suffering from lack of sleep as a result of the late hours at which the aforementioned spouse returns home, followed by early rising to get the children off to school! It is unsurprising that so many MPs' marriages collapse, even where wives and families live in London and therefore maintain daily contact.

Most camels survive the desert ride. In a few cases the privations cause marital breakdown or divorce. In the great majority they are dutifully borne by wives of whom Louisa May Alcott would be proud, so strong is their *Little Women* complex. Yet the burdens, the sheer simple misery of the job, are still resented even by the most dutiful. The attitude is best indicated by the comments of one wife who declined to answer questions on the grounds that she had been brought up to prize loyalty and anything she said would incriminate her husband. She did, however, admit: 'I *will* say I have to bring up a family virtually on my own and have learnt to be self-reliant and used to being at the bottom of my husband's list of priorities.'

The younger generation were more rebellious, though nearly all ended up being just as compliant, in their own way:

I hate the job. I wanted him to do it because I thought we could win against the odds but it's only served to drive us apart and immerse him in a stream of work, meetings, speeches and functions which never ends; while I'm forced to live in a place I don't like where I don't know anyone, away from my friends, my job, and everything I enjoy. The children get all sorts of hassles and abuse at school and just have to take it because they can't tell their father. We never really see each other because weekends are like living in a fish bowl, with a constant stream of people coming to the door, and no chance of a good blazing row to clear the atmosphere; while he's hooked on some stupid idea of service which means putting himself at any inconvenience for people who don't appreciate it. I sometimes think of using my wife's travel warrants to go off and have affairs in London but I suppose we'll just face a limitless future of bickering on for something neither of us any longer really believes in. Until I can persuade him to get out.

VOTE ME
THE FLOATING VOTE
PREVIOUS CAREER
NOT WANTED ON VOYAGE

11 Nunc Dimittis

The length of time served by MPs has increased, is increasing and ought to be diminished. An average of six years between the wars, it was ten by the 1970s and for those who went out on retirement in the seventies it was twenty, a professionalisation of politics produced by a younger age of entry and longer service. Even Members thrown out in the party swings and roundabouts now serve longer, because several of them establish claims to preference in the safer seats which provide the real continuity in the House of Commons.

The trend is not beneficial. A greater turnover would allow more promotions, encourage people to evaluate themselves and the institution and move out, let others make contributions and move on, make the whole body of MPs more active and energetic. The only people who would not like such a shake up would be MPs themselves. As a body they are dedicated to hanging on to their jobs. Our electoral system produces more changes than proportional representation would: a 1 per cent swing from one major party to another changes sixteen to eighteen seats. Yet even so electoral change is exceptional; two-thirds of seats are safe and on average only forty-seven sitting MPs have been defeated in general elections since the war, while fifty-five have stood down, and a further ten have died or retired each year during the life of Parliaments. Thus only a fifth of the House turns over from one Parliament to the next: 7 per cent by defeat, 8 per cent by retirement and 6 per cent through by-elections in between. At times this security of Parliamentary tenure becomes glaring: 93 per cent of the October 1974 Parliament had also been elected in February, the lowest post-war turnover ever. Parliament is becoming addictive. Old MPs never die. They do not even fade away. Not without help.

Ideological or personal oddities can bring an accelerated exit. Incompetence and idleness tend not to get the same treatment. Even MPs who are manifestly incapable are allowed to sit on. One Scottish MP in the late 1960s was acquitted of a shop-lifting charge because, in the judge's view, he was clearly suffering from senile dementia; a Yorkshire MP in the seventies sat on though hardly able to talk; Sydney Silverman towards the end stood to ask a question but could not speak; Bessie Braddock was clearly not at her most acute intellectually, assuring young Members that every time she passed Scotland Yard she was given a secret signal that 'everything was all right'. Sir Arthur Irvine was tottering with snail slowness along the corridors of the House for some time before he died, still MP for Liverpool Edge Hill.

Parliamentary deaths hit the headlines. The 'in Death there is Hope' syndrome means that the parliamentary and political pot is stirred by each one, and the press is dutiful in covering deaths of MPs, if not in covering Parliament itself. The political world waits eagerly for by-elections. Yet, as the SDP have impatiently found, deaths are comparatively rare, and may be getting rarer. Only 15 per cent of MPs die on the (parliamentary) job. In the last Parliament from October 1974 to March 1979, there were only thirty by-elections, of which twenty-two were caused by deaths. In the present Parliament they have been even rarer: strict orders to Tory MPs not to die, on pain that their deaths will not be worth living, have meant only nine by-elections from deaths in the first three years of the Thatcher Government.

Hope will spring eternal. The numbers of by-elections may build up as the strain gathers and the 1979 contingent gets older. Yet there will be no real rush. Contrary to many assumptions, MPs have a better life expectancy than the mass of the population they represent. Indications of stress, strain and exhaustion are deceptive. So are other appearances, such as the Westminster weight problem. Parliament is one of the greatest concentrations of surplus avoirdupois in the land. MPs seem to associate dignity with weight and take their much admired virtue 'bottom' too literally. The job itself imposes irregular and far too substantial eating habits. Perhaps as a matter of courtesy those who dine at someone else's expense so much of the time hesitate to give offence by not consuming all that is so lavishly put before them. After all, food compensates for lack of influence.

So does drink. There is clearly a drink problem even if it is now so over-publicised that 'Order order' is often assumed to mean another round of drinks. MPs are pushed into drinking habits by the need to socialise in London and the constituency, by the demands of an irregular and over-extended existence, by boredom, by killing time through the long watches of the night: a palace with nine bars offers little else to do. There is too much drinking and too large a proportion of Members dependent on it as a prop. Indeed, with whips not averse to a drop and, in the past, though not now, a Mr Speaker who was not necessarily abstemious, it has been very occasionally possible that breathalysers might have pointed to a verdict of alcohol levels over the permitted limit while in charge of the House of Commons. Finally there is an increased, often spectacular, risk from trauma perhaps not unrelated to the fact that many drive, or at least claim, up to 50,000 miles a year. Yet even in their accidents they tend to kill others, not themselves, and the risk is concentrated on those MPs in the 'drive zone' beyond commuter London but nearer than the north, where train is preferable, or Scotland, where most MPs fly.

Such are the myths. Reality is less shocking and none of the problems indicate a serious health problem, merely that such concerns focus on the House 'because it is there' and because Members are exposed to criticism. The real nature of the health problem is being assessed in a full survey of the health of MPs organised by the Department of Health and Social Security. The survey is based on comprehensive medical examination and will culminate in a computer analysis comparing MPs' health and well-being with those overseas parliamentarians who have been similarly studied, and with a control group of civil servants. The study is likely to disappoint would-be vultures by finding that MPs are a healthy lot. They drink too much on average, but the real problem is concentrated on a minority. They are overweight on average, probably with a blood pressure which is rather too high and with a higher incidence of neuroses than the general public, but it is hardly a sign of normality to want to go into politics in the first place. There may well be a higher proportion of homosexuals, certainly practising bachelors. Yet on the whole they are all more healthy than any comparable sample of the middle class, middle aged, who happen to have strong neurotic drives. They also have a rather better life expectancy. Which is perhaps as well. The Conservative Government's threat to close nearby Westminster Hospital, where MPs are taken for emergency treatment, has now receded. Yet there is still no House of Commons medical service, merely a nurse in attendance in office hours and such doctors as happen to get elected; presently Maurice Miller on the Labour side; Gerald Vaughan who also doubles as Minister of Health; and David Owen currently prescribing, somewhat illegibly, for Britain. Excellent as all no doubt are, no one is going to go to them for either Valium or the occasional social disease. It might be preferable to arrange for parliamentary heart attacks to come on somewhere better served, such as DHSS headquarters at the Elephant and Castle, where doctors turned administrators might remember some of their skills. Similarly the nervous breakdowns which MPs are prey to should be booked privately and preferably well away from the constituency. Alternatively if nurses were well enough paid MPs could marry them.

Alarm about the pressures of parliamentary life which built up in the 1970s has promoted a new awareness of the need for physical fitness, typified in the provision of a House of Commons gym, to which seventy Members belong at a fee of £75 a year, use of the RAC swimming pool at £25 a year, the introduction of medical checks and the nurse, additional to Mrs Thatcher, who is now in attendance. There is also a fashion for weight watching, in a place where there is a lot to watch, even a club with a jackpot shared among the best slimmers. Willie Whitelaw lost 28 lbs in his first two years at the Home Office, reversing Rees' and Jenkins' precedents; others like Roy Hattersley jog or take up other forms of exercise, particularly when photographers are present. Cycling is more common and the Cycle Club provides bikes, donated to the House for those too mean to buy one. Yet their awareness of the need for exercise is no greater than in the community at large. Perhaps less so: the irregular life-style makes things more difficult for MPs. The fashion is also too recent to have had any effect on any health figures, or even on the Members' own.

The real reason why MPs are less at risk than the comparable groups at large could be that politicians are self-selecting. Getting there demands staying power and the constitution, perhaps the brains, of an ox. MPs avoid the pent up pressures of those repressed by hierarchies because their job, which can be very hard work, has much more autonomy. They set their own standards and decide their own commitments. This makes them less likely to bottle up pressures. They face nemesis only every five years when across the country redundancies multiply weekly and come quite out of the blue.

Strain is not constant. Every week of the session it builds up. Friday's MP – a crumple-suited, lined-faced, baggy-eyed, pallid lump – is very different from his bright-eyed and bushy-tailed Monday counterpart. October's tanned, lean 'get up and go' man is very different from July's exhausted volcano, for in a long session, with an Opposition harrying the government and wearing it out, Members on both sides seem to age in the process, to go greyer in complexion, to look less and less healthy. On the particularly tough committees, the Finance Bill or controversial major bills, the strain is even worse. At times like this even a cursory examination, using Labour Deputy Chief Whip Walter Harrison's formula, makes it clear that not all will survive. According to it, the symptoms to look for are 'girders in the neck, face like parchment, words not making sense; next week a by-election'. Yet stress lifts. Summer recuperates, and MPs get a much more prolonged dose of recuperation than most.

Timor mortis non conturbat MPs. Yet they do not die on the job, nor are they compelled to retire. At the 1979 election, fifty sitting Members between sixty-one and sixty-five, twenty-four between sixty-six and seventy, and thirteen over seventy, were all returned by grateful electors. A Member in a safe seat can stay on as long as he can persuade his local party to keep him, which often means as long as there is no third party threat. Marcus Lipton was reported to have decided to retire at a ripe age of seventy-eight when he overheard two pensioners in a pub complaining: 'They'd never get away with it if Marcus Lipton were still alive.' Even if MPs are sometimes forced out they have the example of eighty-two-year-old S. O. Davies in Merthyr Tydfil who stood against his own party and won, or David Logan (MP for Liverpool, Scotland from 1929), who died a sitting MP at the age of ninety-two in 1964. Thus the number of MPs not seeking re-election in 1979 was only sixty-one.

Exceptions prove the rule. Few go voluntarily. Nor does disillusionment inevitably lead to dropping out. Even when it does motives are mixed – David Marquand felt the agony and the ecstacy during his on again, off again departure to Salford via Brussels:

> It was quite difficult. I went through an emotional trauma about it and after I decided to do it I suddenly wished I hadn't. I went through a period when I was very sorry . . . I went through terrible withdrawal symptoms for a bit. Now I'm very glad that I left and those withdrawal symptoms disappeared totally . . . Somebody else who left told me that he'd never had any regrets about leaving except for about once in every five years . . . when there's something really dramatic and important going on, and he felt, 'If only I were there I could actually make a difference.' But once every five years is not too bad.

Marquand's career had been blocked by Harold Wilson. Chris

Chataway had got much further when he pulled out and subsequently divorced:

> There were some personal factors in it . . . but I came to a few conclusions. One was that I only had one life . . . and I'd seen the show round twice and I was forty-two and if ever I was going to do anything else this was the only moment. Two was the feeling that the sacrifices one had to make in order to be in politics seriously were really only justified if you felt you were doing something enormously important . . . Thirdly, I felt that the Conservative Party would be likely for a period to swing right and that the sort of policies that the Conservatives would be committed to would be ones I wouldn't have so much enthusiasm for . . . it was a decision that I really made in a fortnight . . . And I haven't regretted it.

Richard Body's reasons seem more materialistic. In fact he stood down in 1959 because he thought he was not ready for the parliamentary career so they were idealistic:

> I was a young barrister just getting going at the age of twenty-seven and MPs were hardly paid in those days: one had no secretary, postage, or anything like that . . . one had to pay it all out of one's salary, which was a very meagre one. And frankly I could not afford to go on as a Member of Parliament when I saw the prospect of being able to earn my livelihood at the Bar and I chose earning what I could at the Bar and at the back of my mind I thought, 'Well, if I can acquire some financial independence as a result of my practice at the Bar then I'll return if I can to the House of Commons.

In 1970, John Smith (Cities of London and Westminster) announced his withdrawal in protest against MPs' working conditions and facilities; on the Labour side, Francis Noel Baker stepped down in Swindon where he was known as the MP for Greece, in 1969, managing to lose Labour the seat in the process; Trevor Park stepped down in SE Derbyshire in 1970; while Chris Chataway went into the City in September 1974 and David Marquand to an EEC job in 1977. Some go on to better things, for election to Parliament is a way of rising in the world. It puts talent on a national market-place. Labour, as the party of the rising men, is particularly prone to this. Alf Robens and Richard Marsh showed the way from humble origins to titles and money though they achieved both through ability rather than on the cash-and-carry basis of Lloyd George's enoblements. Bob Mellish waits his turn and, in 1979, Edmund Dell, transmuted from Manchester City Councillor into a national figure, went out to merchant banking and its occupational hazard, the SDP.

The most common exits are retirement, then defeat. Even then, Members are not disposed to take a forcible ejection as the end. Asked whether they would seek re-election if they lost their present seats, nearly half of the MPs who filled in our questionnaire said they would, a quarter that they would not, and a similar proportion that they did not know but, faced with the reality of defeat, they might. The historical record shows that a large proportion do come back. Some seventy-seven Members were defeated in 1970, sixty-one Labour, eight Conservative, eight waifs and strays. Yet twenty-two of the Labour Members, two of the Conservatives and four of the others had come back into the House within five years. A further twelve, all Labour, had made the attempt but failed. In the two 1974 elections, eighty-two Members were defeated, fifty-six of them Conservatives and only twelve Labour. Some nineteen had got back in five years and eighteen more made the attempt. Of the sixty-five, mostly Labour, MPs defeated in 1979, four: Teddy Taylor (Conservative) who won Southend, Richard Page (Conservative) who moved up in the world to Hertfordshire, Doug Hoyle (Labour) who won Warrington, and Shirley Williams (SDP *née* Labour) in Crosby, have all found their way back into the House in the first few by-elections. Among our sitting MPs, just over a tenth (13 per cent) had been defeated at some stage after first election, and a quarter of these had got back in a year or less, though a third had taken up to four years, another quarter up to six, and a tenth even longer.

Once an MP, always a hopeful. Whether from single-mindedness or simple inability to think of anything better to do is not clear, but losing a seat is both a great blow and often a prelude to trying to get back, as Julian Critchley found when he lost Rochester and Chatham in 1964:

> It's like having a serious operation, losing one's seat . . . Why did I want to get back? . . . First of all, it was very attractive, one had a degree of prestige. One hadn't much income, but as a journalist it certainly helped me to earn some more. And the years '59 to '64 were in retrospect extraordinarily exciting and moving times . . . It was a marvellous period to have sat through, even in a ringside seat. And I had not been trained for anything else. I'm not a barrister or a doctor, I have no professional qualifications. I went and wrote for newspapers and worked for *The Times* but all the time I wanted to get back into politics, at worst to regain my ringside seat and then perhaps to have an opportunity to throw one of

those punches . . . It took me six years from 1964 to 1970 before in fact I did, and that of course was a period of waiting for the postman to come with the invitation from a safe seat that was looking for a new candidate in order to replace the sitting Member. And there were times when I thought I would never in fact get a letter.

John Ellis is a two-time loser. Bristol N.W. in 1970, Brigg and Scunthorpe in 1979 when 2,042 votes for a former Labour Councillor standing as Democratic Labour cost him the seat by 486 votes. It was not his fault in any way, yet:

You feel, 'I have let down all the people who worked for me. Could I have done any more?' At a personal level, something happens in the House of Commons, some national event, and you read about it and think, 'What's the story? What are they all thinking? What are they all doing? I wish I could talk to Fred.'

To get the viewpoint of the victim, a questionnaire was sent to all the Members defeated at the two 1974 and the 1979 elections. Most of those who replied had expected to be beaten, two fifths of them were 'absolutely' or 'pretty certain' they would be, though a similar proportion had thought they had a sporting chance and a fifth had not expected defeat at all. Which did not stop the pain; a sixth were shocked or angry, half emotional or upset, and only a fifth 'resigned', a proportion growing to a third on cooler reflection. Quotations from their comments gives a better impression of their reactions. Most were upset.

I was shattered. I could not believe that I had been rejected on the issue of government relations with the trade unions and that my personal service to the constituency had not counted more.

Shock at such a large swing against me, particularly in view of the hard work done in the constituency over many years. In view of the bigger swings in neighbouring seats, I realised to lose by several hundreds was a grim but reasonably satisfactory result.

I think MPs from minority parties are in a different situation from Tory /Labour MPs. They are more prone to lose seats by national swings and are unlikely to have the establishment contacts to help in job-hunting afterwards. I think too there is an unquestionable sense of being at one's own funeral after a defeat. Friends don't know what to do or say and often, like mourners, do or say totally irrelevant things. The individual's sense of rejection is heightened by the reduction in phone calls, letters, demands on time. It takes some considerable time and strength to readjust and learn to do normal things again like reading, going to the theatre, etc. In my case I painted three rooms in a fortnight before I could finally physically and mentally relax. The change from hyper-activity and a hectic election campaign after demanding parliamentary and constituency duties, to nothing is really quite dramatic. Despite all that, I'll try again.

Yet it is also clear that a substantial minority were relieved, glad to be out of the dirty business of politics or happy to have hung on so long! This sigh of relief came particularly loudly in the Labour Party.

I was philosophical. I'd had a good innings and held a non-Labour seat for twenty-nine years, but profound changes in the social component of the electorate made the result gradually inevitable. No hard feelings. I realised I had kept the seat by sheer meticulous personal service, attracting non-ideological support from farmers, employers, shopkeepers, who were not voting ideologically. In the last two elections I realised that this was wearing thin. There was more concern about ideology, especially fear of the left.

Enormous relief to be rid of the militants in the Labour Party. Cooler reaction was even greater relief . . . My period was blighted by a takeover in my constituency party and a two-year running battle to retain the right to stand as a Labour candidate. It made me less idealistic about the party system.

Yet the minor parties were not immune:

I only stood in February 1974 against my own personal inclination as a result of strong persuasion by former colleagues . . . As I didn't particularly want to get back into the Commons I was not particularly cast down by my defeat. One cannot resign a seat when others have worked so long and so hard for you; and the only decent escape is narrow defeat which can be regarded as 'peace with honour'.

Nine out of ten felt there was nothing they could have done to avert defeat, and even the remainder were scratching round to find what. Nearly half saw national trends as mainly to blame, while a fifth put it down to boundary or population changes, leaving a whole range of miscellaneous causes. Interestingly, nearly a third of Labour men put defeat down to the election promises of the Conservatives, but a third of Conservatives to the impact of the opposite candidate in the constituency. Policy preoccupied the one, personality the other. Hurt oozed out of Labour questionnaires:

Surprise and disappointment and a deep anger at what I felt had been a successful con-trick election – Saatchi and Saatchi, the tax cuts promised, abolish rates, etc. The anger continued but was balanced by the immediately evident family advantages.

Appalled at the success of the Tory campaign locally and nationally, which I had hoped would have been exposed in all its shallowness during four weeks of intense campaigning. Cooler reactions little different, except to have wished that we had gone to the country in October 1978 when my seat would certainly have been held.

With the immediate crisis past, our exes began to reflect upon, in many cases to miss, their previous incarnation. A third found the thing they missed most was being at the centre of things, and another similar proportion said they missed being able to speak out and to influence events. A fifth missed constituency work, and the same proportion the comradeship of other MPs. The thing they were glad to be rid of was the hours: condemned by just over half. Yet this did not stop many wanting to endure them again, for almost half were keen to get back from the first, though nearly a third of these reported that they had become less keen later. This change with time was promptly cancelled out by a further fifth who had not been keen at first but became gradually more so later, which leaves only a fifth who did not want to go back at any stage.

Politics as a life-style seems to have been the main attraction for those who wanted to go back.

People enter politics for all sorts of reasons. Ego and ambition are no doubt common to all, but for those who, in addition, seek to achieve something positive, the political life today is very frustrating. Yet, and even though I have an interesting and highly-paid job, I would go back tomorrow. I am in no rush, and feel no sense of deprivation. I simply feel that politics is where I should be. After over twenty years in local and national office, the habit is very hard to kick. Politics is such a frustrating business today, because so many people believe that what is good for the country can only be what is good for them. Enlightened self-interest has almost totally given way to naked self-interest. However, in spite of believing this, I still feel I could perform a useful role in the political world.

Their feelings were, in fact, almost romantic:

It's a unique job. Your opinion is sought and your views matter, first, where the rules for our society are made and, second, day-to-day on a range of subjects. You might not be very powerful but you have opportunities for influence not easily gained elsewhere . . . I found it harder work and longer hours than I had thought or have ever otherwise worked. I also found it deeply satisfying both to be able to help people and to have a platform for your own deeply-held convictions, and to act as a spokesman for your party and your beliefs.

In fact under half of the defeated candidates had sought selection since, a proportion substantially higher if the 1979 defeats are excluded. They needed determination to seek it for though half of that half tried once, all the rest had to try more, some as many as five or more selections. Ex-MPs are good news and bad. In the political sphere, they have prestige and are more likely to get on to short lists. In fact over half had been selected for a new seat at some stage and four had got back to the Commons, six to the Lords and two to the European Assembly. Yet ex-MPs are bad news on the job front and the most immediate requirement for defeated MPs is to get a job. Chris Chataway was lucky after his 1966 defeat:

Immediately after I was defeated at Lewisham I was asked by the party to take on the leadership of the Inner London Education Authority, which, rather surprisingly, the Conservatives had won in 1967 and so although that was a voluntary job I was doing it fifty or sixty hours a week. It wasn't until late 1968 that I started to look and I really got the second one that I tried for.

That second seat was Chichester, a blue ribbon safe Tory seat. Like him, two fifths of the defeated candidates did not turn the job hunt into a long safari. They were either self-employed or simply carried on full-time with the job they had done part-time while Members, or retired. Others stepped into the Lords or the European Assembly. The remainder began applying for jobs immediately or in a few days and two fifths found it very difficult, only a quarter found it easy. Their difficulties centred on the fact that many employers do not like ex-MPs, a reason given by nearly half the defeated Members.

In 1974 it was comparatively easy to find rather lowly medical employment. Later, when I tried to find a better job, as it was becoming apparent that I was unlikely to find a winnable seat, my political background was an absolute disadvantage. I have frequently been turned down without interview for posts for which, on paper, I must be better qualified by experience than the average. One job I was selected for, subject to transatlantic parent company approval, only to have the local decision reversed 'because of political involvement'. I have approached three management selection firms dealing with medical employment.

Two didn't want to see me, explaining that in the terms of the old cliche, 'nothing was so ex as an ex-MP'.

'I had been a Minister and nobody believed that I was looking for more than a stop-gap before returning to Parliament – a process many employers thought that "the Party would organise"!'

'I was asked if I intended to go back into Parliament. When I said yes interviewers lost interest.'

'Employers were reluctant to take back a former shop steward who they probably were glad to see the back of.'

Job hunting was depressing and frustrating. Yet it was also much more difficult because ex-Members tend to start out at least by looking for a restricted range of jobs. Only a small proportion wanted to go into industry. Most preferred academic or teaching jobs, administrative work, trade union or political jobs. The media were the fifth most popular choice and indeed half a dozen of the 1979 losers went fairly quickly into television, creating the vague possibility of an inverse media balance as last time's government populated the media to influence its coverage of their adversaries in power. Most of the jobs they preferred or set out to look for at first were not those which the Members had done before election. They were attempting to put their parliamentary experience to use. Yet almost half had to lower sights before the search was over. John Ellis lowered his from a temporary job with his union, the Transport and General Workers', to a manual job at British Steel.

> I did my job as MP. I didn't have any other jobs on the side, and I don't go round asking people for favours. So I wanted a job. They've got an employment centre down there and I went along and said, 'I'm looking for a job.' They said, 'There's a job labouring in the medium section mill.' I said, 'Good'. So that's how I came to work for British Steel . . . labouring really . . . with pretty terrible pay . . . We were on £60 top line for a forty-hour week so the gang that I worked with literally worked seven days a week and took home a hundred pounds a week. But they told me when I was employed that you start as a labourer and if there was a chance for other vacancies at the mill then you will be considered for those. We have had some vacancies so I'm now a processman . . . I remember going into the various places in Scunthorpe when I first got the job at British Steel and somebody said, 'I expect they found you a cushy job in the offices.' I said, 'No.' So they said, 'Well, what are you doing?' I said, 'I'm a labourer in the medium section mill.' 'You could have done better for yourself than that, Johnny.'

A few, Hugh Jenkins, Maureen Colquhoun, Brian Sedgemore,

John Tomlinson, Shirley Williams, wrote books. In fact few were much good but it filled time. Books by ex-MPs, however, are a glut on the market, particularly biographical ones, and none made much money.

However, eventually most Members found the kind of job they wanted, even if not at the level they might have preferred, but the search was not short: only a fifth of the job hunters found one in a few days. A third had to wait over six months, well beyond the three months *ex gratia* parliamentary redundancy money, which was £1,724 tax free (in 1979 a quarter of the then salary) and has since increased. Currently a defeated Member under fifty gets six months' salary, over fifty, a year's. The cushion was necessary because in some cases it took over a year to get a job. So only in one respect were they really fortunate: a minority of only one fifth found restrictions placed on political activity by new employers. The rest were at least free to plan their attempt to get back into the House.

Yet not all now wanted to begin such an assault course. Returning to the normal world brought both joys and disappointments which led some to re-evaluate their original intentions; for example, in terms of human satisfactions they found themselves far better off. The new jobs offered more free time and this in turn held out the prospect of a more contented existence with their families, a fact which many put down as the biggest benefit of their new role. Financially many were in much the same position, half (many of them lawyers) better off.

> From every point of view Parliament should be willing to grasp the nettle of MPs' salaries properly. It ought not to be a rich men's or a sponsored men's club. Too many MPs tend to have to look for additional sources of income, which can give too much power to vested interests who are prepared to employ them in a part-time or consultant role. Money was by far the biggest individual worry. I lost a good deal of work at the Bar by being in the House during a period of pretty constant three-line whips. The Heath Government tried to get too much legislation through and overdid the use of three-liners.

Yet two fifths were worse off and the rest were in much the same position financially. Where they really missed out was in two less definable areas. The new jobs were much less interesting: only a quarter found them more satisfying. The jobs also offered less influence on events, and three quarters felt themselves less happy in this respect. The pull back to the Commons was inevitably largely influenced by these reactions to jobs. Among those people who found their current job most satisfying, the desire to get back into Parliament had waned.

Looking over their parliamentary careers, two-thirds of the ex-Members felt that their period in Parliament had been a chance to make a contribution to the country, while half were more vague, classifying it as 'useful experience'. Under half, most of them Labour, regarded it as 'a chance to further the cause of the Party'. This left only two-fifths who were so enthusiastic as to describe it *tout simple* as 'the best part of their lives'. Only minute proportions regarded it as a stepping-stone to something else or positively frustrating. Their likes and dislikes about the House also emerged as they looked back. Overwhelmingly, they opted for dealing with individual problems and for constituency work as the things they had enjoyed most, though even here some were disillusioned: 'The MP is a dogsbody. The only people within the constituency who want to see you are those with a grievance or complaint who need help.'

Committee work, influencing government policy and speaking in the Chamber got more mixed reactions, though on balance ex-MPs found all these areas merely 'fairly' satisfying, a collective description which goes a long way to illustrate the predicament of the MP. It was the more traditional part of the MP's job, questions, both written and oral, committees on bills and Private Member's bills, joined by party committees, which the ex-MPs found least fulfilling, with between a quarter and a third finding each of these opportunities not particularly satisfying and even less saying they were, on the contrary, 'very' satisfactory.

Their answers make it absolutely clear. The satisfactions of the MP's job are overwhelmingly personal, particularly those involved in dealing with individual cases, and social work.

> I found that in spite of all its defects the House of Commons is respected, and its Members always well received in their constituencies. This respect will grow and MPs become progressively more independent of the demands of the party whips and abandon yah-boo politics.

The aspect of their past experience as MPs which in retrospect seemed to the ex-MPs to stand most in need of change was the degree of backbench influence on government policy, mentioned by two fifths of them.

> The lack of democracy prohibits a backbencher from playing any real influential role in the policy making decisions. The Cabinet hands down

the policy (like the tablets of stone) to the Parliamentary Labour Party, where the payroll vote carries the day. A great deal more influence should be exercised by backbenchers over the policy of government. There should be greater accountability by the Cabinet towards the PLP.

Committees on bills were considered unsatisfactory by a third, speaking in the Chamber by over a quarter, and Question Time by the same proportion. A quarter made strong pleas for a greater influence for backbenchers, better procedures for committees, though improved procedures for bills and different hours for the House itself were emphasised by only a seventh. Working as a Minister was given as a major satisfaction by all those who had held the job, while the effect of passing a particular bill or fighting a particular issue tended to stand out for small proportions, all of whom had, however, been intensely involved. Fighting for a party and its cause came very low down the list. Indeed, almost as many mentioned opposing their own party line when necessary. A very few were totally disillusioned: 'Miss? Very little. Perhaps the annual shooting match at Bisley between the Commons and the Lords.'

Asked to look back and sum up their feelings on the role of the MP, two-fifths were predominantly positive: '[Being an MP is] one of the few self-defined activities . . . My basic view is that for any individual deeply imbued with the democratic spirit and committed to the basic values of his party, there is no role which can approach an MP's in job satisfaction.'

One fifth were less pompous and more negative, emphasising such reservations as MPs being cut off from the world, or reduced to being mere social workers. The remainder were pulled both ways, considering MPs could be effective with a better back up, or that they were good as social workers but weak in power and influence. Ex-Members seemed to want to get back, not because of real power or influence but because they had become addicted to something, perhaps a life-style, perhaps a role, perhaps just the feeling of doing an interesting and useful job, even if it lacked influence on policy. The balance between such feelings and the reduced satisfactions from the new jobs may have been the major reason why a return to Parliament still looked attractive.

MPs in safer seats, the House's first-class passengers, have a reasonably predictable career. Those in the marginals travel steerage and become the sacrificial victims of the system. Winning a marginal seat on one swing they can be, and often are, knocked out on the next by national trends largely beyond their control. A different kind of electoral system would provide both a more predictable process, and one on which Members themselves have more influence, and a more rational career pattern as well. Until it does, there are only two ways to compensate for this ritual slaughter of careers and to make it as it should be, more selective and more practical. More generous pension and redundancy payments with a compulsory retiring age could encourage the first-class passengers to sell jobs and allow greater turnover in that log-jammed section of the House. A reformed second Chamber would also allow a sensible career structure to be built up, with people who no longer want to face the hurly-burly, but who still have an important contribution to make, moving up the ladder to make more room downstairs; while others who have lost seats there can be given the choice of the hard drudge to get back or making a contribution through another forum. The major argument for a second Chamber is that it makes political career patterns more manageable.

Abolishing the House of Lords may be good symbolic politics but it is about as useful as abolishing dustbins. There is nowhere else to put the refuse, and more work is thrown on an overstretched cleaning staff. In this case the extra work would fall on an already over-worked House of Commons. There is no argument for a Second Chamber with delaying powers, there is no case for a check on the elective despotism, nor is any possible. Yet there is a very strong case for a second pair of eyes and for a second forum for debate which can mobilise a wider range of opinions. Labour particularly is caught in a vicious circle: declining to give the Lords more to do, lest they become too powerful, when an avowedly toothless Second Chamber could do much to lighten the burdens of the Commons. There is no case for an hereditary Second Chamber and there is no real need for abolition which points to the obvious answer. Just abolish the hereditary element and replace it with an effective Second Chamber, its membership determined by prime ministerial nomination as the life peers now. Such a system of choice would avoid the protracted disputes about elections and competition with the Commons which have held back reform, and such a chamber holds out the prospect of a more dynamic First Chamber by opening up opportunities and encouraging greater mobility among our political elite.

These changes would ensure that the public are better served. They would not be popular either with parties who cannot agree on what to do about the Second Chamber or a public which does not want to give golden handshakes or better pensions to MPs because, if truth be told, it has always begrudged paying MPs at all. Yet politics are becoming more professional and need to be even more so in a modern specialised society. It therefore needs provision for as rational a career structure as can be given in a system answerable to the unpredictable whims of the sovereign people. If we are going to have the political job done it should be done well by those best qualified to do it. We should use their ability in the best possible way.

TUPARTY I
TUPARTY II
Look Upon Our Works, Ye Mighty, And Despair
CENTRIST TOURS

12 As Things Have Been So Shall They Be?

Legislatures around the world are going through identity crises, uncomfortable with their roles, trying to accommodate to increased pressures and changed societies. Nowhere is this crisis more acute than in Britain. The Commons people are grappling with it without the benefits of either understanding it or being able to cope. Parliament represents and reflects Britain. The national forum of an uncertain, unhappy and unsuccessful nation, it is an uneasy, perplexed and not particularly successful institution. The British people are divided and doubting. They have little clear idea of where they are going and confused conflicting sentiments on where they want to go. The Commons people are the same, prone like those they represent to take refuge from present realities in myths and legends of former greatness, ready to abdicate their responsibilities by handing a chunk of their sovereignty to the EEC almost without thinking, or taking the equally escapist stance of blaming others for what is a fault of all. 'If only' as a way of life. In both cases the mighty have fallen. In neither is there any enthusiasm for having the extent of the fall pointed out. Times have changed. Neither the nation nor the institution has changed with it. Both are left floundering and defensive, attempting to keep up with a world with which they can no longer cope.

Most MPs see themselves as working a system of parliamentary democracy: Ministers run departments which carry out policy, government answers to Parliament for it. Problems of scale and inertia may have made the machine more difficult to control, departments may have a will of their own. The Civil Service may be a vested interest. Yet the old interpretation is still assumed to hold in broad outlines. The Thatcher experiment of major policy changes carried through by an obviously reluctant machine helps to prove it, whatever Tony Benn might say. The real problem is not that this traditional system has disintegrated, but that other patterns have grown up alongside and that Parliament is less relevant to any of them.

The structure of British government must now be viewed not as one simple system but as several, all coexisting in the same shell. Each serves a different purpose, each is uppermost for certain functions, all are necessary if the machine is to work. Yet none is dominant and Parliament's role in any of them is confused and curtailed. Thus within the broad framework of parliamentary democracy we also have government by party. Every nation has, in different guises, except Nepal, the only no-party state. In Britain, political parties are national institutions, some say mausoleums. They connect the people to government. They work a mass democracy. The electorate chooses a job lot of Prime Minister, programme, Cabinet and a built-in majority by which the Cabinet controls the House and pushes its programme through. Looked at from another point of view, we have a pressure group democracy. The diverse interests in a modern society are articulated through groups and organisations, and government builds up an elaborate machinery of consultation and involvement to integrate them all. Each department has its clientele of interest groups: institutions, organisations, firms working in a particular area. The framework is topped off by a tripartite series of relationships which at times can resemble a corporate state as government consults the great monolithic interests of the TUC and the CBI and the three do deals, compromise, persuade, bargain. Finally, modern mass communications, and the continuous feedback process built up round them, have endowed us with a framework of plebiscitary democracy of the kind populists might find themselves at home with. Government reads the fever charts of opinion through the polls, the by-elections, and now through referenda, more used in the 1970s than for all the preceding decades of the century. It also speaks directly to the nation through television, putting Ministers in the living-room, just as the people speak to it through the polls.

These four systems coexist where one worked before. None is now visibly dominant. Each modifies the other. In doing so they confuse both participants and public. The diversity has never been made clear to a nation always prone to prefer myths to reality and lacking the remorseless logic of, say, the French in differentiating the real from the sham. No one seems sure what mode is operating at what time, which horse is relevant to what course, which hat participants are wearing. Confused incomprehension characterises most public discussion, and behind the face of government is confusion, with no apparent dominant will or central nerve. We get all the disadvantages of an elective dictatorship and none of the advantages.

This confusion is particularly intense in the case of Parliament. Each of the systems cohabiting within the shell has modified and undermined its power. Government by party means that a House of Commons which in theory controls and checks the executive is in fact controlled by it. Pressure group democracy means that Parliament's role in mobilising consent and charting the limits of the acceptable is transferred to departments who know the crucial views of the interested parties better than the House and can do deals in a way it never could. They present it with proposals already market tested and often immutable: houses of cards which cannot be changed for fear of bringing the whole down. Plebiscitary democracy gives governments a more direct access to the people than they could ever obtain through the baffle and filter of the Commons. The House's job of articulating opinion is downgraded when that opinion can express itself forcibly and directly through the polls and has almost certainly changed since the freeze frame of the attitudes of months, even years, before, which is the Commons. The polls allow opinion to be quantified and measured. Even when the House is performing its natural role as a great echo chamber, amplifying the noises bruiting abroad in the land, the resultant din is of little objective use. Individual MPs when they measure opinions tend to be like cushions bearing the impress of whoever last sat on them, individual, firm, general management committee, constituency chairman or other pressure group.

Once performing real functions, the Commons have been largely restricted to formal ones. Ministers and government formally answer to it. The party debate is formally staged there. Compromises with groups are formally ratified there, Ministers formally announce their intentions, often after briefing the press and providing both advance material and advance interviews, all suitably embargoed. The consent of the community is formally given there, even if the polls show that its real attitude may be very different. The major satisfaction of running the country and participating in the great decisions has been transferred elsewhere. The Commons is a waiting-room or a preparation course for those anxious to pursue them to their new abode. In David Penhaligon's view, it is a talk shop, talking about power:

> The House of Commons is a talk shop, and it's basically designed to let people let off their gripes . . . and as a place where the concerns of a nation can be expressed and I think it does that tolerably well. The idea that it actually controls the executive is one of the more amusing concepts of the House of Commons. It clearly doesn't, and the amount of influence an individual MP has got in our system is really very limited.

For the mass of Members, today's satisfactions are vicarious. MPs are not the holders of power but its residuary legatees, picking it over, tidying it up, telling folk about it. Like street scavengers in Whitehall, they work with the detritus of everything, the paper outpourings of the departments, the torn posters and banners of the party struggle; the muddled, tattered pamphlets of pressure group democracy, even the horse droppings of the constitutional and ceremonial display, while the sounds of the television and radio battle hover in the air and the pollsters throng the streets. Scavengers make their world as tidy as possible without controlling it, create the public impression that someone is there doing something. So do MPs. They participate in each aspect of the multi-faceted system. They do so as the bit part players of the great drama of power, the extras, the crowd scenes, or as Julian Critchley puts it, the gawping spectators:

> A lot of people imagine going into the House is like being a member of Congress: much more glamorous, much more powerful, much more free-ranging than we are. Our eggs are not free-range eggs at all. We're really all brought up in batteries in this place . . . It gives rise to a great deal of frustration, both overt and secret . . . the frustration of sitting if not at the ringside, at least three or four rows back, being splashed occasionally by the water which is thrown over the fighters but not actually being able to get into the ring itself. After a time, there is a tendency to become rather bored and irritated by the whole thing.

To replace one major satisfaction, today's parliamentarian is offered a dazzling array of petty ones. The classical, but in fact short-lived, mid-nineteenth century role of the MP flickers, as it did from 1974–9. Yet the fulfilment of actually counting comes only on those rare occasions when the people stutter instead of speaking clearly and Parliament is left to decide. More normally, MPs face a variety of possible roles and a fragmentation of satisfactions. The machine becomes more complicated and affects the lives of its citizens at a wider range of points, offering enormous and rapidly increasing scope for personal case work, ombudsmaneering, the endless pursuit of ephemera and minutiae, and the intermittent satisfactions of a driving licence wrenched from Swansea, a housing transfer arranged, a social security benefit increased by 50p, a deportation delayed. Even for a former councillor like Bob Litherland it begins to pall:

> I think it's become very pedestrian, the life of an MP. You become more of a welfare worker, a glorified councillor. Quite honestly, sometimes I ask myself what have I done today? What world-shattering effect have I had? And it's very little . . . You feel as though you're just going through the machinery as voting fodder and achieving very little at the end of it.

A limited number can also fulfil themselves through the House itself. They embark on the long plod to committee chairman's panel. They devote themselves to the mole-like existence of the procedural expert, emerging blinking, as Robin Maxwell Hyslop in the hybridity crisis, or Michael English on far too many issues, before going back underground. They work at the difficult job of being 'good House of Commons men', 'sound', or a 'man of bottom', all totally frustrating because of the abdication of ego, initiative and ideas involved.

Government by party offers fewer satisfactions. It provides fulfilment to the ideologues, and to those who get pleasure from the tactics of debate, from political archaeology or low-level name calling. Party is still the ladder of promotion for that majority who see themselves, however misguidedly, as 'ministrables', and the instrument through which they will enforce their will. Yet that will is rarely theirs; it is the local party's, or conference's, or the Prime Minister's, but always someone else's. As for pressure group democracy, it holds out even fewer prospects, though there are the free lunches, a fascination for those who wish to specialise in a subject or even collect a fee as a group spokesman. Some of the more devoted Members, Frank Field on poverty, Charles Irving on mental health, Alf Morris on disablement, Jack Ashley on hearing and handicaps, Robert Kilroy-Silk on prisons, Janet Foulkes on animal welfare, Nigel Spearing on the EEC, Jeremy Bray on econometrics, have built up a real expertise. Others are more content to be used as mouthpieces, putting views or asking questions. What plebiscitary democracy offers is more beguiling; a media platform where MPs are listening to, even the glamour of television. For those over eager to be the clowns in the political circus which the broadcasting organisations stage for the edification of the larger audience outside, there is excitement, vicarious satisfaction, even money.

The real question is not the numbers of roles and satisfactions. There is an obvious plenitude. It is whether they add up to anything worth doing. Can they be combined together, expanded, or built on to provide a satisfying role and a useful career for the Commons people? David Marquand thinks not, after his own disillusioning experience:

> Most backbenchers, given the existing system in the House of Commons, are wasting their time, and that's the real truth of the matter. They're not really achieving very much. Either they realise this and they become very frustrated and fed up; or they don't realise it and they're living in a kind of fantasy world where they think they're doing great things and actually they're not . . . People in lunatic asylums are probably very happy to be in a lunatic asylum. They want it to stay a lunatic asylum. It's the same way in the Palace of Westminster.

Many must secretly agree because MPs themselves have answered 'No' by voting with their feet. If there were a useful, satisfying job in the House, those who do it full-time would be the overwhelming majority. They have also voted with their questionnaires in our survey. There they do not rate themselves as particularly effective. Asked to rate the 'effectiveness of MPs' on a subjective ten-point scale, 35 per cent gave five or less, a high proportion for such a low rating. A further 43 per cent put MPs at points six or seven, leaving only 22 per cent giving MPs (ie themselves) a high rating. These are substantially lower marks than MPs gave to Ministers. There 21 per cent gave half marks or less for ministerial 'effectiveness', 40 per cent gave six or seven points, leaving 39 per cent giving them a very high rating. The taskmasters are better regarded than their humble servants.

Suggesting specific reform proposals to the MPs showed a feeling that all was not well, but there was little agreement on what to do about it: substantial majorities wanted better support facilities and procedural reform (though without specifying what). Around half wanted more emphasis on select committees and better pay, but after that unanimity disintegrated. Only a third wanted full-time MPs, the same proportion televising of Parliament, in both cases with rather more opposed. A 10.00 am to 7.00 pm working day appealed only to just over a quarter, and 'fewer MPs' and longer sessions appealed to even smaller numbers with in each case about twice as many opposed. There is no clear call for reform here, no real idea of how to escape from the trap. George Cunningham still hopes for change forced from outside:

> The thing that's really wrong with British parliamentary democracy is the public, not the House of Commons, because the public doesn't demand from its MPs any degree of independent judgement. You don't get local newspapers saying, 'Here is the voting record of our Member,' because they assume that he's always voted for his own side. So the Member can be a lion in his constituency when he's a mouse in the House. What we need is for the public to force their Members to vote according to some degree of independent judgement.

Yet with those most deeply involved being most divided and the public knowing so little of the realities, such a hope must be forlorn.

Most MPs escape their dilemma by throwing themselves into a welter of work, seeking purpose through activity. This solution offers no escape, though if the work can be channelled and made more effective, it could do. The party domination of the Commons which reached its height in the 1950s has produced an inevitable counter-reaction: backbenchers have begun, painfully slowly, to develop a more independent role. The House has sought compensation for its own decline by turning in on itself, using those powers it still retains more effectively. Both processes involve intense specialisation. The traditional view of parliamentarians is as laymen bringing uninformed judgement to bear on the issues of the day. The new reforms strengthen MPs by connecting them with that body of specialised 'informed' opinion outside which is the real check on governments in a sophisticated democracy because it is the only body qualified to talk to departments on their own terms, or to criticise proposals with genuine effect. MPs are being gradually integrated into this expertise by being given staff and by specialised committees with their own advisers. In this way the House can be a new training ground for specialised talent, and a forum through which government can be forced to justify what it is doing with more than a few throwaway lines. A body of parliamentary expertise can be built up and, more important, given an effective involvement instead of being allowed to dissipate. Those who want to focus themselves more narrowly and pursue the satisfactions of specialisation now can. In this way the whole House is being offered job enrichment and the prospect of being more effective because more professional. At the same time this more professional body of politicians has shown, partly because every problem is now more difficult and divisive if it is approached honestly, a new propensity for independent thought, speech and voting. Both together are gradually transforming the House and making government's life more difficult. To outsiders, MPs still look like party hacks. Perhaps they still are. Yet the House enters the 1980s a better place, working more efficiently, with a new generation of more professional, better educated and, if truth be told, simply better, MPs. It is also more brusque and impersonal, but no matter. It should be even more so. It is more necessary that the House should be good at its job and efficient than that its Members should be able to take refuge from their failure by relaxing into the muggy, vacuous and wholly spurious atmosphere of a matey club.

The changes have taken two decades to achieve. They do not amount to a transformation, merely a new opening. They cannot now be reversed. Yet it is also clear that further progress on this road will not come soon. Developments take time to digest. Members have to adjust to new situations. Governments which control the process of change are no longer certain how to react to a development which would be embarrassing. If there are further advances it is possible that they will have to be forced, not conceded as they have been up to now. If they do they are more likely to arise not so much from the pressures still developing among the backbenchers, not even from concessions by governments who have been notoriously slow to do anything which inconveniences them, but from a change forced on the House itself from outside by the changes in the party system generated by new forces building up in the community at large.

Pressure for structural change in the British political system is becoming stronger. It has been mainly negative up to now, a product of disillusionment. Yet it is still building up. If it continues so it could force structural change on the House of Commons. The political and social geology on which Parliament and the parties rest is never still. Now the tectonic plates are shifting, colliding, thrusting up and down, a tremor in the earth which must produce changes in the structures erected above it.

The class monoliths on which the two main parties rest are disintegrating. Decades of affluence have brought greater mobility, social transformation, new neighbourhoods, new industries, new skills and sub-divisions all weakening class conditioning. New sub-cultures develop, new groups, who do not identify with the old gangs. The great interests have fragmented as finance diverges from industry, distribution from manufacturing. Sellers differ from producers, workers from consumers, union from union, section from section, as each group struggles to improve its lot or defend its position in a competitive society. Men have different interests from women, old workers from younger, race from race, town from country, suburb from city. Tensions impose conflicting roles on individuals as well as between groups. In recession, immediate interest predominates. In affluence, even the present shabby version, roles fragment and individuals wear many hats: as unionists, citizens, householders, taxpayers, beneficiaries, employees, environmentalists, consumers. Each tension softens everyone's position, enmeshing the individual in new and more complex networks. Where parties think they have to appeal to a stable 'vote' and their main job is to get it out, in fact instability and change is now the norm, the settled allegiance exceptional.

This political change supplements social processes. In the 1970s, the political system failed to deliver. Growth faltered, stopped, went into reverse. Faith in parties has declined, along with all attachments and loyalties to them. The proportion of electors describing themselves as 'very strong' party supporters has fallen away steadily. So has the vote for both parties. Their hard-core support, two-fifths of the electorate each in the fifties, may now be only a quarter each. A chorus of complaint and alienation has built up. Widely regarded as the home, possibly the last resting place, of the two-party system, Britain finds itself with the proportion of the electorate committed to those two parties declining to, even below, the same level as in other systems called 'multi-party'. Yet this pattern of crumbling allegiances operates within the strait-jacket of a first-past-the-post electoral system. Such a system works well when there are slight shifts of opinion between two parties. Then it magnifies small movements into larger changes of seats. This beneficial process has chaotic consequences when the shifts themselves grow much bigger. Which they now have, because more of the electorate are foot-loose. Instability is the inevitable result. Britain has had more changes of party in power through the sixties and seventies than most advanced industrial democracies: four of the last six elections have produced changes. It is only a reshuffling of the old cards, for MPs are serving longer, but it has had drastic policy repercussions, more changes of policy and management, more turn-arounds, more often within the same government, shifting as they all do through the phases of government, more promises and more failures all making economic difficulties, and alienation, worse. It has also provided among the more naive politicians a craving for stability and continuity, both of which would in fact be undemocratic and dictatorial, when the real impetus for the instability comes from the people, frustrated as they are by the performance of the politicians.

These trends, social and political, point towards a slow breakdown of the party system. A massive negative protest vote has built up, sloshing now to the Liberals, now elsewhere, currently to the alliance. As it continues and if the alliance can offer something more than mere escapism, the scene may be set for change. All such trends are heightened under a Conservative government, particularly one generating massive depression. If they now push the minor party vote at a general election over that third which produces breakthrough into real parliamentary representation, total electoral uncertainty ensues. One, perhaps both, of the major parties, can be threatened even without the party split which has hitherto been the necessary prelude to breakthrough. No seat can be regarded as safe: a lottery operates. More likely they can give the alliance enough seats to hold the balance of power situation. The Liberals so nearly grasped this in 1974. With the major parties now more unpopular and the third party much stronger, even just a few more seats for the Alliance could put a bigger third party block into a position to dictate terms next time. One of those terms will be proportional representation, which Labour will try to avoid but Conservatives, more inclined to it and always more realistic about power, might well accept.

Neither major party knows how to react to this new situation. Some on both sides attempt to restore old certainties by retreating back to basics. The Thatcherites and their mirror image, the Bennites, build on each other. Yet both only compound the problem by making the parties more sectarian, less attractive, and by vacating the centre ground. Meanwhile with a government pursuing policies which give no indication of working and the Opposition presenting a fractious, unattractive face to the world, the mood of the electorate, hitherto merely negative, could be hardening and undergoing a sea-change. The easy assumption that Labour has merely to pull itself belatedly together and the Tories to tone down their policies, for Bo Peep's wandering sheep to come home dragging their tails behind them, so all can be well again, may be misplaced. Moods can harden into changed attitudes. The hostility is greater than either major party allows, or dares, to understand. To predict is to become a political Petrulenga. Since it involves an assessment of government's determination to persevere, it also involves a measure of abnormal psychology. Without benefit of either it is at least clear that Britain has a multi-party system struggling to be born. Whatever its outcome that struggle promises greater political instability. It therefore threatens certainties in the Commons itself. Safe seats which provide both the ballast and the main recruiting ground for government may be less sure. Parties themselves are threatened, and such an undermining of certainties means they can promise less to their MPs. Minor party representation may well grow so major parties will have more difficulty in governing alone and unaided. Such developments, most of them already foreshadowed in the seventies, could transfer power from Cabinet boardroom to parliamentary shop floor as the unpredictability of the electorate strengthens industrial democracy in the Commons. All bemused Commons people can do is get on with their jobs as best they can and wait to see what happens, hoping to be there after the pack is reshuffled as the new politics begin after the next election, but increasingly uncertain that they will be, because the new uncertainty means that all can hope but few can be sure.

The changes will be partial. If they occur they set us off on a road which leads to electoral reform, for the system cannot fully adjust as long as it remains constrained by an electoral system suited to days of yore and gore. Proportional representation, carefully calculated to translate Britain's fragmenting political preferences into exact political terms, would allow the emerging trends to find their full and natural expression. It would also amplify the consequences for the Commons by weakening the grip of the two majority parties and making coalitions, pacts or 'working arrangements' more likely, thus breaking party domination and completing the emancipation of the backbencher by transferring power from the electorate to the Commons where coalitions would be made or broken. The public will not necessarily like this because the power to make or break governments, to make a clear-cut decision, will have been transferred away from them to the smoke-filled room and the House of Commons. Yet it will also be what an increasing proportion of them have voted for, albeit without realising the fact. It will also be a more finely-tuned machine. At the moment electors have a stark choice: 'Voter, give an honest curse, defend the bad against far worse.' In a more sophisticated electoral system they would have a choice not only between parties but also on what kind of party, which type of candidate they prefer. This could be more crucial than the present ability to opt against Labour but get all the joys of Thatcherism in consequence.

Such projections are futurology. Remorseless projection of trends is as unrealistic as an assumption that new developments will produce their own automatic antibodies. All that is clear is that parliamentary change always follows changes in the wider community. Those wider changes now seem well-established. They do not have to go further to make themselves felt in the Commons but they probably will. To do so is to reinforce the processes of parliamentary change which have already begun, creating the possibility that nineteenth-century patterns could revive: independent MPs, parliamentarians who are more of an elite, more parliamentary power, all within the different confines of a modern mass democracy. This will be a party democracy. Yet the parties could be closer to their continental counterparts, their parliamentary representatives more like their highly professional American brothers, all this combining to give us a Parliament which adjusts better, influences more, and gives a clearer lead to the nation. Government may be less strong. Parliament will be stronger. The Commons people will have become uncommon. Again.

The paen of praise to which anyone frustrated by the present Parliamentary system is driven in welcoming the prospect of such reforms, or indeed any at all, is a tesimony to present frustrations rather than to the possibility of changing basic realities. A Parliament reformed will be one doing a better job more efficiently. Its Members will have a more satisfactory and better focussed existence. They may even find a fulfilment which is presently there only in small doses. Yet Parliament will still be the anteroom, the waiting-room, to power, not its fulcrum. It will be able to audit power, criticise it, unearth and expose its follies and even influence it all in a way it has not done for years. Yet it will never actually exercise it. Only in a system such as the American, with its division of powers and responsibilities, can the legislature have a clear and defined role, a power base of its own within the system. In the British system Parliament cannot have the impossible. It should not try for it.

Moreover, the problem of working even the limited reforms proposed here and fulfilling even these restricted intentions brings us down immediately to the fundamental realities examined in this book, the Commons people. Their lot is not a happy one, try as they might to insulate themselves from it. It could become even less happy. The inscription over the parliamentary portal 'abandon home all ye who enter here' will have to be even more deeply engraved.

The requirements of the job will be even more likely to preclude a normal existence. Parliamentary life will still require the practitioners to live their lives, to have their affairs, accidents, nervous breakdowns and personal problems in a fish bowl. MPs will still be running on a conveyor belt moving too fast for them, still struggling in a disorganised fashion for some not very clear purpose, and still pursuing their own ambitions for power all at the same time. A more useful role might ease some of the problems of sour resignation, engrained hatreds and malevolent bitternesses which arise from collective futility and impotence. Yet it will make the Commons even more a jostling scrum of ambition and thus more impersonal and hardly happier. So this book is dedicated to those who inherit the doubtful prospects of the second decade of Britain's politics of decline, by one who endured something of the first, in the hope that they will find not escape but sublimation in the reform of Parliament which has accompanied the decline.

To do the job of MP properly now demands a peculiarly thick-skinned egomaniac workaholic who has a populist's rapport with people but an intellectual's understanding of problems and issues. We have not got this paragon, although some of the individual characteristics are well scattered about the congregation. We certainly could not breed the parliamentary supermen required by the new situation. If we did, parties would not select them because in their usual perverse fashion, they would still be looking for different things entirely. Electors might become more inclined to pick and choose, less party bound, yet whether they will choose someone with the necessary characteristics to do a job they themselves neither know nor understand is an open question.

Electoral reform is now on the agenda. Yet it is vital that any reform should keep a local tie, a connection with a defined section of the people, even if not necessarily the same artificial areas or the same number of people. The representational role is Parliament's only real strength, the Member's chief joy and his lifeline to those basic realities of places, people, industries, jobs and needs which lie at the base of the whole system. Without such an umbilical the MP is rootless, lost in a universe of facts, arguments, ideas and abstractions. Without it too the MP has no base, the House no function, democracy no roots. The MP is in an impossible situation: feet in the mud, head in the clouds, body subject to a hundred tugging pressures. Yet if he is to do his job he has to accept that predicament. Merely to provide for a more rational, efficient, better organised and more effective Commons, and to do so by taking the MP's feet out of the nasty dirty mud, castrates him. Democracy requires that an MP's job be anomalous, if not impossible. Attempting to do it imposes strain, harassment, upset and inconvenience. This book has illustrated some of each. Doing so is not meant to evoke sympathy. The process is unseemly. If it is not, the job is not being done and it is more important that the impossible be attempted than that 635 ambitious egomaniacs should have a pleasant existence. Make it more efficient. Make them more sensible. But never make the job easy. They do not deserve that, and neither does Britain.

Appendix: The Questionnaires

The material cited in the text is based on three postal questionnaires. These were all numbered so as to enable us to send out reminders, not to check on who said what, since the participants were offered – and got – anonymity and confidentiality. In each case a stamped addressed envelope was sent for the reply and one reminder was sent to those who had not returned their questionnaire. The response rates were:

Survey One

Sent to all sitting MPs except the Speaker, returned by 358 – a response rate of 56 per cent. These were 204 Conservative, 140 Labour, five Liberal, four Ulster Unionist, three Scottish Nationalist, and two (then) SDP. The questionnaire covered thirty-six questions.

Survey Two

Sent to all Members defeated in 1979 and the two 1974 elections – a total of 140. This was returned by seventy-eight, a response rate of 56 per cent. The questionnaire itself asked thirty-nine questions.

Survey Three

Carried out independently by an American research student. Sent to all the wives of all MPs indicated in the standard reference books as being married. It was filled in and returned by 308 wives, while a few more describing themselves as 'ex' returned it diffidently, saying it no longer applied. Since several had to go 'care of' the husband in the House of Commons, a few were also returned by the MP, saying he did not want his wife to fill in questionnaires. No questionnaire was sent to husbands of women Members.

All this material was analysed by Caroline Elliston and Adrian Barker. The figures are quoted in the text in a very generalised way so as not to make the material obtrusive. Some of the many amplifying comments which were so liberally given are also quoted. We wish to thank all those who co-operated in these surveys.

Index